PEACE AND THE PEACEMAKERS

The Treaty of 1783

U NITED S TATES C APITOL H ISTORICAL S OCIETY
Fred Schwengel, President

PERSPECTIVES ON THE AMERICAN REVOLUTION
Ronald Hoffman and Peter J. Albert, Editors

Diplomacy and Revolution: The Franco-American Alliance of 1778

Sovereign States in an Age of Uncertainty

Slavery and Freedom in the Age of the American Revolution

Arms and Independence: The Military Character of the American Revolution

An Uncivil War: The Southern Backcountry during the American Revolution

Peace and the Peacemakers: The Treaty of 1783

Peace and the Peacemakers

The Treaty of 1783

Edited by RONALD HOFFMAN
and PETER J. ALBERT

Published for the

UNITED STATES CAPITOL HISTORICAL SOCIETY

BY THE UNIVERSITY PRESS OF VIRGINIA

Charlottesville

THE UNIVERSITY PRESS OF VIRGINIA
Copyright © 1986 by the Rector and Visitors
of the University of Virginia

First Published 1986

Printed in the United States of America

Library of Congress Cataloging in Publication Data
Main entry under title:

Peace and the peacemakers.

  (Perspective on the American Revolution)
  Includes index.
    1. United States—History—Revolution, 1775–1783 —Peace—Addresses, essays,
lectures. 2. Treaty of Paris (1783)—Addresses, essays, lectures. I. Hoffman, Ronald,
1942– . II. Albert, Peter J. III. Series.
E249.P42 1985   973.3′17   85-10618
ISBN 0-8139-1071-4

This book is dedicated to the memory of
Walter Rundell, Jr.
1928–1982
a founder of the United States Capitol Historical Society
an esteemed colleague, and a valued friend

Contents

CONTENTS

Preface

In 1716, a half century before the beginning of the American Revolutionary adventure that culminated in 1783, a seventy-one-year-old French diplomat named Francois de Callières distilled the experiences of his long and distinguished career under Louis XIV and published them in a remarkable memoir entitled *De la manière de négocier avec les souverains* (On the Manner of Negotiating with Princes). Although a good portion of Callières's activity had taken place in the late seventeenth century, his perception of the nature of diplomacy and the attributes required of its practitioners was so accurate that his small volume soon became a handbook for eighteenth-century diplomats. Indeed, for many diplomats and scholars in the twentieth century, Callières's treatise remains, in the words of Sir Harold Nicolson, "the best manual of diplomatic method ever written."[1] There can be little doubt that a book of such stature influenced, at least to some degree, the men who negotiated the treaty of 1783, and it is appropriate for this reason to review some of its precepts.

While Callières might see no difficulty, the modern reader is struck by a puzzling contradiction in the book's description of diplomatic practice. On the one hand, Callières goes to considerable lengths to assert the importance of dealing in good faith, and he quite firmly eschews deceit as a tool of negotiation. The "good negotiator," he writes,

> will never found the success of his mission on promises which he cannot redeem or on bad faith. It is a capital error, which prevails widely, that a clever negotiator must be a master of the art of deceit. Deceit indeed is but a measure of the smallness of mind of him who employs it, and simply shows that his intelli-

[1] Sir Harold Nicolson, *The Evolution of Diplomacy*, 11th ed. (New York, 1966), p. 85.

ix

PREFACE

gence is too meagrely equipped to enable him to arrive at his
ends by just and reasonable methods. No doubt the art of lying
has been practised with success in diplomacy; but unlike that
honesty which here as elsewhere is the best policy, a lie always
leaves a drop of poison behind, and even the most dazzling diplomatic success gained by dishonesty stands on an insecure
foundation.[2]

Having come down on the side of candor, openness, and
honesty, however, Callières goes on to expound at equal
length upon the value of spies and the uses of bribery: "Well-
chosen spies," he notes, "contribute more than any other
agency to the success of great plans. . . . And as there is no
expense better designed . . . than that which is laid out upon
a secret service, it would be inexcusable for a minister of state
to neglect it." Callières particularly praises the Spanish for
their "wise custom" of placing special funds at the disposal of
their ambassadors for purposes of espionage. "The ambassador," he asserts, "has sometimes been called an honourable
spy because one of his principal occupations is to discover
great secrets." In addition, those who would be successful negotiators should always be poised to take advantage of any
indiscretion by gossips or discontented courtiers, while at the
same time guarding against betrayal by unreliable infor-
mants and double agents.[3]

With regard to bribery, Callières points out that a good
diplomat "must reinforce his own good manners, his insight
of character, and attraction of person by certain expenses."
The reader probably has little doubt what the author means
by "certain expenses," but should there be any confusion,
Callières then gives explicit instructions: "Wherever large
gifts are offered, the giver must take care beforehand to
know that they will be received in the right spirit," for "a gift
presented in the right spirit, at the right moment, by the
right person, may act with tenfold power upon him who re-
ceives it." It is especially important, according to Callières, to

[2] A. F. Whyte, trans., *The Practice of Diplomacy, Being an English Rendering
of François de Callières's "De la manière de négocier avec les souverains"* (London,
1919), p. 31.

[3] Ibid., pp. 26–27.

know whom to approach. Among his recommendations as likely prospects are dancers, "who by the fact of their profession have an *entrée* less formal and in some degree more intimate with the prince than any ambassador can perhaps possess." Similarly, low-ranking officers often respond well to "a timely present" and sometimes "even great ministers of state themselves may not be inaccessible by the same means."[4]

Many pages in Callières's book are devoted to discussing the characteristics of a good negotiator. "These qualities," he writes,

> are an observant mind, a spirit of application which refuses to be distracted by pleasures or frivolous amusements, a sound judgment which takes the measure of things as they are, and which goes straight to its goal by the shortest and most natural paths without wandering into useless refinements and subtleties which as a rule only succeed in repelling those with whom one is dealing. The negotiator must further possess that penetration which enables him to discover the thoughts of men and to know by the least movement of their countenances what passions are stirring within, for such movements are often betrayed even by the most practised negotiator. He must also have a mind so fertile in expedients as easily to smooth away the difficulties which he meets in the course of his duty; he must have presence of mind to find a quick and pregnant reply even to unforeseen surprises, and by such judicious replies he must be able to recover himself when his foot has slipped. An equable humour, a tranquil and patient nature, always ready to listen with attention to those whom he meets; an address always open, genial, civil, agreeable, with easy and ingratiating manners which assist largely in making a favourable impression upon those around him—these things are the indispensable adjuncts to the negotiator's profession. Their opposite, the grave and cold air, a melancholy or rough exterior, may create a first impression which is not easily removed. Above all, [Callières concludes,] the good negotiator must have sufficient control over himself to resist the longing to speak before he has really thought what he shall say.[5]

Finally, Callières warns against some of the pitfalls that lay before aspiring eighteenth-century diplomats. The success

[4] Ibid., pp. 24–26.

[5] Ibid., pp. 18–20.

of any negotiation was closely linked, in Callières's mind, with the social prowess of the diplomat and his ability to project what we would call today an agreeable and attractive "image." In pursuit of this end, Callières asserts that the diplomat "must on no account neglect any opportunity of placing himself . . . in a favourable light in the eyes" of "the ladies of the court . . . for it is well known that the power of feminine charm often extends to cover the weightiest resolutions of state." Callières sagely reminds us that "the greatest events have sometimes followed the toss of a fan or the nod of a head." But let the diplomat beware! While he must assuredly "do all things in his power, by the magnificence of his display, by the polish, attraction, and gallantry of his person," to "engage" the "pleasure" of these ladies, he must be wary "lest he engage his own heart." He "must never forget that Love's companions are Indiscretion and Imprudence, and that the moment he becomes pledged to the whim of a favoured woman, no matter how wise he may be, he runs a grave risk of being no longer master of his own secrets. We have often seen terrible results follow from this kind of weakness into which even the greatest ministers are liable to fall, and we need go no further than our own time for remarkable examples and warnings."[6]

The negotiation of the treaty of 1783 was a momentous development of modern history. It is our hope that these excerpts from François de Callières's volume on diplomacy and the essays contained in this volume will serve to place that seminal event in a more human and accessible perspective. In the opening essays Esmond Wright and Gregg L. Lint explore the objectives of the principal combatants in the Revolutionary War. Wright argues that, up to Yorktown, the British sought a return to the status quo ante bellum and would accept American independence only on the condition of dismemberment. Cornwallis's defeat at Yorktown, together with other reverses, broke the British determination to continue the war and led to the fall of the North ministry and the opening of negotiations. It did not, however, mark

---

[6] Ibid., pp. 23–24.

the end of British reluctance to grant independence to the United States other than on the basis of uti possidetis. According to Wright, the eventual British acceptance of independence, the withdrawal of their forces, and the generous territorial settlement embodied in the Treaty of Paris were founded on the fact that the important negotiators—Shelburne, Oswald, and Franklin—embraced the principles of free trade and were convinced that Great Britain could trade as readily and profitably with an independent United States as with thirteen dependent colonies. Thus, he concludes, the treaty marked the shift in British war aims from a determination to reassert dominion over the former colonies to an attempt to lay the foundation for future reconciliation and trade with the new nation.

Lint treats the interrelation of the American, French, and Spanish war aims. The demand for the recognition of national independence aside, American objectives—principally boundaries and territorial demands, fishing rights, and the navigation of the Mississippi—fluctuated during the war as they were influenced by compromises among state and sectional interests and the vicissitudes of the conflict itself. Moreover, these objectives were not necessarily in harmony with those of France and Spain—the former hoping to improve its position relative to Great Britain and the latter seeking to recover Gibraltar and to maintain Spanish status vis-à-vis the other European powers. In the end, Lint argues, the objectives of the American negotiators themselves played a significant role in the peace settlement and, their government's explicit instructions to the contrary, led these men successfully to undertake separate and secret negotiations with Great Britain.

The next three essays examine the respective negotiators for the United States, Great Britain, and France. James H. Hutson focuses on a common characteristic of the American diplomats—their suspiciousness (or, to use the eighteenth-century term, their jealousy)—and explores the impact of this "diplomacy of jealousy" on the negotiations. The Americans, he writes, manifested a "spectrum of suspicion" that resulted from the coincidence of their personalities (particularly those of Henry Laurens, John Adams, and John Jay) with a political ideology encouraging suspicion in defense of republicanism. Hutson maintains that the excessive distrust displayed by these three commissioners—as opposed to the "covert suspicion" of Benjamin Franklin, which was "carefully calculated and controlled"—could have been disastrous for the negotiations.

Charles R. Ritcheson then studies the men involved in the negotiations on the British side, the earl of Shelburne and Charles James Fox as well as their agents, Richard Oswald, Thomas Grenville, Alleyne Fitzherbert, Benjamin Vaughan, Henry Strachey, and David Hartley. He concentrates in particular on Shelburne, whose reputation has been somewhat rehabilitated, and on Oswald, whose "true character, abilities, shortcomings, and contributions to the making of the peace," he writes, have been misread by historical scholarship. Tracing the course of the negotiations from the spring of 1782 through the signing of the Preliminary Treaty, he concludes that the peace could not have been successfully negotiated without Oswald's efforts and that it marked a significant step in achieving Shelburne's objectives—an end to the Franco-American alliance, the reestablishment of Anglo-American peace and amity, and the reassertion of British economic dominance.

Finally, Jonathan R. Dull looks at the negotiations from the French side. In contrast to Hutson, he finds in the comte de Vergennes and his agent, Gérard de Rayneval, an exemplification of the diplomacy of trust that laid the foundation for peace. He argues that while the peace talks can be seen from one perspective as a contest for advantage among the belligerents, they must also be perceived as a struggle between trust and suspicion; bringing them to a successful conclusion required faith between enemies as well as among allies. It was the establishment of this trust, particularly the trust created between Rayneval and Shelburne during the fall of 1782, that broke the deadlock stalling the negotiations and led to the signing of a general armistice in January 1783.

In the next two essays Marcus Cunliffe and Samuel F. Scott explore the cultural and the military impact of the Revolution. Focusing specifically on the literary aftermath of the war, Cunliffe evaluates contemporary British criticisms of

Preface

"the unexciting nature of American cultural accomplishments" in the postwar era and American counterexplanations for the failure of the post-Revolutionary generation to produce literary masterworks. After reviewing the writings of such authors as Joel Barlow, Noah Webster, J. Hector St. John de Crèvecoeur, Philip Freneau, Charles Brockden Brown, Hugh Henry Brackenridge, Tom Paine, and William Wirt, he concludes that their work was indeed a far cry from the "outpouring of literary genius" predicted at the outset of the Revolution and suggests a number of tentative explanations for the slow emergence of "a major 'American' literature."

Scott assesses the influence of the Revolution on the armies of the great European powers between 1783 and 1789. In Prussia, Austria, and Russia, nations committed to the status quo of autocratic political systems and closed social hierarchies, he finds no evidence that the American Revolution had any military impact. Great Britain's military establishment also rejected the lessons of the American war. In France, however, he argues that the general intellectual ferment and a desire for military reform encouraged the utilization of the American experience to produce such developments as a growing interest in light infantry, changes in the organization and composition of the militia, and attempts to create a more able and professional officer corps.

In the following essay, which is closely related in part to James Hutson's, Bradford Perkins finds little justification for the suspiciousness of the American negotiators and critically evaluates the effectiveness of the tactics that it engendered. In a paper that attempts to demythologize the Americans by analyzing their weaknesses and mistakes, he maintains that they were needlessly alarmist and ineffectually guileful. Their excessive suspicion of the British and then of the French led them to delay the negotiations for nearly two months on the questions of Oswald's commission and the recognition of American independence. They were subsequently forced to negotiate, at times unsuccessfully, on issues that they might have avoided such as the debt question and the loyalist claims. Furthermore, he argues that as far as the western lands were concerned, they settled for minimum territorial demands—the areas south of the Great Lakes and east of the Mississippi—when, if they had grasped the implications of the issue and had pressed the negotiations, they could have won the lands north of the lakes and west of the Nipissing line.

In the volume's concluding essay, Richard B. Morris evaluates the treaty more favorably, both in its impact and its durability. Nevertheless, he writes, the treaty itself "was only a piece of paper, and almost every clause in it required explanation, interpretation, and implementation." The substance of his paper deals with the working out, subsequent to the conclusion of the peace, of such issues as trade between Great Britain and the United States, debts, loyalist claims, the northwest posts, the northeastern boundary question, and the fisheries. He applauds the treaty, however, as the document that provided the basis for the creation of the American republic.

PEACE AND THE PEACEMAKERS

The Treaty of 1783

ESMOND WRIGHT

The British
Objectives, 1780–1783
"If Not Dominion
Then Trade"

GIVEN THE HIGHLY personal character of eighteenth-century British politics, it is impossible to separate the treaty process and the British objectives between 1780 and 1783 from the personalities of the peace commissioners and their intermediaries, that curious ragtag army of benevolent philosophers and unsavory secret and double agents who included playwrights, merchants, and flamboyant adventurers. While I will not be assessing the place of personality in the treaty-making process, I do wish at the outset to stress the role of individuals, not all of whom were holders of political office. The peace owed much to the internationally minded Richard Oswald and Benjamin Vaughan, working as much for their apparent enemy as for their country of origin, and to the fact that throughout his years in Paris, Benjamin Franklin had remained in touch with a number of his old British friends and cronies—among them David Hartley, James Hutton, William Hodgson, William Pulteney, and Thomas Walpole, the London banker—when, in the casual manner of eighteenth-century wartime, they visited the French capital. But not only with Franklin's friends was there a divided allegiance. The secretary of the American commission, Edward Bancroft, was in British pay throughout the war, and Silas Deane and William Carmichael (for a time John Jay's secretary) may well have been so also, so that discussion of the peace terms—or of anything else—did not stay secret long.[1]

[1] For an interesting assessment of Carmichael, see Jonathan R. Dull,

3

PEACE AND THE PEACEMAKERS

To these should be added that even less worthy group of characters who apparently had no true allegiance and who existed like mercenaries in the field, only for pay or for rewards such as seats in Parliament: men like Thomas Digges, whom Franklin called "a very great villain," Paul Wentworth the New Hampshire loyalist, and the glib, unreliable Nathaniel Parker Forth. The maneuvers of these secondary figures—the men of the coulisses—are almost as important as the obvious rivalries of Fox and Shelburne or of Franklin, Jay, and Adams.

Given also the alliance of the American colonies-in-rebellion with the old monarchies of France and Spain, it is equally impossible to separate the American treaty process and British objectives from the struggle with France, which after February 1778 had become once again Britain's major enemy, and from the maritime war being fought outside the continental boundaries of North America that was the corollary of that struggle with France. At key points in the two years between Yorktown (October 1781) and the final peace settlement in September 1783, the already confused pattern of negotiations would be suddenly turned topsy-turvy by news of victories or defeats in a theater of war that stretched from the Newfoundland fisheries and the Caribbean to Gibraltar, Minorca, and the Bay of Bengal. The issue of recognizing the independence of the revolted colonies was for Britain only a small part of the problem of the balance of power in Europe, of seapower and the trade it commanded, and indeed of world leadership. The interdependence of the settlement with America and of those with France and Spain favored delay, for who knew what news tomorrow would bring? In diplomacy, unlike love, fortune favors the dilatory.

Clearly it is not easy to give shape and pattern to such a confused tale. Let me try to do so by putting it into a chronological sequence and by outlining and oversimplifying the stages. For reasons of brevity, I will confine my remarks essentially to the period from 1780 to November 1782 and not attempt a total panorama.

Franklin the Diplomat: The French Mission, American Philosophical Society *Transactions* 72 (1982): 38–41.

First, what were Britain's diplomatic objectives *before* York-town? In essence the nation was fighting a colonial rebellion and seeking a return to the status quo. But with France in the war after 1778, what had started as a colonial struggle had become an international conflict. After Saratoga, Sir Jeffery Amherst, the former British commander in chief, estimated that victory in America would require an army of 40,000 men, and, since this was impossible, he recommended a naval war only. The entry of France into the war had driven the British commander in chief in America, Sir Henry Clinton, to evacuate Philadelphia and fall back on New York, and to post 5,000 men to the West Indies and another 3,000 to St. Augustine and West Florida. Lord North's Conciliatory Propositions of February 1778 made a number of surrenders, especially of the right to tax. The Coercive Acts were to be withdrawn and the colonists would be allowed to raise their own revenues, maintain their own army, and, if they chose, keep the Continental Congress in being as a subordinate branch of the imperial Parliament. Furthermore, a commission, headed by the earl of Carlisle but directed in fact by William Eden, was sent to Philadelphia empowered to offer anything short of independence. All that Britain sought to retain was the power to regulate external trade. The commission's arrival was mistimed, however, since by then Clinton was evacuating Philadelphia and the American treaty with France was already signed. Congress refused to negotiate except on a basis of independence and a withdrawal of British forces.

Paradoxically, Britain as negotiator in 1778 was somewhat more fortunate elsewhere than in Philadelphia. Spain had originally hoped to use the war to recover Gibraltar, but without formal participation and without loss of life. The idea in 1778–79 was for Spain to mediate between Britain and France, arranging a truce and being rewarded with Gibraltar. Why should what the Spanish foreign minister, the conde de Floridablanca, called "a pile of stones" separate the two states? Only when Britain refused did Spain sign the Convention of Aranjuez (April 12, 1779), which bound it to an alliance with France. When the British rejected a Spanish ultimatum, the terms of the convention brought Spain into the war (June 21, 1779). In America, Bernardo de Galvez, the energetic governor of Louisiana, pushed the British out of West Florida, captured Mobile and Pensacola, and secured control of the Mississippi River. But the Spanish would not sign a treaty with the Americans. John Jay, sent as American agent to Madrid at the beginning of 1780, became increasingly frustrated. Since Spain would not recognize American independence, Spanish diplomats treated him politely but coolly; only the lice in Spanish inns gave him a warm welcome. In 1780, to his frantic annoyance, the government in Madrid held talks with a British peace mission. The Spanish preference was for an end to the fighting on the basis of uti possidetis: that is, everybody holding on to whatever territory they then occupied. Second, there would be no formal recognition of American independence. Finally, since Spain's concern in North America was to retain control of the Mississippi, the Spanish suggested confining the new nation to the Appalachians as a western boundary. Spain had restive colonies of her own and vast territories, and entertained no sympathy for the cause of colonial revolt. Moreover, Spanish hopes were concentrated on gaining possession of Gibraltar, so Floridablanca's design was to get rid of the American issue in order to pave the way for a settlement with Britain on Spanish terms. The conversations that took place in Madrid—conducted for Britain by Richard Cumberland, and with an Irish priest Thomas Hussey as go-between—broke down in the spring of 1781, however, because of George III's refusal to consider any concessions to his rebellious subjects.[2]

It was not only Spain that was a reluctant ally of the Americans; some Frenchmen were also unenthusiastic about the war. As Richard B. Morris has demonstrated, there was a covert suggestion to Britain in 1780 about a compromise settlement that would have conceded the independence of New England alone. The intermediary was no less than Jacques Necker, the French director-general of finances, who made the approach through a Swiss intermediary to Lord

[2] Sir John Fortescue, ed., *The Correspondence of King George the Third from 1760 to December 1783*, 6 vols. (London, 1927–28), 5:142; also see Samuel Flagg Bemis, *The Hussey-Cumberland Mission and American Independence* (Princeton, 1931).

Mountstuart, the British ambassador at Turin. Necker acted without the knowledge of the comte de Vergennes, the French foreign minister,[3] but George III again turned it down: any notion of independence was still anathema to him—even just the independence of the Boston that had caused all the trouble in the first place.

Meanwhile, for various reasons every nation in Europe was busy calculating how to benefit from the war. Several, in particular Austria and Russia, were willing to act as mediators. Vergennes had given a stony response to the Anglo-Spanish talks, but by the beginning of 1781 he was longing for peace. The war had been going badly almost everywhere. He would recommend one more major campaign, but it was to be the last. If matters did not improve, Vergennes was ready to put forward a scheme similar to the one discussed in Madrid. It would call for a cease-fire, preliminary to a peace treaty, with each side accepting the actual war map as of January 1781. France would appear guilty of bad faith sponsoring such a suggestion, so Vergennes wanted it to come from Austro-Russian mediators, who were to meet in Vienna.

As things turned out, largely because of Yorktown, the Vienna conference never took place, and it remains one of the intriguing might-have-beens of history. The "treaty of Vienna" mediators would, it seems, have recommended a one-year truce, leaving the British in possession of most of Maine, New York City, and Long Island, the coastline and much of the interior of the Carolinas and Georgia, and their forts at Niagara, Detroit, and elsewhere, which dominated the Great Lakes country and the Old Northwest. The empress of Russia, reported Sir James Harris, the British ambassador, was "strongly against the independence of America." In a note dated May 20, 1781, sent to Britain, France, and Spain, but not to the United States, Vergennes outlined a procedure for "negotiation at Vienna." He did not mention the uti possidetis idea, but he did refer to his ally as "the American Colonies," and suggested that Britain and the "colonies" should deal directly with one another. The clear implication was that

[3] Richard B. Morris, *The Peacemakers: The Great Powers and American Independence* (New York, 1965), pp. 88–111.

7

the Americans would not necessarily gain independence, and that no one would intervene to support them.

Coupled with these maneuvers was Vergennes's subtle and effective pressure upon Congress itself during 1781. Conrad Alexandre Gérard had been replaced as French minister to the United States by the chevalier de La Luzerne. La Luzerne was a man of great gifts, and he spread money as well and as lavishly as advice. He boasted to Vergennes that Gen. John Sullivan was in his pocket and that he had handpicked Robert R. Livingston to be secretary for foreign affairs. It was La Luzerne who now sought—unsuccessfully—to sell the idea of dismemberment to members of the Congress. He stressed the French interest in Canada and questioned the American claim to a share of the Newfoundland fisheries.

Thus, whether it was the voice of Sir James Yorke, the British minister at The Hague, or of Sir James Harris in St. Petersburg, or of Lord Stormont in Whitehall, and whether it would be necessary to bribe Russia by offering cash to assist the transport of troops from Siberia to Russian forts in California, and to bribe Austria by supporting the plan to open up the Scheldt—whoever's the voice and whatever the bribes, it seemed clear that America would not get its independence. Or, to use Stormont's words to Simolin, the Russian ambassador in London, just a few days before the news of Yorktown, Britain would not recognize the independence of America until the French took the Tower of London, and she would exchange Gibraltar only for Madrid. When in doubt—it is the oldest trick in the cutting of Gordian knots—when in doubt, partition. It had been good enough for Belgium, Vergennes wrote to La Luzerne in Philadelphia: the Americans must accept it.

The loss of Cornwallis's army of 7,000 men at Yorktown on October 19, 1781, four years to the day after Burgoyne's surrender at Saratoga, ended, it seemed—and it is usually said—any remaining British hopes for outright military victory on the American mainland. Did it end the plan to partition? That it was an outright victory was by no means clear at the time. Word of it, to be sure, came as a shock to Lord North. And the comte de Maurepas, on his deathbed in

Paris, could say, "Now I die content." Congress was swept by a wave of euphoria and thought the war won.

There was, however, no such certainty for George Washington. He still commanded an army short of food, clothing, medical supplies, and ammunition. Fighting continued in the South, and Nathanael Greene, the American commander there, put a blockade round Savannah; some 15,000 loyalists were moving first to Georgia and then, expecting it to remain British, to Florida and safety. In December, George III replaced Sir Henry Clinton with Sir Guy Carleton as commander in chief in America. The king gave no evidence of any change in attitude. "I trust," he wrote, "that neither Lord George Germain nor any member of the Cabinet will suppose that it makes the smallest alteration in those principles of my conduct which have directed me in past time, and which will always continue to animate me under every event in the prosecution of the present contest." Nevertheless, despite Washington's warnings against any relaxation of effort, after Yorktown America became a bystander in the war as news poured in of further British disasters—the loss of St. Eustatius, the Dutch supply point in the Caribbean which Admiral Rodney had captured in 1781; the loss of Nevis, St. Kitts, and Montserrat in the West Indies; and then Minorca. With each loss the ministerial majority in the House of Commons fell, and as Charles Stedman, the contemporary British historian, put it, the war was now "generally disrelished." Only three islands in the West Indies remained to Britain. In this sense Yorktown does represent the end of Stage One of the peacemaking.[4]

Stage Two began in February 1782. Edmund Burke wrote to Franklin, whom earlier he had called "the philosopher, my friend, and the lover of his species," with the news that the House of Commons had, on February 27, approved by nineteen votes Gen. Henry Conway's motion condemning the

[4] Henry B. Wheatley, ed., *The Historical and Posthumous Memoirs of Sir Nathaniel William Wraxall, 1772–1784*, 5 vols. (London, 1884), 2:137–42; Richard Grenville, duke of Buckingham and Chandos, *Memoirs of the Court and Cabinets of George the Third*, 4 vols. (London, 1853–55), 1:23; Morris, *Peacemakers*, pp. 249–53.

"offensive War in America" and calling for direct peace negotiations with "the revolted colonies." "I congratulate you, as the friend of America, I trust, as not the enemy of England; I am sure, as the friend of mankind; on the resolution of the House of Commons, carried by a majority of nineteen at two o'clock this morning, in a very full house. . . . I trust it will lead to a speedy peace between the two branches of the British nation, perhaps to a general peace; and that our happiness may be an introduction to that of the world at large. I most sincerely congratulate you on the event." On March 15 the Government's majority on a direct vote of confidence was down to nine—the country gentlemen at last were turning.[5]

The king's defenses in Parliament were crumbling, or, as the earl of Sandwich put it, "the rats increase." The rats included Burke and Charles James Fox, John Dunning, and now the young William Pitt in the Commons, calling for North's resignation. The earl of Shelburne in the Lords was more cautious; "the Jesuit of Berkeley Square" was still a supporter of the crown and emphasized the importance of timing, of the moment to be seized—the customary language of caution. He would not use a word like *independence*, knowing how much it would irritate the king who was now openly considering abdication and a return to Hanover. Instead he talked of "the two branches of the British nation," but with "one purse and one sword." Confronted with revolution in Ireland as well as in America, he saw that no form of effective association with either an independent North America or with a self-governing Ireland would be possible without a substantial abandonment of mercantilist principles. He had, in other words, become a free trader.

Aware of the immense resources of the North American continent, Shelburne was afraid not only of the colonies' total independence but of their instincts toward republicanism, for he was always a loyal king's man. In this sense he was, in 1782, intellectually where Franklin had been twenty years before. Unlike Fox and the Whigs, he believed that European stability depended on Britain working in alliance with

---

[5] Thomas W. Copeland, ed., *The Correspondence of Edmund Burke*, 10 vols. (Chicago, 1958–78), 4:362, 418–19.

France. As a result, he espoused peace in 1782, but on the basis of the ground possessed. This accorded with the king's views, for at the end of February, George III wrote Lord North that he was now prepared to negotiate peace on the principle of uti possidetis, but would treat only with the separate provinces, to detach them from the alliance with France. The king's position was still rigid, but for the first time he was talking of peace negotiations. George III as well as the House of Commons was weakening.

A few days later, on March 4, Parliament adopted a resolution that all but called for the end of the war and the recognition of the independence of "the revolted colonies." In a desperate move the king sent an envoy to Paris to see Vergennes and formally propose peace "on the ground possessed." Vergennes stiffly replied that Louis XVI would consider an honorable peace only if the British dealt on an equal basis with the ally of France, America. Vergennes's reply left Lord North and the king with no more room for maneuver. On March 20, with the opposition raising a storm in the Commons, North held a last, painful meeting with the king and told him that he now had no choice left but to resign. His ministry had lost all credit, as well as control, in the House.

Even in the final moments of North's government, the British objectives held: if independence, it was to be only on the basis of uti possidetis, and by the separation of one enemy, France, from the other, America. But none of the emissaries employed—the unreliable and bankrupt Thomas Digges to John Adams in Amsterdam, Nathaniel Parker Forth to Vergennes, and Paul Wentworth to The Hague— was held in enough respect to get more than the most cursory of hearings. At this point, however, one of Franklin's many contacts, Lord Cholmondeley, carried a message of greeting and pleasantries from Franklin to Lord Shelburne, not knowing how well-timed it was.

The king, still tempted by the idea of abdication, would not replace Lord North with any of those who had publicly spoken in favor of independence, and so ruled out men like the duke of Richmond or Fox. Fox, in any event, had too much influence over the prince of Wales. The king decided

to turn to Shelburne, who had always—in the imperial tradition of Pitt the Elder—opposed independence, though he
moderated his views under the impact of successive British
defeats. Like Pitt, he was also a believer in the royal prerog-
ative. Shelburne hoped that diplomacy might be able to work
out a compromise that would keep Britain and America
united, under one king, in one empire, but each with its own
sovereign parliament. This would offer America the "Irish
solution," then being negotiated in March of 1782. When
Shelburne became involved in the negotiations, he was emphatic that whatever the outcome——independence or
reunion or the Irish variant, one, two, or even three parlia-
ments—it must not be a disguise for a reemergence of
French colonies in North America, where after all a French
army was being successful. He was aware of the strength of
British feeling against independence and of British concern
over the fate and property of the loyalists. Moreover, if there
was to be a settlement and a genuine reconciliation, Americans and their spokesmen in Paris must appreciate how little
time was available or how few were their sympathizers in Parliament or near the king.

Shelburne hesitated, however, about accepting the king's
offer to head the ministry. He was not a party leader and had
no "connection" to head or with which to bargain. He was by
nature aloof and secretive and took pride in "keeping the
secrets of the King." As a result he had many enemies and
few friends—he was more suitable, perhaps, for diplomacy
than for Parliamentary intrigue. It had been twenty years
since he had sat in the Commons, and he did not sense its
many moods and had few spokesmen there except Isaac
Barré. It would be almost impossible for him to be prime
minister, he explained to the monarch. Instead of himself,
he suggested the name of Rockingham. The marquess of
Rockingham had many friends among the opposition as well
as in the court party. He was the man who, in 1766, had led
the ministry that repealed the Stamp Act and might be favorably remembered by the Americans. George III was cool toward Rockingham, but he finally yielded, on the condition
that Shelburne would accept the portfolio of secretary of
state for Home, Irish, and Colonial Affairs, the key post for

dealing with the Americans so long as they were not independent. This was a revamped edition of the old secretary-ship for the Southern Department. The post of secretary of state for Foreign (that is, European) Affairs—the old North-ern Department—was given to one of the leaders of the opposition, Charles James Fox, who had supported Franklin in his efforts to seek a compromise in 1774–75. Fox favored prompt and unqualified recognition of American independence not only to force France to terms but to give himself control over *all* peacemaking. He saw the administration as having two parts, "one belonging to the King, the other to the public," by which he meant himself; moreover, he intended to give a "good stout blow to the influence of the Crown," that is, Shelburne. Tension between the two men was exacerbated by the fact that while peace with America was Shelburne's province, peace with France was Fox's, and each would have his own agent in the negotiations. Basically the two differed in their views. Fox wanted a peace with America concluded quickly so that France without an ally would make peace—that is, he wished to concede independence and talk later about boundaries, debts, and the loyalists. Fox described himself in a wider setting as Fox Populi—his phrase, not mine—and saw himself in his bibulous moments, which were frequent, as leader of an English revolution on Irish and American lines. To Shelburne in 1781–82 Fox's French policy was defeatism: could independence not be joined with a new Anglo-American accord? As a policy this duality was a guarantee of confusion and, in the end, of chaos.

George III continued to consult regularly with Shelburne, instead of his prime minister, giving Shelburne tremendous power without the burden of being the chief executive of the government. This closeness to the king nourished the suspicion of Shelburne that, in the end, destroyed his career. Shelburne for his part lost no time in answering Franklin's friendly letter. He had been waiting for it and was ready to respond by sending an agent to talk to Franklin. Simultaneously, he selected another agent to meet with John Adams in Holland, for British spies had reported that Adams was willing to talk confidentially with the British about a separate peace. Shelburne's emissary to Adams was none other than Henry Laurens, the American peace commissioner released from the Tower and on parole in London.

To meet with Franklin, Shelburne chose a Scottish merchant, Richard Oswald, who had made a fortune in the slave trade and as a commissary to Brunswick's army as long ago as 1756–57—Oswald at seventy-six was a year older than Franklin. Through his wife, the only daughter and heiress of Alexander Ramsey of Jamaica, he had estates and relatives in North America and the West Indies. Oswald had had an American agent for that trade (a thirty-year-old acquaintanceship), to whom he had paid a 10 percent commission on each cargo of slaves: none other again than the same Henry Laurens. For this was a small world. He stood bail for £50,000 for Laurens's release from the Tower. Oswald was also a friend of the economist Adam Smith, was familiar with Smith's work and with the writings of the physiocrats of Paris, and was felt to be the ideal man to sound out Franklin. It was Adam Smith, in fact, who first introduced Oswald to Shelburne. Oswald's strengths were that he was honest, old, with no ambitions, and an open admirer of Franklin. His weakness was that he was totally unversed in diplomacy; he had quixotic notions, like an alliance with Russia, that would allow Russian troops to garrison New York and would reward Russia with bits of California and Mexico, not a policy attractive to Spain. According to Vincent Harlow, his importance in shaping the settlement between Britain and the United States has been greatly exaggerated. Oswald was unusually sympathetic to American propositions. His ideas about the strategy of the peace negotiations are revealed in an undated memorandum to Shelburne written about this time. "I always supposed we must satisfy the Americans," he wrote, "in such a manner as to have a chance of soothing them into neutrality." If the colonies could be satisfied by a grant of independence, then Oswald "submitted to better judges whether it ought not to be done without delay as an introductive preliminary to a general peace." Thus the gratitude of the Americans would be "brought to trial." Then it would be seen whether they would stand by their allies or drop out of the war, allowing Britain to turn all its force against the three remaining belligerents. The first order of business, Oswald advised, was to sound out the American commissioners to find out how they stood on a separate peace.[6]

Nevertheless, Oswald was more than a mere intermediary. He told Franklin what he thought would be acceptable. He played down Shelburne's preference for an America divided into north and south and moderated a number of Shelburne's assertions—for example, that he would never give up the loyalists (a point on which Franklin felt especially strongly), that British ships should be allowed to trade with every port in America as in the past, and that America must end all connection with France.

It was Oswald's free trade sentiments that brought him close to Franklin—if America were independent, British trade would profit. It was commercial empire, not territorial jurisdiction, that mattered to the liberals. In his Journal entry of May 6, 1782, Oswald set down his private opinion on the subject. Had he been an American, he declared, he would have insisted for the sake of future peace that all the settled parts of the continent, including Canada, Nova Scotia, Newfoundland, and East Florida, must "be brought under the cover of one and the same political constitution." This was the major step: from partition and from the loose ties of continuing political association to, now, independence. As for the thirteen colonies—"The more these States extend themselves in Population and Cultivation, the better it will be for England. While they have such immense expansion of vacant Lands behind them to be taken into Appropriation at almost no expense, they will never become Manufacturers. . . . the States will, therefore, for Centuries to come, continue extending themselves backwards, and according as they produce, they will consume and be in a condition to pay for the material of consumption . . . so that a Nation who has a free and safe access to their Ports . . . will never fail to profit by their Correspondence."[7] Great Britain and Ireland were

---

[6] Vincent T. Harlow, *The Founding of the Second British Empire, 1763–1793*, 2 vols. (London, 1952–64), 1:245–46; Morris, *Peacemakers*, pp. 248–81.

[7] Richard Oswald, Journal, F.O. 95/511, no. 4 and no. 7, Public Record Office.

ideally situated for this purpose. The loss of the thirteen colonies was "of no great consequence," provided that in separating from the mother country they did not continue in a political confederation. In that event an American Congress would be able to direct their naval power, which could be a threat to Britain. This ultimately became Shelburne's policy, and from it came a total independence for the new United States. Franklin noted in his Journal of Negotiation for Peace on April 15:

> All I could learn was that the new ministry sincerely wished for peace; that they considered the object of the war, to France and America, as obtained; that if the independence of the United States was agreed to, there was no other point in dispute, and therefore nothing to hinder a pacification; that they were ready to treat of peace, but he [Oswald] intimated that if France should insist upon terms too humiliating to England, they would still continue the war, having yet great strength and many resources left. I let him know that America would not treat but in concert with France, and that, my colleagues not being here, I could do nothing of importance in the affair; but that, if he pleased, I would present him to M. de Vergennes, Secretary of State for Foreign Affairs.[8]

Almost to the end Franklin kept Vergennes informed of his discussions. He recounted the earlier visit of Lord Cholmondeley, then the letters from Shelburne and Laurens introducing Oswald. He loyally and fully summarized his entire talk with Oswald. Any move toward a separate peace or any division would sabotage the alliance and risk losing all that had been won.

On April 18 Oswald came to Passy to join Franklin for a trip to Versailles to open conversations with Vergennes. Vergennes told Oswald exactly what Franklin had told him, that the allies would not deal separately and would not negotiate anything but a general peace for all parties. Through Oswald, Franklin stressed, first, that the Americans were officially accredited to talk of peace and that Oswald should be

[8] Albert Henry Smyth, ed., *The Writings of Benjamin Franklin*, 10 vols. (New York, 1905–7), 8:463.

so accredited by the British government to enter specific negotiations, and, second, that peace must be founded on genuine reconciliation, which, in turn, should be based on fair and just reparations for injuries and losses suffered. As evidence of this he appealed for exchanges of prisoners—not a new theme with him—and he even pressed the hope of the cession of Canada. He reminded Oswald of a previous conversation in which Oswald had remarked that it had been politic of France to cede Canada to Britain in the peace after the Seven Years' War. Would it not now, asked Franklin, be politic of Britain to return this favor to America? Franklin felt that Oswald had been "much struck with my discourse." It was, to be sure, a very curious suggestion since he knew of the continuing French interest in Canada and he knew that Vergennes was opposed to the American acquisition of what had been a French province. If the Vienna arbitration had come off, it was France that might have retained Canada. The Old Magician had limits to his loyalty; Britain might be wise to be generous.

At the same time he was approaching Franklin through Oswald, Shelburne sent instructions to Sir Guy Carleton, his commander in chief in America, and to Adm. Robert Digby, his naval commander, to try their luck in direct negotiations with George Washington, Congress, and the governors of the thirteen states. They received their instructions on April 4, within days of Oswald's memorandum to Shelburne underlining the purposes of these moves: "I always supposed we must satisfy the Americans in such a manner as to have a chance of soothing them into neutrality." There was here a sad illusion that he was still seen in America as the liberal he perceived himself to be, an illusion that Henry Laurens never shared. As the latter wrote to Vergennes, he need have no worries, "Leur ancienne popularité n'existe plus dans ce pays." In any event General Carleton sent a messenger to Washington, bearing copies of the resolution of the House of Commons in favor of peace and independence. He proposed a simple armistice on land warfare along the Atlantic coast settlements. This would, of course, leave the British free to conduct naval warfare, to seek out and destroy the French fleet, and to remain in control of American waters.

Washington would not hear of any separate British-American agreement, let alone what Carleton was proposing. He refused to send the British dispatch on to the Congress or to engage in a one-sided truce. Congress, for its part, passed a resolution condemning the "insidious steps which the Court of London is proposing." Carleton came back to Washington again, promising that American independence would be recognized by Britain "in the first instance" and informing him that negotiations for peace with France were already underway. But Washington and Congress saw through this as completely as they had the first time. They let it be known, without ambiguity, that all negotiations would be carried on in Paris, with the American peace commissioners working loyally with the French.

If it had to be a concession of independence, Shelburne believed that it should be done generously by Britain so that there might be in return a possibility of federal transatlantic union facilitating free trade. Behind the liberal spirit, however, there was a British caution: America must—by persuasion or by territorial concessions—be kept out of the grip of France, and the final shape of the treaty must be drawn while Shelburne himself was in a position to get it through Parliament.

On April 23 the cabinet decided to send Richard Oswald back to Paris with authority to name that city as the place for holding the peace negotiations and to set a timetable with Franklin for the start of the negotiations. Oswald was instructed "to represent to him that the principal points in contemplation are the allowance of independence to America, upon Great Britain being restored to the situation she was placed in by the Treaty of 1763." On the other hand, the cabinet refrained from conferring plenipotentiary powers upon Oswald and instead authorized Charles James Fox as foreign secretary to propose to the king a person who would begin direct negotiations with Vergennes. The king, who thoroughly agreed with Shelburne on the necessity of having Oswald in Paris as "a useful check on that part of the negotiation that is in other hands," approved the letter the Scot was to take to Franklin. The king even indicated that it would be proper for Shelburne to talk with Fox's emissary to Vergennes. Oswald returned to Paris on May 4 and, to Franklin's surprise, did not carry precise terms of peace but instead conveyed a letter from Shelburne that merely confirmed that the Scot was to settle with Franklin "the preliminaries of time and place," and informed the doctor that the foreign secretary would soon send over a "proper person" to confer with Vergennes. Then he added a note that Franklin instantly recognized as a major tactic to separate the French and the Americans. He said that the peace would be based on "the allowing of American independence, on condition that England be put into the same situation that she was left by the peace of 1763." He also reported that Thomas Grenville, son of the former chancellor of the Exchequer, was coming over to Paris as Fox's agent.

Franklin, behind his disappointment, found Grenville to be "a sensible, judicious, intelligent, good-tempered and well-instructed young man." Grenville was, of course, Fox's man. To the duc de Lauzun, Fox had made a pious profession of peace, writing, "Please God that it is near." Fox had instructed his envoy to name Paris for the peace talks, provided Vienna and Petersburg would not be offended. Grenville was to use his discretion in stating peace terms and was to be prepared to accede to the "complete independency of the Thirteen American states," including the cession of New York, Charleston, and the entire province of Georgia. Otherwise matters were to be restored to the situation as it obtained under the Treaty of Paris of 1763. In addition, he was told to sound out Franklin on the chances for a separate peace with America should the general negotiations be broken off, as "his countrymen" would then "be engaged in a war" in which they could have "no interest whatever either immediate or remote." Central to the peacemaking of 1782 and 1783 was this anti-Bourbon position of the Foxite Whigs, and central to understanding the confused negotiations is the question whether the recognition of American independence should be part of the treaty with France or be separately negotiated and conceded. France wanted it to appear a gift from herself and to limit its extent within the Allegheny Mountains, so that Canada might be French and the valley of the Mississippi, Spanish. To the British negotiators the western boundary would be the Mississippi and would thus include what Britain had acquired from France in 1763, with the exception of Canada, which would remain British. And there were other thorny problems to be settled: northern and southern boundaries and the claims of merchants and of loyalists.

To Vergennes, when they met on May 9, Grenville said that, with Britain conceding America its independence, France was expected to restore the conquests she had made of British islands and receive back her own islands of St. Pierre and Miquelon, two tiny fishing posts off the coast of Canada. It was, as a result, a cool meeting. After receiving Grenville's report, the British cabinet agreed on May 18 to vest him with full powers to negotiate a peace on the basis of the Treaty of Paris and American independence.

At this point the British argument was strengthened, for on May 18 news reached London from Rodney's fleet in the West Indies. The British caught up with the French on April 12 off the Saintes, an island group lying between Guadeloupe and Santo Domingo. Seven French battleships were captured. The single greatest French loss was the capture of Admiral de Grasse himself and his 110-gun flagship, the *Ville de Paris*. Britain regained the control of the Atlantic she had lost in 1781. She still held New York and Charleston. The defeat made France a good deal more tractable in the peace talks and made Franklin's negotiating position easier, for Vergennes had had the idea of using this peace treaty to undo some of the losses sustained to Britain in the treaty of 1763, particularly in Africa and Asia. After the Battle of the Saintes, Vergennes abandoned that idea and laid down no more demands that it would have been difficult for Franklin to support.

Twenty years before, such a victory would have led Pitt the Elder to abandon all peace negotiations—had he ever begun them. On this occasion, however, while the victory strengthened the British negotiators, it was not fully exploited, since the negotiators formed two distinct teams, each answerable to distinct leaders. Fox wanted his man Grenville to be in sole charge, and he wanted him to be empowered "to propose the independence of America in the first instance instead of making it a condition of a general treaty." The cabinet, how-ever, impressed by the ease of the Oswald-Franklin relation-ship, thought it unwise not to send Oswald back—that is, it preferred to pursue Fox's policy but through Shelburne's man. Indeed, Shelburne's private briefing of Oswald stressed "the propriety of making Peace either general or separate the price of Independence," and the king was assured that only by paying such an awful price—the concession of inde-pendence—would peace be secured. Grenville for his part sought a negotiation with France that would omit all refer-ence to the United States. When he heard Oswald refer to Franklin's pressing upon Shelburne the case for the cession of Canada—always a theme of Franklin's and not entirely playful—he voiced to his master, Fox, his suspicions that Os-wald was, in fact, dealing secretly, and by Shelburne's direc-tion behind his back, with Franklin. Fox's suspicions of his colleague hardly needed this further fostering.

Toward the end of May, Grenville called on Franklin to say that he had received full powers to deal on peace terms with France and her allies. France, however, would have to agree to send a minister with the same powers to London. Accord-ing to Vergennes, Grenville had presented his official powers and they had related only to France, with no mention of the United States. Vergennes had coldly informed Grenville that France would not treat for the United States and that the Briton must have official powers to negotiate with Franklin or there would be no negotiations. Ally was—it seemed—totally loyal to ally.

Grenville came to see Franklin on Saturday, June 1. He revealed to Franklin secret instructions he had received to acknowledge the independence of America unconditionally *before* the commencement of a peace conference. He argued that, France being America's only treaty ally, America was under no obligation to coordinate its peace aims with those of Spain or Holland, the other belligerents. He pointed out that it would make things difficult for Britain if it had to sat-isfy in turn each of four belligerents, each of them holding out until all four got the terms they wanted. When they met on June 3, Franklin told Oswald, as he had already men-tioned on several occasions to Grenville, that "the best way to come at a general peace, was to treat separately with each party, and under distinct commissions to one and the same, or different persons."

By mid-June, Fox was on the verge of a dangerous course that was quite out of line with cabinet policy. He was ready to grant American independence even without a treaty of peace, which would have produced dangers of mental imbalance in the king and in any case ran counter to Britain's renewed strength at sea. He wanted total control of the peace negotiations. He was about to resign office when again events took command and gave him no alternative. Lord Rockingham, never robust, died on July 1, 1782, in the influenza epidemic. The king promptly appointed Shelburne first lord of the Treasury; Shelburne's hour had come, for the cabinet was loyal to him. Fox thereupon resigned, and the twenty-two-year-old William Pitt became chancellor of the Exchequer. So, reluctantly but at last firmly, Shelburne abandoned his hopes of reunion with America. If independence was to be granted—and to be a secure independence—it would be done generously. The treaty had of course to be approved by the House of Commons and so there would need to be concessions by America: discussion was thus prolonged on indemnification for property confiscated and on debts due to merchants; indeed the British efforts on behalf of the loyalists almost brought the negotiations to an end. But Shelburne's objective was now clear.

In July 1782 he expressed it clearly: "I have never made a Secret of the deep concern I feel in the Separation of Countries united by Blood, by Principles, Habits, and every tie short of Territorial Proximity. But you very well know that I have long since given it up *decidedly* tho' *reluctantly*: and the same motives which made me perhaps the last to give up all Hope of Reunion, make me most anxious, if it is given up, that it should be done *decidedly*, so as to avoid all future Risque of Enmity, and lay the Foundation of a new Connection better adapted to the present Temper and the Interest of both Countries."[9]

[9] Also see the variant reading in Fortescue, ed., *Correspondence of George the Third*, 6:91.

External events still favored Britain—by mid-October came the news of the relief of Gibraltar—but now it was too late. The outcome of the negotiations, reached by the end of October, was a host of compromises. On paper at least the American delegates accepted responsibility for repaying debts due to British subjects. On the fisheries question Henry Strachey and Oswald went beyond their instructions and conceded the "Liberty" to dry and cure fish in the "unsettled parts" of the Magdalene Islands and Labrador; they also granted freedom to fish off the Newfoundland Banks, in the Gulf of St. Lawrence, and all other places where the inhabitants of both countries had been in the habit of fishing. The boundary question was deferred for a later commission, but confusion reigned for two generations over the St. Croix boundary in the north and over that of Florida and the Yazoo in the south. As to the loyalists, Article VI promised an end to prosecutions and confiscations, but the initiative lay with the states; all that Congress would be asked to do was "earnestly recommend" to the legislatures of the individual American states the restitution of confiscated estates and property. Both parties were aware that this provision was worth very little. It owed much to the compromising skills of Oswald, once again very lenient toward the "enemy," and Franklin's bitterness over loyalism.

The Preliminary Treaty of peace with America, or more accurately "the treaty of peace proposed to be concluded" (November 1782), was thus Shelburne's, Oswald's—and Franklin's—handiwork and was in being before Shelburne's fall in February 1783 to the infamous Fox-North coalition. Indeed, its date was primarily due to Shelburne's party and Parliamentary weakness: he wanted it through before Parliament convened, a date originally set at November 26 but delayed until December 5. He well knew that then his real trial would come, as indeed it did. To meet it, he insisted on holding on to Gibraltar, at Florida's—and the loyalists'—expense.

There is a certain continuity in all political operations. I was for three-and-one-half years a member of Parliament as a Conservative, not in the 1780s but in the mid-1960s, and was waiting to be called to make my maiden speech. I was quietly rehearsing my remarks to Selwyn Lloyd, my next-door neighbor, and said, looking at the Labour benches opposite, "The enemy." He said: "No, Esmond. The gentlemen on the other side are your political opponents. Your enemies you will find on your own side of the House." Shelburne could have said it too.

This would seem to be the place and the time, November 30, 1782, to end this scene setting. Four Americans and an elderly Scot signed their names to a preliminary treaty. Its terms had to be approved by two governments and by America's French ally; and, for it to be binding, Britain had also to make a separate settlement with France as well as with Spain. Congress did not receive the document until March 13, 1783, and ratified it on April 15. The agreed treaty was signed in Paris on September 3 before going back to the United States for a formal ratification by the Continental Congress on January 14, 1784. By that time Shelburne had been out of office eleven months. He had had only eight months at the top, and for more than half of them Parliament had not been in session. He did, however, use it decisively. The United States emerged, however federal in its thinking, a single undivided state, "free, Sovereign and independent," from the Mississippi to the fishing grounds off Nova Scotia and Newfoundland, from the Great Lakes to the northern boundary of Florida (which Britain did now return to Spain) but without any definition of where those boundaries were. The United States had conceded the right to fish in Canadian waters, and off the Newfoundland banks as "heretofore," and British subjects were to share with Americans the right to navigate the Mississippi. The settlement all but ignored the claims of Britain's Indian allies and white loyalists, although it was left to the thirteen state legislatures to treat the loyalists fairly. America, in other words, got almost everything it sought. The king declared a holiday and asked for prayers of thanksgiving for peace. Vergennes could not comprehend the reasons for British generosity. There was dancing in the streets of Paris.

There is in history, or at least in chronology, no inherent logic—or justice. If Shelburne was, on the British side, the author of the treaty of 1783, it was in the final stages David Hartley's achievement as Fox's emissary in Paris. And Fox was Lord North's mischievous ally, taking over in April 1783, and not then, if ever, the liberal of the Whig mythology. He defeated the American Intercourse Bill and Shelburne's dreams. He had not, it is assumed, read Adam Smith.[10] By 1783 opinion was being made by Lord Sheffield's nationalistic tract *Observations on the Commerce of the American States.* Big concessions in territory were made to the new republic, but the United States was outside the empire and would be firmly excluded from the carrying trade to the British West Indies (Order in Council, July 2, 1783). It was that empire of the seas, not least the Caribbean and Newfoundland, with its fish and its role as nursery of seamen, that still mattered. If the future lay with an industrial Britain dominating the Seven Seas, its prosperity and security both in the eighteenth and nineteenth centuries depended on its naval predominance; nationalism *and* mercantilism in 1783 were still powerful forces. And Shelburne never became the hero of the story, liberal though his views had been both in 1763 and in 1782. It is never wise—at least politically—to acquire a reputation for indecisiveness or to be associated with what critics could describe as a national humiliation.

What conclusions arise? Government was royal. Britain, which meant the king, was reluctant to make peace with the colonies. Even as late as Yorktown, the objective was to avoid independence, and to try either by "Vienna's" intervention or by Spain's to settle for a smaller United States, for a continent divided. And this in the knowledge that both France and Spain, one with interest in the St. Lawrence and the other with ambitions in the west, would prefer a smaller American republic to a vast new society. Gibraltar mattered—mattered more than Florida—and to secure the former meant abandoning the latter and the 10,000 or more loyalists streaming there in 1782 and 1783 in the pathetic belief that they would be safe. The news that Gibraltar was still British came just too late to harden Oswald's stance. France was still the real enemy. Certainly, to quote the Amer-

[10] Charles R. Ritcheson, *Aftermath of Revolution: British Policy toward the United States, 1783–1795* (Dallas, 1969), p. 7.

ican commander in chief who was to become the first president of a great and federal republic, speaking on the eighth
anniversary of Lexington, a "stupendous fabric of freedom
and empire" would arise on "the broad basis of independency." Yet it owed its origins to the world of the old diplomacy. Spain in the end kept the Floridas and Minorca and
for the next twelve years controlled the mouth of the Mississippi. Britain retained Gibraltar and doubled her national
debt. France acquired a few West Indian islands, the prestige
of defeating the old enemy and dividing the English-
speaking world—and a condition of near-bankruptcy that
would bring a real revolution in its train.

But, royal in form and European in its primary objectives,
British government was also parliamentary. There fell on
whoever was primus in that Parliament an appallingly intri-
cate task. However willing in the end Shelburne was to accept
American independence—his phrase to Franklin in August
was "the most unequivocal Acknowledgement of American
Independency"—he had to play the role of parliamentary
juggler, a role in which he was inept. Though by nature more
courtier than combatant, he found it difficult (as he told Gérard de Rayneval) to talk to the king. As a later and more
skillful prime minister put it, in talking to royalty it was essential to lay flattery on with a trowel. The king had to be
told that his resources were infinite and that France was on
the edge of collapse, but in the end it might yet be necessary
to concede independence to the Americans. As late as September 1782 his language to the king was still dexterous and
even evasive of the central issue. "As to the General Measure," he wrote on September 15, "I am as clearly of opinion
against a Peace as I ever was against American Independence, till in fact the Resolutions of the House of Commons
decided the point. I am very clear that Your Majesty has
within Your Dominions Resources of every kind, if they be
brought forth. But Your Majesty knows, what I am mortify'd
to allude to, better than any of your subjects, the State of
both Army and Navy; the few subjects capable of supplying
what is wanted in regard to both Services; the State of Ireland and that of the House of Commons." He remained to

the end the courtier and the diplomat, not the parliamentary leader.[11]

There is, I think, yet another conclusion. Clearly the individual negotiators were of major importance—but I leave it to others to make the point. They mattered, however, because through the long years of war, many of them as Franklin's friends kept in touch with him, and in this sense the treaty was, first and last, his achievement, as Jonathan R. Dull has demonstrated.[12] All of his contacts in the House of Commons were men interested in power. Shelburne skated dexterously around the king's unwillingness to accept American independence. Others like Fox were, behind the liberal talk, men greedy for place and power. What in the end made a treaty possible was the broad acceptance of those principles of free trade that all of the actual negotiators—particularly Franklin, Shelburne, Oswald, and Vaughan—shared.[13] They were ready to admit an American independence, even of a continental America, because they believed that it would be good for Britain, who could trade as easily and profitably with a politically independent America as with her colonies of twenty years before. Shelburne and Oswald, as Adam Smith's men, knew this too. They believed that, given free trade, given American industrial backwardness and its dependence still on British manufacturers, there would still be a transatlantic world of trade and prosperity, even if no longer a unified world in politics. And in this, though they could not foresee Napoleon, they were right, as Lord Shef-

---

[11] Fortescue, ed., *Correspondence of George the Third*, 6:125.

[12] Dull, *Franklin the Diplomat.*

[13] Vaughan is as interesting as Oswald, and his choice indicated both Shelburne's skill in selecting agents and the extensive nature of the Anglo-American network. Born in Jamaica of a planter father and a Bostonian mother, educated as a Nonconformist and at Cambridge, a distant relative of Laurens and an editor of Franklin's writings, he was tailor-made. He was still a believer in Anglo-American union, from circumstances of birth as well as radical conviction. But—like his mentor—he had few friends and won little approval. To Oswald he was an officious busybody. He would end his days in Maine, but only after a spell in a French jail during the Revolution.

field was not. They preferred, in Shelburne's phrase, "trade to dominion." But, thanks to Napoleon and despite the American war and its losses, by 1815 a powerful British trading empire would reemerge almost as if the loss of her American colonies really did not matter after all.

In the end the terms were remarkably generous, as Vergennes noted. They were the result, not of the French alliance, but of British generosity. They were much more generous than either France or Spain would have wished, with the loyalists and the idea of partition abandoned, and the states not only free and independent but stretching from the Canadian border to Georgia. Shelburne had dreamed of a continuing relationship based on the ties of blood, trade, and strategy. Whether politically linked or not, what mattered was that there must be no links between the Americas and France. As he told Rayneval in their near-frank exchanges at Bowood in September 1782, it was Europe that was primary to both of them.

To put it cynically, the opening words of the final treaty of peace are "In the name of the most Holy but Undivided Trinity," yet Shelburne said that only three people mattered in making the peace, and he meant Vergennes, himself, and Rayneval as their mediator. This, as he knew, flattered the third. Despite the European-centeredness of Shelburne, the effective trio were Franklin, Oswald, and Shelburne, a far from holy and very divided trinity. What really consolidated the terms of the Treaty of Paris and averted a renewal of French and Spanish ambitions in the Mississippi Valley and the St. Lawrence that would have blocked American expansion west was the growing weakness of the French government and the dramatic coming of the French Revolution and Napoleon. For twenty-two years, 1793–1815, Britain and France were wholly preoccupied with their renewed rivalry in war. But to an independent America there was now offered, not burden and bloodshed, but opportunity. Out of these long years of almost undisturbed development emerged a totally free and greatly augmented United States, with the Louisiana Purchase giving her almost unlimited access to the West and the French menace permanently removed, and for Britain a new trading empire, worldwide, and such dominion over the seas as no other power had ever enjoyed. But it was, unfortunately, an empire without America.

GREGG L. LINT

Preparing for Peace
The Objectives of
the United States,
France, and Spain in
the War of the
American Revolution

THE WAR OF the American Revolution was a conflict between the Old World and the New. It was, of course, primarily a struggle by the American colonies to achieve confirmation of their independence from Great Britain. But it was also a struggle by the Americans to obtain a peace treaty achieving objectives that were, in some cases, at odds with those of France and Spain. In an examination of this tripartite conflict among the United States, France, and Spain, the goals of each party must first be defined and then the differing perceptions of the path to peace explored.

The accurate determination of national objectives, here, peace objectives, is a difficult process for the historian. One must identify the individuals or groups he believes to have been the most instrumental in determining foreign policy, and upon that basis define what he perceives to have been the interest of a given nation at a specific time. This is a subjective process, however, and the question arises whether the definition is truly representative of the national interest or is only the view of a relatively small elite.

For France and Spain this task is made easier because both

countries were relatively unified and homogeneous. Their policies were rooted in the past and were largely aimed at reversing their present circumstances and restoring faded glory. There was little new in either their objectives or the means by which they were to be achieved. Moreover, the two foreign ministers, the comte de Vergennes and the conde de Floridablanca, were essentially the sole enunciators of foreign policy, and even if they occasionally resorted to questionable justifications for their policies, it was still clear what they believed their ultimate objectives to be.

With the United States the undertaking is more difficult. Representing thirteen independent states, the members of the Continental Congress were themselves divided on foreign policy. A vital objective to one section or interest group was unimportant to another, and thus the peace ultimatums adopted by Congress were the product of compromise. This situation was complicated by the fact that it would not be Congress that negotiated the peace but rather its peace commissioners, 3,000 miles away and far more aware of the realities of and opportunities presented by the European political situation. Thus a second set of objectives, those of the commissioners, came to equal and then surpass in importance those of the Congress, a result of both the disorderly (when compared with the French or Spanish) American political system and the decision to negotiate in Europe. It was a situation which France did not take into consideration but which ultimately became the decisive factor in the peace negotiations.

The Declaration of Independence asserted that the United States was an independent, sovereign state. To this extent, independence itself was not an issue for Americans or, in a strict sense, an objective to be achieved in the peace. It was as true for Americans in 1776 as it was for John Adams in 1781 that "there are no 'American Colonies' at war with Great Britain. The power at war is the United States of America. No American Colonies have any representatives in Europe, unless Nova Scotia, or Quebec, or some West Indian Islands may have an agent in London."[1] The basic issue of the An-

[1] "Answer of the Minister Plenipotentiary of the United States to the

glo-American war for the United States became, therefore, not the achievement, but rather the confirmation of independence and thus the legitimacy of the new American government. This was to be achieved, first, by the agreement of Britain to treat with American negotiators as representatives of a sovereign state and, second, by a precise statement acknowledging that condition in a treaty of peace. Although a fine point, it was of fundamental importance and was recognized as such by the Continental Congress in its responses to the Howe and Carlisle peace commissions and in its instructions to the American peace commissioners. Despite the fact that it was later modified in response to the pressures of war on alliance politics, it was upon that basis that the treaty of 1783 was concluded.

Except for this political decision concerning the basis upon which negotiations could begin, the Continental Congress made no formal attempt to define its objectives before February 1779. This was true even for such fundamental issues as boundaries. Before the conclusion of the Franco-American treaties in 1778, this was probably due to the assumption that peace negotiations would take place in America and that when they began Congress could respond directly. It may also reflect a reluctance to raise issues that would divide Congress along sectional lines, as happened with the Newfoundland fisheries. With the conclusion of the alliance, however, it became clear that the treaty would be negotiated in Europe by peace commissioners named by Congress and that, accordingly, the American peace ultimatums would have to be defined in advance.

Despite the new situation, Congress might not have undertaken the task even then without French intervention. In October 1778 Vergennes instructed Conrad Alexandre Gérard to press for congressional action and outlined his position on the various American objectives then being informally discussed. Gérard placed the demand before Congress in his

Articles to Serve as a Basis to the Negotiations for the Re-establishment of Peace," enclosed in John Adams to the comte de Vergennes, July 13, 1781, Francis Wharton, ed., *The Revolutionary Diplomatic Correspondence of the United States*, 6 vols. (Washington, D.C., 1889), 4:571–73.

letter of February 9, 1779.[2] Ostensibly, Gérard's request reflected France's desire that the United States be prepared for negotiations in the event that the then ongoing Spanish mediation effort succeeded. There was, however, another motive: France wished to limit American objectives in order to bring them into line with her own and to remove obstacles to Spain's entry into the war.

As presented to Congress, the Spanish mediation became a straw man. In October 1778, when the instructions under which Gérard acted were composed, Vergennes could have had few illusions about the probable success of the Spanish effort or that a favorable outcome was likely to be in the French interest.[3] From Vergennes's point of view the mediation was important as a means to force Congress to draw up a formal set of ultimatums; these, unlike the various unofficial American objectives, would be amenable to French influence and binding on Congress.

From the standpoint of American interests, Congress was in a poor position to undertake a formal consideration of peace terms on the expectation that they would be used in negotiations resulting from the mediation. None of the letters from the American commissioners in Europe had mentioned the Spanish effort, much less its chances for success.[4] Congress was thus forced to rely on information provided by

[2] Conrad Alexandre Gérard to the president of Congress, Feb. 9, 1779, ibid., 3:39–40.

[3] Vergennes to Gérard, Oct. 26, 1778, John J. Meng, ed., *Despatches and Instructions of Conrad Alexandre Gérard, 1778–1780* (Baltimore, 1939), pp. 355–62.

[4] See letters from Benjamin Franklin, Arthur Lee, and Adams, as joint commissioners and as individuals, to the president of Congress and the Committee for Foreign Affairs between April 1778 and February 1779 in Wharton, ed., *Revolutionary Diplomatic Correspondence*, vols. 2 and 3. The first word that Congress received concerning the mediation from any of its representatives in Europe was Franklin's letter to the Committee for Foreign Affairs of May 26 (ibid., 3:195). Franklin, however, had been aware of the mediation since at least December 1778, when he had been consulted by Vergennes concerning the Spanish proposal of a long truce. Franklin's opinion had been that it would be acceptable to Congress (Meng, ed., *Despatches of Gérard*, p. 451).

Gérard. One is struck by the confidence of many members of Congress in the ultimate success of the Spanish effort and their belief that any delay in establishing ultimatums would unnecessarily prolong the war, all seemingly based on the information supplied by the French minister with no confirmation from their own commissioners.

On February 23, 1779, a congressional committee presented a draft report on American peace objectives that, in light of later changes, represents the most determined effort by that body to serve the fundamental interests of the United States. The report declared that the United States was not to join the mediation without a prior acknowledgment of independence by Britain. Negotiations could then proceed with the American commissioners insisting on boundaries extending north to Canada and including the portion of present-day Ontario between Lakes Ontario and Huron, west to the Mississippi, and south to the Floridas; evacuation of all places held by British forces; acknowledgment of American fishing rights on the Grand Banks; free commerce to some port on the Mississippi south of the boundary; and, if its allies would support it by continuing hostilities, the cession or independence of Nova Scotia. Nova Scotia could be given up if the fisheries could not be otherwise obtained; if neither could be achieved, then Bermuda was to be claimed. The report also provided that if adequate compensation was made, the United States would not engage in trade with the East Indies or in slaves, would not allow settlement beyond the treaty boundaries, would cede Florida to Spain if ceded to the United States by Britain, and would enter into a reciprocal guarantee of possessions. It would not agree to a truce except during the negotiations.[5]

Except for the portion dealing with British recognition of American independence, these objectives were in conflict with those of France and Spain. The basic problems concerned Canada, the Newfoundland fishery, and western boundaries, none of which were explicitly dealt with in the treaties of 1778. The French position was made clear on May

[5] Worthington C. Ford et al., eds., *Journals of the Continental Congress, 1774–1789*, 34 vols. (Washington, D.C., 1904–37), 13:239–44.

22, 1779, when Gérard informed Congress that France was committed only to the achievement of British recognition of American independence and would not prolong the war to achieve ends not specifically mentioned in the Franco-American treaties. He added that the boundaries could not be settled until the final peace treaty, and thus the French guarantee of American territory could not come into force until such time as peace was concluded.[6]

There had been an awareness of the probable conflict between French and American objectives long before Congress formally defined the latter in 1779. In a memorandum written in April 1776, Vergennes stated that it was "very probable that as a result of events we could recover a part of the possessions which England took away from us in America, such as the shore fishery, that of the Gulf of St. Lawrence, Cape Breton Island, etc. etc. We are not speaking of Canada."[7] Vergennes could renounce Canada because France lacked the resources to regain it, the general belief that the economic return was not worth the effort of reconquest, and the knowledge that such an undertaking would alienate the Americans. A formal renunciation was proposed by the United States in the Model Treaty, or treaty plan, of 1776 and was accepted by France in the alliance of 1778.[8]

For the United States this was an important concession. Canada had long been a major American goal, as was indicated by the unsuccessful Arnold expedition of 1775. Samuel

[6] Gérard to the president of Congress, May 22, 1779, Wharton, ed., *Revolutionary Diplomatic Correspondence*, 3:175–78.

[7] "Réflexions," [Apr. 1776], Henri Doniol, ed., *Histoire de la participation de la France à l'établissement des Etats-Unis d'Amérique*, 5 vols. and supplement (Paris, 1886–99), 1:243–49. English translation from Orville T. Murphy, "The Comte de Vergennes, the Newfoundland Fisheries, and the Peace Negotiation of 1783: A Reconsideration," *Canadian Historical Review* 46 (1965):32–46. For the dating, see John J. Meng, "A Footnote to Secret Aid in the Revolution," *American Historical Review* 43 (1938):791–95.

[8] "Plan of Treaties as Adopted," [Sept. 17, 1776], Art. 9, in Robert J. Taylor et al., eds., *Papers of John Adams*, 6 vols. to date (Cambridge, Mass., 1977–), 4:292; "Treaty of Alliance," Feb. 6, 1778, Art. 6, Hunter Miller, ed., *Treaties and Other International Acts of the United States of America*, 8 vols. (Washington, D.C., 1931–48), 2:38.

Chase, member of a congressional committee sent to Canada to gain Canadian support, declared in 1776 that "I think the Success of the War will, in a great Measure, depend on securing Canada to our Confederation."[9] On February 7, 1779, only two days before Gérard approached Congress on defining its ultimatums, William Whipple stated that the United States should accept nothing short of independence, but "even that, in my judgement ought not to satisfy us unless she [Britain] will quit all pretenses to Canada and Nova Scotia."[10] For John Adams, Canada was necessary because "we shall have perpetual wars with Britain while she has a foot of ground in America."[11]

France's renunciation of Canada did not mean that it favored substituting American for British rule, however. Vergennes informed Gérard on March 29, 1778, less than two months after signature of the Franco-American treaties, that France wished Canada to remain in British hands to assure American dependence on French support.[12] And on October 26, 1778, Vergennes wrote to Gérard that "it would be . . . very useful if Congress's ultimatum included . . . a renunciation of Canada and Nova Scotia or at least Canada." Peace should not depend on so secondary a cause as Canada.[13]

The French position regarding Canada had a significant impact. The draft ultimatums called for the cession of Nova Scotia, and, as stated, the boundaries included a large portion of present-day Ontario, but the remainder of Canada was not an objective. This was not due to any lessening of Canada's perceived importance as a means to finally eject Britain from North America, for it was designated a desir-

[9] Samuel Chase to Adams, Jan. 12, 1776, Taylor et al., eds., *Papers of John Adams*, 4:400.

[10] William Whipple to Josiah Bartlett, Feb. 7, 1779, Edmund Cody Burnett, ed., *Letters of Members of the Continental Congress*, 8 vols. (Washington, D.C., 1921–36), 4:59–60.

[11] Adams to James Lovell, July 26, 1778, Taylor et al., eds., *Papers of John Adams*, 6:321.

[12] Vergennes to Gérard, Mar. 29, 1778, Meng, ed., *Despatches of Gérard*, p. 129.

[13] Ibid., Vergennes to Gérard, Oct. 26, 1778, p. 359.

able object in the instructions adopted on August 14 and sent to John Adams on September 29.[14] Instead, it presumably reflected a desire to avoid raising an issue that could only be divisive in view of Gérard's forceful statement of the French position. An additional restraint on Congress may have been the recently canceled expedition against Canada. Such an operation could only succeed with French help, and there was concern, notably on the part of George Washington, that, because of the large French population there and in spite of France's renunciation, a victory might lead to the re-establishment of France in North America.[15]

Vergennes's memorandum of 1776 had also called for the restoration of French rights to the Newfoundland fishery lost in the peace treaty of 1763. The United States, however, saw the issue as one in which, at the very least, American fishing rights would be recognized as being of the same extent enjoyed before the Revolution. This was true even when the question of the fisheries was later relegated to the status of an object to be pursued in a proposed Anglo-American commercial treaty rather than a peace ultimatum.[16] The first draft of the treaty plan of 1776 had contained nothing concerning French fishing rights, and later drafts restricted it to those permitted under the treaty of 1763. Moreover, the territorial renunciation called for in the treaty plan had included the island of Newfoundland.[17] The revision of the plan in December 1776 offered France more, but still envisaged a share at least equal to that of France, proposing a division of the fishery and the island; this was still a far cry from the exclusive rights sought by Vergennes.[18]

[14] Ford et al., eds., *Journals of the Continental Congress*, 14:957–60.

[15] George Washington to Henry Laurens, Nov. 14, 1778, John C. Fitzpatrick, ed., *The Writings of George Washington*, 39 vols. (Washington, D.C., 1931–44), 13:254–57.

[16] Ford et al., eds., *Journals of the Continental Congress*, 14:960–62.

[17] "Plan of Treaties," [ante July 18, 1776], Art. 8; "Committee Report on a Plan of Treaties," [Aug. 27, 1776], Arts. 2 and 8; "Plan of Treaties as Adopted," [Sept. 17, 1776], Arts. 3 and 9, Taylor et al., eds., *Papers of John Adams*, 4:267–68, 279, 280, 291, 292.

[18] Ford et al., eds., *Journals of the Continental Congress*, 6:1055–56.

As concluded, the treaties of 1778 did not mention the acquisition of fishing rights, but this was no accident. France renounced its right to acquire territory in North America, but did not rule out expanding its fishing rights or even excluding the Americans from the fishery. The treaty of amity and commerce provided for exclusive fishing rights on the coasts and in places held by either party, and the United States agreed not to "disturb the Subjects, of the most Christian King in the Enjoyment and Exercise of the Right of Fishery on the Grand Banks of Newfoundland" or as established by the Treaty of Utrecht.[19] France did not commit itself to help the United States gain a share of the Newfoundland fishery or to allow Americans to retain the rights that had been enjoyed as British subjects. In his instruction to Gérard of October 26, 1778, Vergennes stated that he did not know whether Britain could be persuaded to admit the Americans to the Newfoundland fishery, but that in any event they already had a long coast and enough opportunity for fishing without extending it to the north, and, therefore, he favored a renunciation of the fishery in the ultimatums to be prepared by Congress.[20]

With regard to the western boundary, Vergennes, in his instruction of October 26, was unsure of the precise Spanish position. He doubted whether Spain would accept American claims to the Mississippi and thought that Congress should consider the interests of Spain in drawing up its ultimatums. Gérard was directed to accept guidance on the matter from the unofficial Spanish representative at Philadelphia, Don Juan de Miralles.[21] Congress already had indicated the extent of its probable willingness to satisfy Spain. Revised instructions regarding the treaty plan, which were adopted in December 1776, provided that if Spain would join the war, the United States would "assist in reducing to the possession of Spain the town and harbour of Pensacola, *provided the citi-*

[19] "Treaty of Amity and Commerce," Feb. 6, 1778, Arts. 9 and 10, Miller, ed., *Treaties*, 2:9–10.

[20] Vergennes to Gérard, Oct. 26, 1778, Meng, ed., *Despatches of Gérard*, p. 359.

[21] Ibid., pp. 359–60.

zens and inhabitants of the United States shall have the free and uninterrupted navigation of the Mississippi and use of the harbour of Pensacola."[22] The United States had even been willing to go to war with Portugal if such were desired by Spain. Any hopes that such concessions, or indeed any others that Congress was likely to make, would satisfy Spain vanished when Gérard met with that body on February 15, 1779, and, according to William Henry Drayton, stated that "Spain wishes to see the territorial claims of the United States terminated. She wishes to have the navigation of the Mississippi shut, and possession of the Floridas."[23]

Considering France's position on Canada and the fisheries and its desire that the United States recognize Spanish interests in its peace ultimatums, it is not strange that Congress's instructions to John Adams of September 29, 1779, differed from those proposed by its committee on February 23. What is remarkable is that French pressure and the acrimonious debate, inside Congress and outside of it, which stretched over six months, did not produce greater changes. The requirement that American independence be recognized before negotiations could begin as well as the provision defining boundaries remained. Free navigation of the Mississippi became an objective to be sought by John Jay in a treaty with Spain, and the acquisition of Canada and Nova Scotia became desirable objects in a peace treaty rather than ultimatums.[24] Although not an ultimatum, the confirmation of American fishing rights was to be a major objective in an Anglo-American commercial treaty.[25] The proposal for such a treaty was in line with the long-term American objective of seeking to widen its trading opportunities, but it was more immediately the result of the need to compromise over the question of the fisheries in order to obtain any ultimatums at

[22] Ford et al., eds., *Journals of the Continental Congress*, 6:1057 (italics in original).

[23] William Henry Drayton, Memorandum of Conference with the Minister of France, Feb. 15, 1779, Burnett, ed., *Letters of Members*, 4:70.

[24] Ford et al., eds., *Journals of the Continental Congress*, 14:957–60.

[25] Ibid., pp. 960–62.

all. Such a solution was satisfactory to France since the negotiation of a commercial treaty seemed a doubtful undertaking and thus was unlikely to affect France's own interests or objectives.

It is significant, however, that no specific American objective was formally renounced. That, together with the appointment of John Adams as the sole American peace commissioner, indicated that there were limits to France's ability to influence the American position regarding peace negotiations.

On April 12, even as debates in Congress continued over American peace objectives, France and Spain signed the Convention of Aranjuez that brought Spain into the war.[26] A Spanish belligerency had always been an objective of the United States and France, as can be seen in the secret article of the alliance, but more so for the French than the Americans.[27] This was evident from the limited concessions that the United States was willing to make to accommodate Spanish interests as opposed to the concerted French effort to limit American territorial acquisitions and ultimately was borne out by the terms of the Convention. There, because it needed the Spanish fleet, France undertook commitments in support of Spain that went far beyond what it expected from Spain, even to the extent of agreeing to terms that, if not directly in conflict with the Franco-American alliance, violated its spirit.

The Convention of Aranjuez is a clear exposition of French and Spanish objectives. The document confirmed mutual obligations under the Family Compact and the commitment of each nation to the combined operation for the invasion of England. France was unable to obtain even a tacit recognition by Spain of American independence with the result that in Article IV Spain promised only to do nothing regarding the article concerning independence in the Franco-American treaty of alliance without informing

[26] "Projet et texte de la convention," Apr. 12, 1779, Doniol, ed., *Participation de la France*, 3:803–10.

[27] Treaty of Alliance, Feb. 6, 1778, Act Separate and Secret, Miller, ed., *Treaties*, 2:45–46.

France. Article V set down the French aims, of which the most significant in terms of the Franco-American alliance was the "expulsion of the English from the island and the fishery of Newfoundland," to which in the event of success Spain was to be admitted. Additional objectives were the removal of the British commissioner from Dunkirk, unrestricted access to the East Indies, the restoration of Senegal, "unrevocable possession of the Island of Dominica," and the abrogation of the Anglo-French treaty of commerce signed at Utrecht in 1713. On the Spanish side, Article VII called for the restoration of Gibraltar, capture of the river and fort at Mobile, restoration of Pensacola and the coast of Florida on the Bahama Channel, expulsion of the British from the Bay of Honduras, revocation of British rights to cut dyewood on the coast of Campeche, and the recovery of Minorca. Finally, Article IX provided that the two powers would not make peace until Gibraltar had been taken.

For each of the three nations the peace objectives were but part of a larger policy. For France and Spain a favorable treaty would mark the end of an undertaking, for the United States a beginning. France hoped to reverse its position vis-à-vis Britain resulting from its defeat in the Seven Years' War and formalized in the Treaty of Paris of 1763. Spain sought to recover its lost territory, particularly Gibraltar, and to slow, if not reverse, its slide to the rank of a second-rate power. The United States sought to establish its independence and provide for its future prosperity by seeking trade with all nations while rejecting involvement in European political rivalries.

The French policy was dangerous, made even more so by the far more limited objectives of its allies. In essence, the United States sought recognition of its independence and Spain wanted Gibraltar. France was committed to both objectives, even promising not to make peace until they were attained. The United States and Spain, however, were under no obligations to each other and were committed only to the achievement of constituent parts of the larger French plan to gain a decisive victory over Britain. It was questionable whether either the United States or Spain would continue the war past the point at which a peace embodying their objectives became possible. A victory decisive enough to satisfy France and materially alter the balance of power depended as much on French perceptions as on material gain, and, moreover, it is doubtful whether such an outcome would have served either American or Spanish interests or have been permitted by the other European powers. Certainly the two mediation efforts, first by Spain and later by Austria and Russia, can be seen as attempts to limit the objectives of the belligerents and thus preserve a workable balance of power.

The American Revolution seemed an opportunity for France to engage Britain on favorable terms and, initially, at little risk. According to prevailing mercantilist thought, the separation of the colonies from the mother country would deprive Great Britain of a trade—fully one-third of the total according to some sources—that could not be made up elsewhere. Britain would thus be so weakened that it would be reduced, perhaps, to the level of a second-rate power. The prospect of such an outcome, particularly if it promised to enhance French commerce by permitting entry into the American market, induced France to assume the objective of American independence as its own, despite the obvious incongruity of an absolute monarchy supporting the revolt of subjects against their king.

The initial French commitment was small, but soon expanded. Turgot, the finance minister, warned, prophetically as it turned out, that although clandestine aid could be provided at relatively little risk, it could not long continue, even in the absence of an open and declared Anglo-French war, without severely straining French finances.[28] Vergennes, either not understanding or ignoring France's financial plight, saw the small initial cost of the aid as of no importance. Even if the Americans were overcome, the extent to which the war could be prolonged would increase British expenditures and the defeated colonies would be considerably less lucrative and governable than previously. For Vergennes,

---

[28] Orville T. Murphy, *Charles Gravier, Comte de Vergennes: French Diplomacy in the Age of Revolution, 1719–1787* (Albany, N.Y., 1982), pp. 253–54.

financial considerations were always opposed to "reasons of state" and it was the latter that "assured triumphs."[29]

The moment of truth came with the arrival of news concerning the battles at Saratoga and Germantown. The outcome of those engagements permitted the American commissioners to argue that Britain might now be willing to negotiate and that the absence of a more substantial French commitment forced the United States to look with favor on such an opportunity.[30] At that point, according to a memorandum of January 13, 1778, unsigned but presumably reflecting his thoughts, Vergennes saw only two possible options: total abandonment or full support. Abandonment was unacceptable because "England will take advantage of it by making a reconciliation, and in that case she will either preserve her supremacy wholly or partially, or she will gain an ally. Now it is known that she is disposed to sacrifice that supremacy and propose simply a sort of family compact, that is to say, a league against the House of Bourbon. The result of this will be that the Americans will become our perpetual enemies, and we must expect to see them turn all their efforts against our possessions, and against those of Spain."[31]

The decision to grant the United States formal recognition and a treaty flowed from this assessment, but both that decision and the sincerity with which it was made are questionable. In the aftermath of Saratoga and Germantown there was no reason to believe that the United States would accept a peace on any terms less than full independence, and the possibility of an Anglo-American alliance against France was totally devoid of substance. Nor was there any indication that the North ministry, much less George III, was about to make

[29] Orville T. Murphy, "Charles Gravier de Vergennes: Profile of an Old Regime Diplomat," *Political Science Quarterly* 83 (1968):403.

[30] Samuel Flagg Bemis, *The Diplomacy of the American Revolution* (New York, 1935), pp. 58–60.

[31] "Considerations upon the Necessity of France Declaring at Once for the American Colonies, Even without the Concurrence of Spain," Jan. 13, 1778, in Edward S. Corwin, *French Policy and the American Alliance of 1778* (Princeton, 1916), p. 399.

a serious offer. Indeed, in April 1778, before it received word of the treaties, Congress rejected Lord North's conciliatory bills and thus the efforts of the later Carlisle Commission, declaring that it would not negotiate without prior recognition of independence and withdrawal of British forces from America.[32] Of even more significance was the fact that France, through its clandestine aid, was achieving its purposes. Despite the absence of any formal Franco-American ties, the war was continuing, Britain's attention was focused on America rather than Europe, and the British were expending vast funds to continue the war. Moreover, a treaty with the United States meant an Anglo-French war and a great increase in French expenditures.

Vergennes's experience and available intelligence should have indicated that an American withdrawal was very unlikely. For the United States, France was the only port in the storm, the only conceivable source for the money and arms necessary to continue the war. If such was not apparent and Vergennes seriously believed that the United States might settle with Britain for less than independence, and if, for that reason, he sought a treaty, he was embarking on a course fraught with dangers. Was there any reason to think, for example, that if British recognition was offered, the United States would not accept it, thus leaving France to fight Britain alone?

Regardless of this potential danger, it is clear that Vergennes believed the time had come to act. He needed to reassure Louis XVI that French policy toward America was correct, and his outline of the consequences of an Anglo-American rapprochement was well calculated to do that as well as justify deeper involvement. What was probably more important, however, was that events in Europe threatened to divert French attention from America and thus undermine the policy that Vergennes had been pursuing since 1776, and that reflected the long-standing French desire to overturn the treaty of 1763. Too much effort and prestige had been spent to allow it to be abandoned at a time when the possibil-

[32] Ford et al., eds., *Journals of the Continental Congress*, 10:374–80, 11:614–15.

ities for success seemed greater than at any time previously. The policy had developed a life of its own, and for Vergennes to have let it be terminated would have endangered his position in the French government. Certainly the degree to which Vergennes had tied his fate to the American policy is indicated by his refusal to meddle in the Bavarian succession crisis, which almost certainly would have resulted in greater immediate gain for France at far less risk than would result from the certainty of an Anglo-French war if the American policy continued.[33]

If Vergennes's assessment was unrealistic in the short run, it contained an element of truth in the event of a protracted war. When the treaty plan of 1776 was drafted, Congress expected that opening the American market would be enough to induce France to provide aid without a political or military alliance, but France needed a stronger attachment and thus the alliance was concluded.[34] The initial lack of enthusiasm by the United States for such an agreement raised questions about its long-term commitment, and France might well be uneasy because the achievement of its objectives depended to a considerable degree on American adherence to the alliance. Of even more significance was the fact that the United States was fighting the war less to defeat Great Britain than to maintain its independence until Britain would agree to end the conflict and confirm what already existed. Such a recognition was Britain's to give regardless of French participation in the war, and, considering the enthusiasm on all sides in Britain for a war with France, it was never outside the realm of possibility that it would be granted. This was not a problem in late 1777 or 1778, but it always loomed as a possibility, one which Vergennes continually had to consider.[35]

[33] Bemis, *Diplomacy of the American Revolution*, pp. 70–74.

[34] Taylor et al., eds., *Papers of John Adams*, 4:261.

[35] Two examples will indicate the degree to which such a possibility preyed on Vergennes's mind. In July 1778 he submitted to the American commissioners reports that Britain was about to offer the United States independence in return for a separate peace and an alliance against France. Franklin and Adams reassured him and then immediately wrote

Statements by Benjamin Franklin and John Adams, both of whom were involved in the drafting of the treaty plan and would become peace commissioners, lend credence to French fears. On May 4, 1779, Franklin informed David Hartley of the obligation not to sign a separate peace and the absence of any American desire to be freed from its obligations to France. But, he declared, "powers who have made a firm, solid league, evidently useful to both, can never be prevailed with to dissolve it for the vague expectation of another *in nubibus,* nor even on the certainty that another will be proposed, without knowing what are to be its articles."[36] The implication was that if Britain were willing to make an acceptable offer, the United States, despite any obligations to France, would be willing to consider it. In 1780, after Vergennes had rejected his plan to disclose formally his commissions to Britain, John Adams observed that the alliance with France would last no longer than the war and that, in effect, it was in Britain's interest to make peace as soon as possible so as to remove the threat posed by it.[37]

If France had doubts about the United States as an instrument to achieve its objectives, the Convention of Aranjuez posed questions about the American reliance on France. The

to inform Congress that the French alliance was in effect and that any such agreement with Britain was unthinkable. Lee, apparently believing it an unwarranted intrusion by France as well as unnecessary, refused to sign the letter (Taylor et al., eds., *Papers of John Adams,* 6:312). On Dec. 7, 1778, Gérard asked Congress to declare publicly its fidelity to the French alliance and specifically that it had not reserved the right to negotiate separately with Britain. Congress complied with the request on Jan. 14, 1779 (Wharton, ed., *Revolutionary Diplomatic Correspondence,* 2:855; Ford et al., eds., *Journals of the Continental Congress,* 13:61–62). In neither case did Vergennes's apprehensions have any basis in fact.

[36] Franklin to David Hartley, May 4, 1779, Wharton, ed., *Revolutionary Diplomatic Correspondence,* 3:155.

[37] James H. Hutson, comp. and ed., *Letters from a Distinguished American: Twelve Essays by John Adams on American Foreign Policy, 1780* (Washington, D.C., 1978), p. 23. Adams's view of the treaty takes on added significance because, although the letters were published in *Parker's General Advertiser and Morning Intelligencer* in 1782, the essays were originally written in 1780, soon after Adams arrived in France as minister to negotiate the peace.

obligation not to make peace until Gibraltar was taken put France in a curious situation. The United States could not be expected to delay peace for that objective since it did not constitute one of the provisions of the treaty of alliance. Nor could Spain be expected to continue the war until American independence was recognized since the Convention of Aranjuez put it under no obligation to do so even tacitly, and such an outcome ran against its own interests. At the point at which either the United States obtained recognition of its independence or Spain took Gibraltar, France would be faced with the question of what to do in regard to its other ally. This was what in fact happened in 1782 with the signature by the American peace commissioners of the preliminary articles, and what might have occurred in 1780 had the Hussey-Cumberland negotiations resulted in a British cession of Gibraltar. The problem would be particularly serious if the Americans won recognition because France, with its long-standing commitments under the Family Compact, would find it much more difficult to impose an alternative solution on Spain and might find itself fighting the British for a considerable time after its alliance with the United States had lapsed. Finally, the Convention of Aranjuez was an explicit statement of objectives, while the Franco-American alliance was definite only on the question of independence, which could be achieved either formally or tacitly, the rest being open to interpretation. Thus, to the extent that Spain during the course of the war achieved its objectives, the greater would be the limits placed by France on those to be achieved for the United States.

Despite the urgency with which Congress had been pressed to define its objectives in 1779, once adopted they were of little use. The Spanish mediation failed, and there was no prospect of an acceptable British offer. The instructions, however, were in the hands of John Adams, a man whom Vergennes distrusted insofar as any negotiations with Britain were concerned. Ultimately, Adams's proposal to disclose his commissions to the British, the protraction of the war with no prospect of decisive victory, uneasiness regarding Spain following its apparent effort to make a separate peace through the Hussey-Cumberland mission, and the offer of an Austro-Russian mediation led Vergennes to seek other American commissioners to negotiate the peace and to attempt to exert much tighter control over any negotiations that might take place.

For the United States the continuation of the war influenced its conception of what was possible in a peace. In February 1781, following Virginia's acquiescence, Jay was instructed to agree to a treaty with Spain that did not contain a provision guaranteeing the right to free navigation on the Mississippi.[38] By June 1781 Adams had been joined by additional peace commissioners and new instructions were issued. No longer was recognition of the United States a prerequisite to negotiations, nor were the boundaries delineated in previous instructions to be regarded as an ultimatum. Even a truce was permissible if peace could be obtained in no other way. Most importantly, the new instructions declared that "you are to make the most candid and confidential communication upon all subjects to the ministers of our generous ally, the King of France; to undertake nothing in the negotiations for peace or truce without their knowledge and concurrence; and ultimately to govern yourselves by their advice and opinion."[39]

When these instructions were adopted they were understandable. There were genuine doubts in the minds of many members of Congress about the ability of the United States to continue the war, and, in any case, it could not do so without continued aid from France. Despite this, France in demanding such instructions overplayed its hand and created the conditions most conducive to producing the situation it feared. It would not be a Congress under the domination of a French minister, naively accepting his interpretation of events, that would negotiate the peace but rather peace commissioners 3,000 miles away. Franklin might be seen by some

[38] Thomas P. Abernethy, *Western Lands and the American Revolution* (New York, 1937), p. 280; "Instructions to Mr. Jay as to Mississippi River," Feb. 15, 1781, Wharton, ed., *Revolutionary Diplomatic Correspondence*, 4:257.

[39] "Instructions to the Commissioners for the Peace," Wharton, ed., *Revolutionary Diplomatic Correspondence*, 4:504–5.

as too eager to appease France, but he was an experienced diplomat and an expansionist, well aware of where American interests lay. Certainly it was questionable whether Adams, if he received support from others and if conditions warranted it, would feel himself bound by the instructions. But it was Jay who provided the strongest evidence that Vergennes's policy was in jeopardy. Writing to the president of Congress on September 20, 1781, he declared that "as an American I feel an interest in the dignity of my country, which renders it difficult for me to reconcile myself to the idea of the sovereign independent States of America submitting, in the persons of their ministers, to be absolutely governed by the advice and opinions of the servants of another sovereign, especially in a case of such national importance." Moreover, the instructions put "out of the power of your ministers to improve those chances and opportunities which in the normal course of human affairs happens more or less frequently to all men."[40]

The question posed by the new instructions, addressed by Jay and ultimately settled by the separate negotiations leading to the peace treaty of 1783, was that of legitimacy. The United States could accept aid from France and even guidance as to its objectives, but to allow France to determine the terms under which it was to exist, which was what the peace treaty was about, meant that the United States became a creature of France. Whatever standing it would have on the world stage would then be dependent upon continued French support. Such dependence was in line with French policy, but could not be accepted by the United States, particularly in view of its desire to remain outside the political system of Europe, enjoy the benefits of neutrality in its wars, and, for all intents and purposes, terminate the alliance with France at the end of the war.

It was also an important domestic issue. After the victory at Yorktown some members of Congress sought to modify the instructions of 1781 to bring them into line with Ameri-

[40] John Jay to the president of Congress, Sept. 20, 1781, ibid., pp. 716–17.

can interests.[41] This was not done because of the implications for the French alliance while the war continued and French aid remained necessary. It showed, however, an awareness that the terms of a peace treaty would be important domestically, particularly if it appeared that concessions had been made unnecessarily and sectional interests had been needlessly sacrificed. If such were perceived to be the case, then it would have a profound effect on the acceptance of the treaty and possibly even the continued cohesion of the United States under the Articles of Confederation.

The decision of Adams, Franklin, and Jay to negotiate separately and secretly had a profound effect on the achievement of peace objectives. The United States did not obtain Canada and Nova Scotia, but, by reverting to the objectives of 1779, it achieved almost everything else. The French believed that Britain bought, rather than negotiated, a peace, but there was a logic to the British concessions.[42] Once the decision had been made to grant independence and begin serious negotiations, there was little reason to limit American boundaries to the Proclamation Line or to restrict access to the fisheries. Indeed, one can discern a certain desire for revenge, for by setting the boundary on the Mississippi and sharing the right to the free navigation of the river derived from the treaty of 1763, Britain left Spain with exactly the problem that it and France had hoped to avoid through the limitation of American objectives. By granting the Americans extensive fishing rights on the Grand Banks of Newfoundland, Britain worked a division of the fishery between itself and the United States, leaving France no better off than it had been before.

France and Spain found themselves in essentially the same position that they had occupied vis-à-vis Great Britain before the war began. France did achieve the separation of the

[41] William C. Stinchcombe, *The American Revolution and the French Alliance* (Syracuse, 1969), pp. 170–82.

[42] Richard B. Morris, *The Peacemakers: The Great Powers and American Independence* (New York, 1965), p. 383. For the negotiations, see ibid., chs. 18–28, Murphy, *Charles Gravier, Comte de Vergennes*, chs. 29–31, and Stetson Conn, *Gibraltar in British Diplomacy in the Eighteenth Century* (New Haven, 1942), ch. 9.

American colonies from Britain and the removal of the British commissioner from Dunkirk, but it was unable to achieve an exclusive access to the fisheries and made no major gains in the West Indies. Also it had been unable to achieve the decisive victory that it needed to reverse the results of the treaty of 1763, and ended the war in far worse financial condition than at the start. Spain gained Minorca, but even with French help, it could not conquer Gibraltar, an object that Spain might still have obtained had it been willing to give up something suitable in return, such as Puerto Rico.

The preliminary peace treaty signed in 1782 was a triumph for American self-interest, made necessary by the conflict between the objectives of the United States and those of France and Spain. For the United States the Franco-American alliance and its tenuous connection with Spain were viable only so long as they provided a means to achieve the short-term objectives set down in the ultimatums of 1779 and did not permanently prevent the new nation from pursuing the long-term objective of remaining apart from European political affairs, with neutrality the foundation of its foreign policy. The instructions of 1781, in the minds of the American negotiators, threatened the achievement of both sets of objectives. Therefore, a separate peace was concluded in violation of the alliance, dashing French hopes of exerting significant influence over the future policies of the United States and, for all intents and purposes, ending the French alliance.

JAMES H. HUTSON

The American Negotiators

The Diplomacy of Jealousy

WE KNOW A great deal about the Americans who negotiated the peace treaties of 1782 and 1783: John Adams, Benjamin Franklin, John Jay, and Henry Laurens. Teams of scholars are publishing their papers in meticulously prepared multivolume editions. Not long ago they were principals in a Broadway play. John Adams has recently starred in a television series that is rerun nearly as often as "I Love Lucy."

Since Adams has become so familiar, you will recognize the accuracy of the following descriptions. He was, writes one biographer, a "Puritan," "a devout Christian and stern republican," "austerely virtuous," possessed of an "intense nature, hot temper, and acerbic tongue," a man of diligence who loathed "balls, concerts or horse races."[1] According to another scholar he was "a model of virtue both in private and public affairs," "one of those epitomes of abstract propriety who existed and prospered in the early history of the United States"; a man of "profound piety and unbreakable religious faith . . . with the strongest and most affectionate attachment for domestic life"; he was vain, "obstinate, indefatigable and dogmatical."[2] Accurate portraits of Adams, are they not? No,

---

[1] Laura Frech, "The Career of Henry Laurens in the Continental Congress, 1777–1779," Ph.D. diss., University of North Carolina, 1972, pp. 469, 3, 7, 366, 6.

[2] Samuel Flagg Bemis, *Jay's Treaty: A Study in Commerce and Diplomacy* (1923; rev. ed., New Haven, 1962), p. 281; John Vardill to William Eden, Apr. 11, 1778, Benjamin Franklin Stevens, comp., *B. F. Stevens's Facsimiles of Manuscripts in European Archives Relating to America, 1773–1783*, 25 vols. (London, 1889–98), 4: no. 438.

they are not. The first writer is describing Henry Laurens, the second John Jay.

The purpose of playing this trick, of indulging in what the eighteenth century would have called a piece of low cunning, is to demonstrate that there were similarities in the personalities of Adams, Jay, and Laurens (Franklin we will defer for the time being). This paper will focus on the common personality traits of the peacemakers and explore how these traits shaped the negotiations that established the independence of the United States.

Henry Strachey—an undersecretary of state in the Colonial Office whom Lord Shelburne sent to Paris in October 1782 to stiffen Richard Oswald's negotiating posture—was one of the earliest observers of a collective personality trait among the American negotiators. Frustrated by haggling with John Adams and John Jay, Strachey griped that "these Americans are the greatest quibblers that I have ever seen."[3] This complaint articulated the exasperation of a man dealing with two of the toughest, shrewdest lawyers in the United States. Adams and Jay were both chief justices of their respective states before they were diplomats, and they brought to the peace negotiations the litigious approach of the attorney become jurist. They could be called lawyerlike personalities, not because they were born disputatious, but because the discipline of their profession produced habits and attitudes peculiar to the bar. Jay's character, wrote an old friend in 1778, was "much perverted by the study of the Law."[4] His refusal to negotiate with Oswald in August and September 1782 until the latter's commission was altered to include the United States by name has been censured by many diplomatic historians as unduly "legalistic" and counterproductive[5] and may be cited as the primary example of the lawyer's personality influencing the negotiations, as it continued to do in October and November, when Adams, now joined with

[3] Quoted in Frank Monaghan, *John Jay: Defender of Liberty* . . . (1935; reprint ed., New York, 1972), p. 199.

[4] Vardill to Eden, Apr. 11, 1778, Stevens, ed., *Facsimiles*, 4: no. 438.

[5] Samuel Flagg Bemis, *The Diplomacy of the American Revolution* (New York, 1935), p. 210.

Jay, wearied Strachey by battling to dot every *i* and cross every *t*.

Adams and Jay were only half of the peace commission. Their colleagues, Laurens and Franklin, were not lawyers and had no desire to be. Franklin, in particular, found the contentiousness of the legal fraternity tiresome. Therefore, it would be difficult to argue that being "legalistic" was the most conspicuous feature of the personalities of the peace negotiators. What appears to be far more pervasive in their personalities was suspicion.

Suspicion takes several forms. Sometimes it is specific, grounded in prejudice and indoctrination. An example is the colonial Americans' fears of France, nurtured by British Francophobia that distorted every aspect of the French nation from its honor—it was said to be utterly perfidious—to its manhood—Frenchmen were depicted as "dwarfs, pale, ugly specimens who lived exclusively on frogs and snails."[6] Such an intellectual environment implanted in the minds of Americans maturing before the War of Independence the conviction that France was, as the youthful John Adams declared, an "ambitious and faithless Nation," an attitude that survived the signing of the French alliance.[7] Although residues of this ancient suspicion played on all the American peace negotiators in 1782–83—and on none more than on descendants of Huguenots like Jay and Laurens—I do not refer to it when I assert that suspicion was the dominant characteristic of the peacemakers. I refer to a more generalized suspicion that encompassed not only a hereditary enemy but friends, colleagues, countrymen, and even mankind in general.

Such an attitude appeared in its extreme form in Arthur Lee, one of the original commissioners to France. Lee gloried in his suspiciousness. "He has Confidence in nobody," fretted John Adams. "He believes all Men selfish—And, no

[6] Ronald Hoffman and Peter J. Albert, eds., *Diplomacy and Revolution: The Franco-American Alliance of 1778* (Charlottesville, Va., 1981), p. 14.

[7] Lyman H. Butterfield, ed., *Diary and Autobiography of John Adams*, 4 vols. (Cambridge, Mass., 1961–66), 1:36.

Man honest or sincere."[8] Adams relates that he tried to argue
Lee out of these ideas, but failed. (Before Adams quit the
diplomatic service, his own suspicions rivaled Lee's.) Those
with a psychological orientation will trace attitudes like suspicion back to an individual's childhood. Arthur Lee's latest
biographer, who leans to the view that Lee was paranoid in
the clinical sense, has argued that youthful psychological
traumas fostered his later suspicions, which he then accommodated in a congenial political ideology.[9] Whether the same
process was at work in the lives of the peace negotiators is a
question beyond the ken of this paper. What is clear is that
American Revolutionary leaders subscribed to a political ideology that put a premium on suspicion or, to give it its eighteenth-century name, jealousy. If this ideology did not
"create" the jealousy of the peacemakers, it certainly sustained it.

The ideology of the Revolution has been authoritatively
described in the last two decades by Bernard Bailyn and Gordon S. Wood.[10] It can be called opposition, or "country," ideology become republicanism. A major tenet of this ideology
was the "propulsiveness" of power, the idea that anyone
holding power would seek to increase it, would turn tyrant
and enslave his fellow citizens, if he could. Therefore, jealousy, which comprehended both suspicion and vigilance, was
a civic duty, the first line of defense against possible abuses
of power.[11]

As the British Parliament appeared to be implementing a
systematic strategy of oppression in the colonies in the 1760s

[8] Ibid., 2:347.

[9] Louis Potts, *Arthur Lee: Virtuous Revolutionary* (Baton Rouge, 1981), pp.
12–14, 135, 145, 174, 199, 225.

[10] Bernard Bailyn, *The Ideological Origins of the American Revolution* (Cambridge, Mass., 1967); Gordon S. Wood, *The Creation of the American Republic, 1776–1787* (Chapel Hill, 1969).

[11] See James H. Hutson, "The Origins of 'The Paranoid Style in American Politics': Public Jealousy from the Age of Walpole to the Age of Jackson," in David D. Hall, John M. Murrin, and Thad W. Tate, eds., *Saints and
Revolutionaries in Early American History* (New York, 1984), p. 336.

and 1770s, American leaders implored their countrymen to be jealous. "A perpetual jealousy . . . is absolutely requisite," urged John Dickinson in his famous *Letters from a Farmer in Pennsylvania* (1768). Tribunes of the people in every colony demanded "watchful, hawk-eyed jealousy."[12] The result was that by 1773 a leading patriot observed that "jealousy and suspicion . . . had become the very basis of American politics." Far from diminishing jealousy, independence enhanced it, for independent America espoused republicanism and republicanism put a premium on jealousy. Like virtue, simplicity, and frugality, it was an indispensable republican quality.

Extolled and encouraged, "republican jealousy" luxuriated after 1776. "Jealousy was prevalent in Republicks," asserted Silas Deane in 1777, "and its greatest degree was now excited in America."[13] No one, friend or foe, foreigner or neighbor, was immune from it. Everyone was suspect. "Tyranny," wrote Benjamin Rush in 1778, "can now enter our country only in the shape of a whig. All our jealousy should be of ourselves." "The jealousy of the people in this country," Noah Webster observed, "is directed against themselves." "The people of this country," agreed another, "turn their fears and jealousies against themselves." It was, as a New Englander said simply, "a time of jealousy."[14] This orgy of jealousy produced a reaction in the 1780s when some Americans, convinced that jealousy impeded efficient government, began to denounce it as a "little, mean, and sneaky temper" and to suggest that it had become pathological—a "delirium of the imagination," a "strange madness."[15] Nevertheless, it was in the floodtide of jealousy of the late 1760s and 1770s that the political careers of Laurens, Jay, and

[12] Ibid., pp. 343, 346.

[13] Paul Wentworth to Eden, Dec. 22, 1777, Stevens, ed. *Facsimiles*, 2: no. 234. See also David Ramsay's observations about the "extreme jealousy of new republics" (Ramsay, *History of the United States*, 3 vols. [Philadelphia, 1816–17], 3:xi).

[14] Hutson, "Origins of 'The Paranoid Style,'" pp. 350–52; Christopher Collier, *Roger Sherman's Connecticut* (Middletown, 1971), p. 224.

[15] "S.C.," *Pennsylvania Gazette*, July 9, 1783; Hutson, "Origins of 'The Paranoid Style,'" pp. 354–55.

Adams were launched. The fulsome suspicion of those days left its mark on their personalities.

It did not, of course, produce identical results, for it was operating on different individuals with different temperaments and convictions. Jay, for example, and Adams and Laurens belonged to competing political groups in the Continental Congress. They had, said Adams in 1782, been members of "different sects."[16] The Adams-Laurens sect has received a number of labels from contemporaries and historians: enemies assailed it as the "Lee-Adams junto"; Conrad Alexandre Gérard, the first French minister to the United States, called it the "Party of the East" and the "anti-gallican" faction; historians in the progressive tradition have described its members as "radicals" as opposed to the "conservatives" with whom Jay was affiliated. H. James Henderson has recently designated it the "Party of the Revolution," by which he means to indicate that it was more committed to republican ideological purity than its opponents.[17] Its members placed a higher value on jealousy than did their adversaries—"it is a spirit," declared Arthur Lee, that "we ought to respect even in its excesses"—and were more willing to indulge it.[18] Therefore, there was a difference in the jealousy of Jay, Adams, and Laurens. If Arthur Lee, who left Europe in 1780, and Franklin are added to the group, we may say that there was a spectrum of suspicion in American diplomats, running from Lee through Laurens and Adams, falling off slightly at Jay, and ending with Franklin at its weakest point.

We are now ready to examine the cargoes of suspicions that the American commissioners brought to the peace talks, beginning with Henry Laurens. Because he arrived last at the negotiations and contributed least, Laurens has not attracted

[16] See James H. Hutson, *John Adams and the Diplomacy of the American Revolution* (Lexington, Ky., 1980), p. 118; for Laurens's membership with Adams in the "Eastern Party" in Congress, see H. James Henderson, *Party Politics in the Continental Congress* (New York, 1974), pp. 103, 165, 174.

[17] Henderson, *Party Politics*, pp. 109, 182.

[18] *An Appeal to the Justice and Interests of the People of Great Britain in the Present Dispute with America* (London, 1774), p. 62.

the attention of diplomatic historians. His activities in the peace commission are interesting, nevertheless—if only to connoisseurs of the bizarre—and graphically illustrate the thesis of this paper. That Laurens was temperamentally unsuited for diplomacy—he was described as "garrulous and peevish" in April 1782—has been conceded by historians but excused because of the trauma inflicted by a long, rigorous imprisonment in the Tower of London.[19] Even before Laurens left America in 1780, however, he displayed a personality that made his choice as a peace negotiator egregiously ill-considered. Laurens seems to have been exceptionally bellicose; at the Continental Congress in January 1779 he fought a duel with John Penn of North Carolina whom he had baited on the floor of the house by taunting him with a doggerel: "Poor little Penny, poor little penny, sing tan-tarra-ra-ra."[20] He engaged in a running argument with Secretary Charles Thomson, at one point squaring off to fight—or rather to kick—him.[21] He feuded with the North Carolina delegation in 1779, accusing it of engaging in a "settled Plan ... to hunt me down." With his colleague William Henry Drayton he quarreled throughout 1779, suspecting Drayton of "deliberately deceiving him and laying traps for him."[22]

Laurens's belligerent suspiciousness was easily inflamed when maneuvering for peace began in the spring of 1782. On May 11, 1782, he left London and traveled to the Netherlands to explore the possibility of executing the minister plenipotentiary's powers that Congress had granted him in 1779 and that Adams was exercising in his stead. Following Laurens into Holland was an anonymous letter, whose authorship has never been established. Dispatched by Laurens's friend Edward Bridgen, the letter warned "Adams envious of every superior merit has much labour'd clandestinely in

[19] Richard B. Morris, *The Peacemakers: The Great Powers and American Independence* (New York, 1965), p. 516.

[20] Edmund Cody Burnett, ed., *Letters of Members of the Continental Congress*, 8 vols. (Washington, D.C., 1921–36), 4:403.

[21] Ibid., p. 399.

[22] Frech, "Career of Henry Laurens," pp. 425–42.

injuring Franklin and Laurens to secure his situation and answer further ends."[23] Bridgen sent another copy of the letter, dated May 3, 1782, to Edmund Jenings, a confidant and unofficial adviser of John Adams living at the time in Brussels. Jenings, as Bridgen evidently anticipated he would, sent the letter on to Adams in the Netherlands.

Laurens conferred with Adams during the first days of June. Because Adams still considered him a British prisoner on parole, he refused to divulge anything about the Dutch mission. Laurens was offended by Adams's reserve. According to Jenings, who saw Laurens for a week in Brussels just after he left the Netherlands, the South Carolinian was "confused by rage" over Adams's treatment of him.[24] Jenings and Laurens discussed the anonymous letter in Brussels. Ever suspicious, Laurens began to play with the idea that Jenings, though professing to be Adams's friend, had written it. Jenings claimed later that Laurens developed these suspicions by displacing upon him his anger and frustration with Adams. As the summer passed, Laurens's suspicions of Jenings grew stronger as the evidence against him grew weaker. Because Jenings had written Laurens twice at Adams's request—once about the anonymous letter—Laurens concluded that he was "intermeddling" and that his "impertinent officiousness" suggested guilt.[25] Additional "proof" of Jenings's culpability was hearsay evidence supplied and then repudiated by Bridgen, and handwriting analysis of another anonymous letter that Laurens believed implicated Jenings, but that no fewer than five other Americans concluded established his innocence. By the end of the summer of 1782 Laurens confessed that the affair of the anonymous letter had "rather wound me up." In fact, at-

[23] James H. Hutson, comp. and ed., *Letters from a Distinguished American: Twelve Essays by John Adams on American Foreign Policy, 1780* (Washington, D.C., 1978), p. 53.

[24] Edmund Jenings, *A Full Manifestation of What Mr. Henry Laurens Falsely Denominates Candor in Himself and Tricks in Mr. Edmund Jenings* (London, 1783), p. 47.

[25] For this and the following quotations in this paragraph, see Hutson, *Letters from a Distinguished American,* pp. 56, 57, 62–63.

tempting to prove his suspicions of Jenings became his consuming passion during the negotiations for a preliminary and definitive peace.

Laurens appeared at the preliminary negotiations at the very last moment, on November 29, the day before they concluded. On the thirtieth, after the preliminaries were signed, he briefed Adams on the anonymous letter, laying out at length his suspicions of Jenings, which Adams neither then nor at any subsequent time accepted. Late on the evening of the thirtieth, Adams called on Jenings, who was now in Paris, and relayed Laurens's charges.[26] After conducting their own preliminary negotiations, Jenings and Laurens, with the assistance of intermediaries, were apparently reconciled at a meeting in Paris on January 6, 1783. But Laurens's suspicions of Jenings were too strong and by March 1783, having acquired an additional scrap of dubious evidence and having nearly precipitated a duel between Jenings and William Lee, the South Carolinian was back on the attack.[27]

On March 6, 1783, Laurens wrote Adams an exposé of Jenings "to undeceive you and to prevent, if possible, the progress of further evils, from his influence over or interference in our Councils and deliberations." Jenings, Laurens continued, had ingratiated himself with Adams "by an excess of flattery."[28] Adams ignored this insult and brushed aside Laurens's indictment of Jenings. On March 26 Laurens responded with an angry letter, scoring Adams's gullibility.

Both Laurens and Jenings were now in London. Although Laurens was still a member of the peace commission and was supposedly acting as an intermediary with the British ministry during the definitive negotiations, he spent most of his time trying to prove his case against Jenings. In the summer of 1783 the two men went public with their quarrel, Jenings producing a pamphlet on July 7, 1783, and Laurens replying from Bath with a long recitation of his suspicions on Septem-

[26] Edmund Jenings, *The Candor of Henry Laurens, Esq.; Manifested by His Behaviour to Mr. Edmund Jenings* (London, 1783), p. 6.

[27] Hutson, *Letters from a Distinguished American*, pp. 59–60.

[28] Ibid., p. 60.

ber 3, 1783, the day his colleagues in Paris signed the definitive treaty. Later in the year Jenings published a tedious rejoinder.

The quarrel continued to seethe in 1784. Laurens bared his hostility to Adams in a letter of February 3, 1784, in which he complained of Adams's "contempt" and warned him not to "mistake forbearance for tameness which you might play with; nor can I in any other manner reconcile your conduct with the hazard attending it." The "hazard" with which Laurens threatened Adams—a duel—did not materialize. Nor, fortunately, did a duel that Laurens and Jenings were on the verge of fighting in London in May 1784. In 1783 Laurens had informed Adams that the "grand view" of the writer of the anonymous letter was to "excite jealousy and by degrees to produce animosity among us all."[29] With such suspicious and combustible material as the American peace negotiators, very little skill was needed to strike the spark that would shower animosities all around.

If Adams treated Laurens with restraint, it was probably because the full force of his anger and suspicion was focused on Benjamin Franklin and the comte de Vergennes, the French foreign minister. Adams was a man of turbulent emotions—he suffered what a recent writer has described as three nervous breakdowns between 1771 and 1783—who as early as 1765 extolled a "jealous Watchful Spirit" and who made it his business to practice what he preached.[30] Adams spent parts of 1778 and 1779 as a commissioner at the court of France. During that period he grew envious and suspicious of Franklin, suspicious to the point of believing that the Doctor and his friends contrived to arrange his capture at sea by the British as he sailed to America in the summer of 1779.[31] No sooner was Adams in Massachusetts than he was elected by Congress to return to Europe as minister plenipotentiary to negotiate treaties of peace and commerce with Britain. Immediately—months before Franklin could have

[29] Ibid., pp. 64, 60.

[30] Peter Shaw, *The Character of John Adams* (Chapel Hill, 1976), pp. 64–66, 150–51, 186–91; Hutson, *John Adams*, p. 35.

[31] Hutson, *John Adams*, pp. 48–50.

learned of the appointment—Adams convinced himself that upon his return to Europe the Sage would try to "starve him out" of the Continent by refusing to pay his salary.[32] Back in France, Adams intensified and expanded his suspicions of Franklin until they reached extraordinary heights by the summer of 1782.

Adams's relationship with the comte de Vergennes did not have a happier issue. The two men could not agree on the posture and policy that France and America should adopt toward each other. By July 1780 Adams suspected that the comte's attitude toward the United States was malevolent. French policy, he was persuaded, was designed to "keep us poor. Depress us. Keep us weak"; above all, to keep America dependent on France so she could be manipulated as France pleased.[33] As these suspicions mounted, they merged with Adams's suspicions of Franklin to forge his conviction that Vergennes and the Doctor had joined forces against him. Thus, when Adams traveled to Holland in July 1780 "to try," as he declared to Franklin, "whether something might not be done to render us less dependent on France," his suspicions of the Doctor and Vergennes had ripened into something like a paranoid conviction that he was the object of a malign conspiracy. He was, he claimed, "pursued into Holland by the intrigues of Vergennes and Franklin, and was embarrassed and thwarted, both in my negotiations for a loan and in those of a political nature, by their friends, agents, and spies, as much, at least, as I ever had been in France."[34]

In the Netherlands, where Adams served from the summer of 1780 until the fall of 1782, he experienced the putative persecutions of Franklin and Vergennes intensely. Their object, he continued to believe, was to keep the United States dependent on France by preventing Adams from procuring a Dutch recognition of American independence. This assumption was false—France would have welcomed a Dutch

[32] Ibid., p. 54.

[33] Ibid., p. 69.

[34] Ibid., pp. 72–74.

recognition of the United States—just as was his conviction that Franklin and Vergennes wanted to humiliate him personally by scheming to thwart him. Nevertheless, Adams writhed under the pain of what he believed to be Franklin's "assassination upon my Character," motivated by "base Jealousy" and "sordid Envy" and suffered "a miserable state of health by anxiety of mind . . . menaced with an axe and hurdle in London, threatened with starvation from Passy; and having frequently suggested to my recollection, the butcher's knife, with which the De Witts had been cut up at the Hague."[35]

When the prospect for peace negotiations emerged in 1782 Adams viewed Franklin and Vergennes and their alleged policy of keeping the United States weak and dependent with fear and loathing. "Knowing that I should have the Count and the Doctor to combat almost in every step of the negotiation for peace," he later wrote, "I thought I should be useless and my situation very unpleasant. This prospect staggered my fortitude for a moment and I thought of resigning."[36] But Adams remained in Europe and heeded John Jay's summons of September 28, 1782, to come to Paris and join the negotiations. Adams arrived in Paris on October 26, 1782. So suspicious was he of Franklin and Vergennes, so alienated from them was he, that he evidently intended to avoid them until a confrontation was forced upon him.

Matthew Ridley, deputed by Maryland to borrow money in Europe, visited Adams on October 29 and reminded him that courtesy required that he call on Franklin. "There was no necessity," Adams exploded. "After the usage he had received from him he could not bear to go near him. . . . He said the D[octor] might come to him. I [Ridley] told him that . . . the last comer always paid the first visit. He replied the Dr. was to come to him. He was first in the Com[missio]n. I ask[ed] him how the D was to know he was here unless he went to him. He replied that was true, he did not think of that and would go. Afterwards when pulling on his Coat he

35 Ibid., pp. 100–101.

36 Ibid., p. 115.

said he would not, he could not bear to go where the D was. With much persuasion I got him at length to go."[37] With no one cajoling Adams to see Vergennes, he eluded the French minister more successfully. He was in Paris a full two weeks before the comte discovered "from the Returns of the Police" that he was in town.

Worked up to such a pitch of suspicion himself, Adams would embrace a man like Jay, erstwhile adversary though he was, whose own suspicions had independently brought him to a similar point of view about France, if not about Franklin. Scholars have stressed Jay's suspiciousness. Though hardly a republican ideologue of the Adams-Lee stripe, Jay was not immune to the ideology of the Revolution and seems to have agreed with Samuel Adams and his cohorts that jealousy was beneficent. Thus, we find him delivering the following charge to a grand jury in Ulster County, New York, in September 1777: "Vice, ignorance, the want of vigilance will be the only enemies able to destroy [liberty]. Against these be forever jealous."[38] Be suspicious, Jay advised, of the lack of suspicion. James Madison, Jay's collaborator on the *Federalist*, affirmed Jay's jealousy in a famous interview with Jared Sparks in 1830, in which he stated that Jay "had two strong traits of character, suspicion and religious bigotry."[39] Although in 1967 Richard B. Morris denounced the notion that Jay was "of an inordinately suspicious nature," Morris's own edition of Jay's papers betrays his jealousy so strongly that a distinguished reviewer in 1980 pronounced Jay "cantankerous, stubborn, and suspicious."[40]

All writers agree that Jay's Huguenot background inspired him with "an inherited suspicion of France."[41] When he ar-

[37] Ibid., p. 118.

[38] Monaghan, *John Jay*, p. 101.

[39] Irving Brant, *James Madison*, vol. 5, *James Madison: Commander in Chief, 1812–1836* (Indianapolis, 1961), p. 502.

[40] Richard B. Morris, *The American Revolution Reconsidered* (New York, 1967), p. 117; Alexander DeConde, "Cantankerous Diplomat of Independence," *Reviews in American History* 8(1980):485.

[41] Monaghan, *John Jay*, p. 186.

rived in Paris on June 23, 1782, to join Franklin in conducting the peace negotiations, Jay was smarting from months of
studied humiliation administered to him by Spanish diplomats, which he was inclined to ascribe to the French.[42]
Therefore, Jay was unwilling to give France the benefit of the
doubt. In fact, he was prepared to put the worst possible interpretation on her conduct.

Soon after his arrival in Paris, Jay came down with influenza and was unable to assist Franklin in the negotiations
until the beginning of August. At his first working meeting
with Vergennes on August 10, 1782, Jay's suspicions of
France were inflamed by observations of the comte's deputy,
Gérard de Rayneval, on the extent of American western
claims. Jay leaped to the conclusion that France wanted to
keep the United States weak by limiting its size, that she
should not, therefore, be trusted, and that the American negotiators should, if necessary, flout their instructions of June
15, 1781, which enjoined them to communicate with the
French ministry and rely on its advice in negotiating with the
British. In a famous gesture, Jay, his agitation growing as he
talked to Franklin, hurled his pipe into the fireplace and asserted that he would break his instructions with as few re-
grets as he would a farthing pipe.[43]

Jay's anxieties about France grew as the negotiations pro-
gressed, culminating in his extraordinary decision in September to send Benjamin Vaughan on a second mission to
Lord Shelburne to counteract Rayneval. Controlling the negotiations in September and October—Franklin was incapac-
itated by kidney stones—Jay permitted his suspicions of
France to dictate his negotiating strategy—silent treatment
for the ally and a "conciliatory line," approaching in some
instances flirtatiousness, toward the enemy.[44] Adams, who arrived in Paris on October 26, endorsed his colleague's conduct. On October 28 Jay and he had an interview—almost a
joint confessional—in which they shared their suspicions,

[42] Ibid.

[43] Morris, *Peacemakers*, pp. 308–10.

[44] Ibid., p. 311.

formed at Versailles and in the Netherlands, that France was attempting to keep the United States weak and dependent. "It is impossible," Adams later wrote, "for any man but Mr. Jay and myself to conceive our mutual feelings upon this sudden discovery that we had both formed the same opinion of the policy of the Comte Vergennes."[45]

Adams improved on Jay's suspicions. Where Jay believed that France merely wanted to weaken the United States by limiting its western boundaries and fishing rights, Adams concluded that the French objective in these and other cases—their support of restitution for the loyalists, for example—was to sow the seeds of future wars between the United States and neighboring powers, so that America would be compelled to rely on French protection and become a client of Versailles. Concerning the western boundary, Adams believed that France wanted it drawn in the most controversial way to provoke hostilities between the United States and Spain. Had this really been true, France's policy would have been to set her oldest and newest allies against each other, exposing herself to their conflicting claims with the alienation of one or the other the certain result.[46] So diabolically manipulative did France seem to Adams that he suspected she had planted emissaries at the Court of St. James's, who persuaded the British ministry to issue the famous Order in Council of July 2, 1783, excluding American shipping from West Indian ports. Adams firmly believed that this celebrated measure, which pointed a dagger at the heart of American commerce, was adopted upon the "advice and desire" of France.[47] Holding these views, it was perhaps inevitable that Adams should attribute the anonymous letter that so exercised Henry Laurens to a plot concerted by France and Franklin.[48]

Adams and Jay, their suspicions ascendant, dominated the

[45] *Boston Patriot*, July 27, 1811.

[46] Hutson, *John Adams*, pp. 120–22.

[47] Ibid., p. 122.

[48] John Adams to Edmund Jenings, Apr. 18–21, 1783, Adams Papers, microfilm, reel 108.

remainder of the negotiations. The preliminaries, signed on November 30 and re-signed as the definitive treaty on September 3, 1783, constituted, in the opinion of the dean of American diplomatic historians, "the greatest victory in the annals of American diplomacy."[49] The implication of Samuel Flagg Bemis's pronouncement is provocative. Does it mean that suspicion is indispensable to diplomacy and that the greater the suspicion the greater the chances of success? Should we seek our diplomats at St. Elizabeth's Hospital rather than at the State Department?

The historical record shows that, in dealing with France, American negotiators had much to be suspicious about. Whether one subscribes to the conventional historical view that France was willing to betray the United States at the peace table by thwarting its legitimate aspirations or to the revisionist view that France was more indifferent than hostile to American claims,[50] the fact is that had American negotiators naively trusted their fortunes to France, they would have come away from the negotiations with far less than they did. Up with suspicion, then; the more, the better.

But the case is not quite so simple. The negotiations of Adams and Jay display instances in which their excessive suspiciousness could have been disastrous for the United States. Jay's vindictive suspiciousness of Spain encouraged him to persuade the British to capture West Florida from her and led him to offer Britain, as a secret peace article, expanded boundaries for the province in the event she acquired it. A British presence in Florida would, of course, have been pernicious for the United States. Jealous of what he took to be French persecution, Adams in the Netherlands tried to negotiate over the head of the French ambassador by presenting against the comte de la Vauguyon's express wishes the famous memorial of May 4, 1781. The memorial had no chance of helping the allied cause and might have brought Russia into the war on Britain's side. The suspicion that motivated Jay and Adams in France soured their relations with

[49] Bemis, *Diplomacy of the American Revolution*, p. 256.

[50] Alexander DeConde, "The French Alliance in Historical Speculation," in Hoffman and Albert, eds., *Diplomacy and Revolution*, pp. 21–26.

French officials. This observation applies to Adams more than to Jay, but it is difficult to believe that either man could have reconciled Vergennes to American conduct at the peace negotiations as Franklin did in December 1782, even as he obtained a French loan of six million livres for the bankrupt government of the Confederation.

And this brings us to Franklin. It has been the fashion of recent writers to focus on the inconsistencies in the Doctor's character. Behind his professions of universal benevolence they find a demanding and, at times, a cruel husband and father.[51] Behind his professions of diligence they find a dallier. He is even exposed as a poor sport in chess. These writers are not inspired by Franklin's contemporaries like Adams and Arthur Lee, who angrily assailed the contradictions in his life-style or by British opponents who branded him Dr. Doubleface. Yet the effect of the new scholarship is to reinforce the old rancor and to create the impression that Franklin was a hypocrite or a plastic man, a manipulator of various personas, as another recent writer describes him.[52]

Franklin's diplomatic conduct seems to be consistent with a personality whose stock in trade was inscrutability and craft. He did not give the appearance of being suspicious. His writings yield little praise for jealousy and little that indicates a commitment to republican ideology. He seems, in fact, to have ostentatiously repudiated suspicion. He was profuse in his declarations of trust for France, and he made the famous comment about receiving with equanimity the news that all his servants were enemy spies. Franklin, however, set the example of negotiating with the British without communicating with the French, when he presented confidential articles of peace to Richard Oswald early in the summer of 1782. From this action one infers that Franklin may have been just as suspicious of the French as his colleagues, but more willing to disguise his feelings. Covert suspicion,

[51] This is one of the points raised continually in Alfred O. Aldridge, *Benjamin Franklin: Philosopher and Man* (Philadelphia, 1965), pp. 126, 155, 215–16, 243–44.

[52] This is the thesis of Paul Conner, *Poor Richard's Politicks* (New York, 1965).

carefully calculated and controlled, could be exercised, Franklin must have perceived, without alienating the French, on whom the well-being of the United States depended.

No good diplomat in the eighteenth century would have suspended his suspiciousness, just as no good diplomat today should. But to broadcast it, even to the enemy, as Adams and Jay did, and to be possessed by it at the expense of one's good judgment, as both of them on occasion were, abused what was a potentially valuable resource. This is how Franklin evaluated jealousy, and this was the way it was assessed in the United States as the ardor of the Revolution began to diminish. By the late 1780s John Adams himself had tempered his jealousy.[53] But in 1782 the imprint of republican ideology was still strong on him, on Laurens, and, to a somewhat lesser degree, on Jay. Jealousy, a product of that ideology, guided them as they negotiated for peace. We should be glad today that it did. But we should also be glad that the wise and subtle Benjamin Franklin was present in Paris in 1782 to keep his jealous colleagues from ruining a cause they all loved.

[53] Hutson, *John Adams*, p. 35.

CHARLES R. RITCHESON

Britain's Peacemakers 1782–1783
"To an Astonishing Degree Unfit for the Task"?

AT A PARTICULARLY tense moment in September 1782 the earl of Shelburne, chief minister of the crown, accepted the urgent advice of Richard Oswald to amend his commission to negotiate peace with America. The "Colonies and Plantations" became the newly styled "Thirteen United States of America." Intended to soothe American anxieties, the step involved great risk. Cabinet colleagues doubted its legality. The king was restive. A powerful opposition was certain when the prorogued Parliament reassembled. The American response could not be foretold. "Having said and done everything which has been desired," a worried Shelburne wrote to Oswald, "there is nothing left for me to trouble you with except to add that we have put the greatest confidence, I believe, was ever placed in Man, in the American Commissioners." If an honorable peace did not ensue, "our heads will answer for it, and deservedly."[1] Both men escaped the ultimate experience on Tower Green; but Lecky's savaging of Oswald with the words quoted in the title of this essay show condign punishment wrought by the instrument proverbially mightier than the headsman's sword.[2]

Denunciation of Lord Shelburne reached even greater

[1] Sept. 23, 1782, Shelburne Papers, LXXI, fol. 123, William L. Clements Library, University of Michigan, Ann Arbor.

[2] W. E. H. Lecky, *A History of England in the Eighteenth Century*, new ed., 7 vols. (London, 1892), 5:158.

heights of bitterness, although his critics tended to dwell not on incapacity but on hypocrisy, duplicity, mendacity, overweening ambition, and the manipulation of the power of the crown to circumvent Parliament. A hundred and seventy years later Vincent T. Harlow, building upon the earlier works of Clarence W. Alvord, provided a considerable measure of rehabilitation for "the Jesuit of Berkeley Square."[3] The earl discerned the shape of the future, the argument ran, more distant, indeed, than he hoped. Still, free trade, Shelburne's great vision in 1782, triumphed in the nineteenth century, and the British-American reconciliation that he strove so valiantly to reestablish during the peace negotiations emerged with great force in the twentieth. The visionary, Harlow concluded, was closer to truth than the realist. Although the thesis rests in part on assumptions that appear questionable—the doctrine of eventual justification, for example, and Shelburne's supreme dedication to free trade—it is sounder by far than partisan attacks during the earl's lifetime and the nationalistic nineteenth-century American interpretation that remains influential to this day.[4]

Harlow did not extend his reappraisal to Richard Oswald, however. The duke of Richmond angrily told George III in 1782 that the Scot was just another American commissioner. Lecky, Sir George Lewis, the *Dictionary of National Biography*, and others have transformed Richmond's charge into convention. It deserves reexamination.

Oswald was the principal but not the sole British agent in the negotiation of the Preliminary Treaty. Toward the end, indeed, he played a secondary role and was forbidden to sign a treaty without express approval of others on the Paris scene. This constitutes no defense, of course, but it does sug-

---

[3] Vincent T. Harlow, *The Founding of the Second British Empire, 1763–1793*, 2 vols. (London, 1952–64); Clarence W. Alvord, *Lord Shelburne and the Founding of British-American Goodwill* (Oxford, 1926), and *The Mississippi Valley in British Politics*, 2 vols. (Cleveland, 1917). George III's epithet for the earl comes from the 1760s.

[4] Harlow, *Founding of the Second British Empire*, 1:311. For a critique of Harlow's interpretation of Shelburne see Charles R. Ritcheson, "The Earl of Shelburne and Peace with America, 1782–1783: Vision and Reality," *International History Review* 5 (1983): 322–45.

gest a broader approach than mere condemnation of Oswald. Sent to Paris in April 1782 to gauge the sincerity of Benjamin Franklin's professions of peace, Oswald was soon joined by Thomas Grenville, son of the Stamp Act's champion, who represented Foreign Secretary Charles James Fox. When the marquess of Rockingham died on July 1, Shelburne succeeded to the Treasury, Fox resigned, and Grenville returned home. Alleyne Fitzherbert, whose sponsor seems to have been the new home secretary, Thomas Townshend, was dispatched from the Brussels mission to take up negotiations with the Continental belligerents. At the end of July, Oswald was commissioned to treat with the Americans. Shelburne intended to give him a colleague, Richard "Omniscient" Jackson, member of Parliament and sometime advocate at the Board of Trade who would have provided much-needed expert assistance. Jackson declined the appointment, apparently for reasons of health, and Oswald functioned as sole British envoy until October.[5] In July, Shelburne had thought fit to send his young personal friend Benjamin Vaughan to Paris in a private capacity to assure the Americans that the new ministry remained committed to independence. Vaughan managed to prolong a four-day assignment for six months by citing his intimate relations with the Americans. In the autumn Oswald fell foul of his London principals, and Henry Strachey, member of Parliament and undersecretary in Townshend's office, was ordered into the fray. With the preliminaries signed on November 30 and Shelburne driven from office the following February, the Fox-North coalition ministry sent David Hartley to make a definitive treaty, which proved to be essentially the preliminaries with new date and signatures. A second assignment, to make a commercial treaty with America, was aborted by the Order in Council of July 2, 1783. Finally, the duke of

[5] John Jay, *The Peace Negotiations of 1782 and 1783* (New York, 1889), p. 112, reprinted from Justin Winsor, ed., *Narrative and Critical History of America*, 8 vols. (Boston, 1884–89), 7:89–184. Also see the earl of Shelburne to Richard Oswald, June 30, 1782, F.O. 27/2, fols. 153–55, Public Record Office. Shelburne was writing on the very day Fox was beaten in the cabinet. Richard Jackson to Shelburne, Sept. 29, 1782, Shelburne Papers, Bowood, Calnes, Wiltshire.

Manchester, Britain's first postwar ambassador to France, signed a definitive treaty with the Continental powers identical to Fitzherbert's earlier accords. This minor duty discharged, his Grace may be excused further scrutiny.

Putting aside considerations of Richard Oswald for a moment (and the duke of Manchester forever), the remaining five—Grenville, Fitzherbert, Vaughan, Strachey, and Hartley—possessed very considerable experience with America. They sincerely desired an end to the war and believed in varying degrees that conciliation of America was necessary and reconciliation highly desirable. None thought in terms of abject surrender, however, or a "diplomacy of defeat." Hartley and Vaughan knew Franklin intimately and admired him enormously, and by 1782 both had taken public positions sympathetic to the American cause. Grenville and Strachey tended to follow the Old Whig line in Parliament and must be reckoned as critics of the North ministry and supporters of American independence. Fitzherbert had no obvious political connections, a status most fitting for a professional diplomat. In Brussels, however, he gathered much intelligence on Continental attitudes toward the rebellion that served him well in his subsequent negotiations.[6]

Four of the negotiators (including Oswald) came from the geographical fringes of British life where Dissent, a frequent element in pro-American sympathies, was strong; but it does not appear that religious nonconformity figured to the slightest degree in British diplomacy in 1782. Oswald, Hartley, and Strachey had Scottish backgrounds. Vaughan, born in Jamaica of a Bostonian mother, came from Welsh stock. Fitzherbert and Grenville, by contrast, belonged to the English social and political Establishment.

---

[6] George H. Guttridge, *David Hartley, M.P.: An Advocate of Conciliation* (Berkeley, 1926), p. 237. Of his forty-four speeches to the House of Commons, thirty-six were on American affairs and the remainder contained allusions to them. On Vaughan, see John H. Sheppard, *Reminiscences of the Vaughan Family, and More Particularly of Benjamin Vaughan* (Boston, 1865), the *Dictionary of National Biography*, and William Vaughan, *Tracts on Docks and Commerce* (London, 1839), introduction. There are two volumes of his correspondence with Shelburne at Bowood. For Fitzherbert's activities in Brussels see his dispatches in C.O. 5/231, P.R.O.

Of the six, there were four who could claim some sort of official status. Grenville, Hartley, and Strachey sat in the Commons, and the last was an experienced and respected bureaucrat. Fitzherbert, a man of cool and uncommon good sense, was well launched on a successful diplomatic career. Grenville's future also lay in diplomacy, although his debut in Paris in the spring of 1782 could have been read reasonably but inaccurately as a poor augury. Strachey alone encountered the rebels in their native habitat. In 1776 Lord North persuaded him much against his better judgment to become secretary to the Howe peace commission. In New York he composed some notably unsuccessful exhortations to unrepentant enemies of the crown, but the unpleasant experience left no discernible mark six years later. Vaughan lacked any public character but held a very considerable private advantage, the patronage of the earl of Shelburne, whom he served occasionally as unofficial secretary and who introduced him to Franklin at Bowood. Grenville, loyal friend of Fox, and Hartley, whose Old Whig ideology made him the foe of Toryism, real or suspected, detested Shelburne. Both paid in the coin of disappointment, Hartley because Shelburne chose Oswald for the Paris mission, and Grenville in circumstances described below.

Four had important economic ties with America. Hartley, Vaughan, and Oswald had trading interests, although by 1782 Oswald was retired with a large fortune.[7] In addition, Oswald and Strachey owned much real estate in the colonies. Strachey, who numbered among his ancestors the first secretary of the colony of Virginia and a last surviving relative of the American line who died in the Old Dominion in 1756, had land in West Florida.[8] Oswald's much more extensive

---

[7] W. Stitt Robinson, Jr., in the essay accompanying his edition of Oswald's 1781 *Memorandum on the Folly of Invading Virginia, the Strategic Importance of Portsmouth, and the Need for Civilian Control of the Military* ([Charlottesville, Va., 1953], p. 35), states that Oswald's private fortune was much in excess of £250,000.

[8] Despite the best efforts of his friend Governor Tonyn, Strachey lost the property through rebel confiscation (see C. R. Sanders, *The Strachey Family, 1588–1932* [Durham, N.C., 1953], pp. 76–77).

property came to him at least in part from a lucky second marriage, and included holdings in the southern colonies and the West Indies. Several tracts lay in West Florida, too, one of some 8,000 acres. In happier days the Scot had contemplated founding his own colony there, an intriguing possibility that encourages speculation about its role in the war. It is impossible to prove self-interest in the two landowners' intercourse with the government, but it is not without significance that both, particularly Oswald, tried hard to focus British wartime efforts on the South.[9]

In 1782 Grenville was twenty-six years old, Fitzherbert twenty-nine, and Vaughan thirty-one. Strachey and Hartley were in vigorous middle age. Oswald, by far the oldest, was 75. The near half century separating him from Grenville explains much in human terms about their difficult relations in Paris. Oswald's venerable age was significant for another reason. He had accumulated fifty years' commercial experience with America including six years' residence in Virginia where he met and befriended Henry Laurens, the future member of the American peace commission.[10]

It is often thought that free trade doctrine played an important role in Britain's peacemaking. Fitzherbert, Strachey, and Grenville may be ruled out of the discussion at once. Professionally engaged in the public service or, in Grenville's case, soon to be, they were pragmatists, not ideologues; the instruments of policy, not its makers. Hartley certainly agitated for a liberal trade treaty with America in 1783 and

---

[9] Robinson, ed., *Memorandum*, pp. 35, 44–52; Sanders, *Strachey Family*, p. 77. Oswald's dealings with John Jay, looking to a British reconquest of the province of West Florida from the occupying Spaniards, are treated below.

[10] Benjamin Franklin Stevens, comp., *B. F. Stevens's Facsimiles of Manuscripts in European Archives Relating to America, 1773–1783*, 25 vols. (London, 1889–98), 10: no. 959, notes. In 1781 Oswald testified to his attachment to Laurens by posting a £2,000 bond to secure his release from the Tower. (The £50,000 figure given in the *Dictionary of National Biography* is a gross exaggeration [see Robinson, ed., *Memorandum*, p. 37]). To return the favor, Laurens wrote a warm letter of introduction to Franklin that Oswald carried to Paris on his first visit.

would gladly have renounced the Acts of Trade and Navigation to get it.[11] His overriding concern was not the rearrange-
ment of international trade, however, but the constitutional
crisis he saw at home and overseas. Political radicalism did
not translate into free trade economics. In Hartley's voluminous writings there is not a single discussion of Adam Smith's
work, let alone an application of the free trade theory to
America. Kept out of the peace process by Shelburne, he re-
joiced in 1783 at his chance to set all things right. Instead, he
suffered bitter disappointment and public humiliation when,
without warning, the Fox-North coalition imposed its July
Order in Council excluding American vessels from the West
Indian carrying trade. Vainly imagining he might yet negotiate a British-American economic union, Hartley lingered in
Paris sacrificing both dignity and reputation. The Americans, who rightly saw the July Order as the triumph of the
old mercantile system, treated him with pity scarcely distin-
guishable from bemused contempt. The younger William
Pitt's exasperated foreign secretary, the marquess of Carmarthen, brutally canceled his powers while the unhappy man
was still at his post.[12]

Vaughan, whose gadfly radicalism came to extend to economics as well as politics, became a free trader with all the
gusto his irrepressible and immature nature could muster,
but his pamphlet on the subject appeared long after peace
was made. At any event, he never possessed the means, intellectual or diplomatic, to make a major intervention in the
negotiations, and had as much influence on great events as
he did on the lunar tides. The truth finally dawned on the
"inveterate busybody" himself. On December 31 Shelburne
wrote to Vaughan, who should have been in London long
since. The letter has not survived, but the response makes
the nature of his lordship's message clear. "I presume from
the tenor of it," the young man wrote, "that your lordship
foresees that my farther stay here may prove frivolous; which

[11] Guttridge, *Hartley*, pp. 266–67.

[12] The primary original source for the Hartley mission is F.O. 4/2,
America, ser. I, P.R.O.

indeed I had myself begun to suspect."[13] Vaughan and Hartley shared much: admiration for America as the defender of
liberty and hope of the world, a belief that British welfare
required reconciliation with the new nation, and utter inabil-
ity to forward these objectives in any significant way. As for
free trade, whatever Hartley failed to think or Vaughan
thought about it was irrelevant.

What about Oswald? It has been asserted and frequently
repeated that Shelburne chose him for the Paris mission because they were both free traders.[14] This is not the case.
Much significance has been wrongly attached to Adam
Smith's introduction of the two men some years before 1782.
The economist was merely performing a courtesy to his
friend, Richard's older brother, the Rev. James Oswald.[15]
Shelburne's own connection with Smith was familial (his
younger brother passed some of his student days as a paying
guest in Smith's household), cool, and distant. There is not a
shred of direct or credible evidence to show the great Glas-
wegian influenced his thinking in the slightest. It cannot be
demonstrated that the earl ever read the *Wealth of Nations*,
and his views on free trade are, in fact, suspect. In the elo-

[13] See his pamphlet *New and Old Principles of Trade Compared, or a Treatise
on the Principles of Commerce between Nations* (London, 1788), and Benjamin
Vaughan to Shelburne, Jan. 5, 1783, Shelburne Papers, Bowood. My treat-
ment of Vaughan is based principally on eleven of his letters to Shelburne
(preserved at Bowood in typescript), which date from October 1782 to
February 1783. The king's attitude emerges in his letter to Shelburne,
Nov. 3, 1782, in the Shelburne Papers, Bowood, in which he also criticizes
Vaughan's literary style, surely an example of pot and kettle. Also see
George III to Shelburne, Aug. 12, 1782, Add. Mss. 34523, fols. 365–72,
British Museum, and Harlow, *Founding of the Second British Empire*, 1:272–
74, 264 n. 78, 305–6. Harlow uses the phrase "inveterate busybody."

[14] Lecky, *History of England*, 5:152; Robinson, ed., *Memorandum*, pp. 38–
39; Lord Edmond Fitzmaurice, *Life of William, Earl of Shelburne*, 2 vols.
(London, 1912), 2:119–20, and Harlow, *Founding of the Second British Empire*, 1:276.

[15] E. C. Mossner and I. D. Ross, eds., *The Correspondence of Adam Smith*
(Oxford, 1977), p. 88n; Sir George Lewis, *Essays on the Administrations of
Great Britain from 1783 to 1830* (London, 1864), pp. 81–84.

quent apologia to the Lords in February 1783 Shelburne inveighed against commercial monopoly and praised trade over dominion but, at the end, he rested his defense of the treaties on Britain's distressed and impotent condition. In private correspondence, to be sure, he boasted that the accords were "pervaded" by the great principle of "General Freedom of Commerce." Even a casual reading, however, is sufficient to demonstrate his mistake. The boundary settlement may indicate an indifference to dominion compared with trade, and a provision in the French treaty certainly provided the genesis of the liberal commercial treaty of 1786. But even if the two articles are accepted for purposes of argument as evidence of radical economic thought, they can scarcely be thought to "pervade" the treaties. To maintain the contrary raises a real question, not about Shelburne's sincerity, but about the quality of his understanding of economics. Correspondence with his mentor, the Abbé Morellet, who by the earl's own testimony converted him to laissez-faire in 1771, creates the uneasy suspicion that the second-rate philosophe provided little more than the vocabulary of a fashionable radical chic. The two friends seemed to use "free trade" and "liberté du commerce" as pebbles to skip across the Channel without reference to the profundities below the surface. It must also be noted that Shelburne's talk in 1782 about lowering British trade barriers for French and American benefit furnished a remarkably convenient supplement to a diplomatic arsenal singularly bereft of major weaponry.[16]

---

[16] Shelburne made the remark to the Abbé Morellet (Fitzmaurice, *Life of Shelburne*, 1:430). The Morellet-Shelburne material is preserved at Bowood; Lord Edmond Fitzmaurice edited much of it in his *Morellet-Shelburne Letters* (Paris, 1898). Harlow, *Founding of the Second British Empire*, 1:433–34, provides a brilliant insight into Shelburne's personality but fails to reconcile the two antipathetic strains in the speech of February 1783. The Abbé's comment on Adam Smith's *Wealth of Nations* furnishes a notable example of an endemic superficiality: "Cette forme ne vous plaira peut-être pas," he wrote to Shelburne, "mais pour moi . . . l'ouvrage me fait grand plaisir" (Mar. 12, 1776, Fitzmaurice, ed., *Morellet-Shelburne Letters*, p. 106).

Harlow is quite correct in using the term *Zollverein* to describe Shelburne's aspiration for a postwar settlement with America, but the term

The case against Richard Oswald as a free trader is even stronger. He never held himself to be a supporter of radical economic theories and went to Paris because he was a man of practical affairs, not of abstract thought.[17] Neither his public nor private papers afford the slightest reason to think that he ever considered abandoning the mercantile system from which he had so signally benefited for over fifty years. In 1795 Benjamin Vaughan, by then both a resident of America and a rabid free trader, sent James Monroe a long panegyric of the old Scot, dead for a decade. It contained not a word about free trade principles.[18]

When it is asked what Richard Oswald wanted in the way of peace with America, the usual answer is that he wanted what Dr. Franklin wanted. The "ingenuous soul" of "transparent candour" was a "simple-minded, well-meaning man," "to an astonishing degree unfit for the task" in Paris because Franklin could make upon him the impression of his choice. The word *senility* is rarely spoken, but it hovers close at hand.[19] These interpretations are serious misreadings of the man's true character, abilities, shortcomings, and contributions to the making of the peace. Oswald was in reality a complex personality, thoroughly mercantilist, and hostile toward Revolutionary America. Under an exterior of modest affability and jocular good nature, he was, if a colloquialism may be employed, a tough and wily old bird. He could be brutal. In

---

(which the earl would not have recognized) is not synonymous with *free trade* or *laissez-faire*. Further, it is well known that Smith had important reservations about the value of Britain's trade with America compared with her trade with Europe.

[17] Shelburne to Benjamin Franklin, Apr. 6, 1782, Fitzmaurice, *Life of Shelburne*, 2:119–20.

[18] The letter, dated Sept. 18, 1795, is in the Monroe Papers, Library of Congress, and is quoted in Robinson, ed., *Memorandum*, pp. 39–40.

[19] The quotations are from Harlow, *Founding of the Second British Empire*, 1:276, 439, Lord John Russell, ed., *Memoirs and Correspondence of Charles James Fox*, 4 vols. (London, 1853), 1:344, Lewis, *Administrations of Great Britain*, p. 33, and Lecky, *History of England*, 5:158. Samuel Eliot Morison called Oswald "senile" during a lecture in his famous course on colonial and Revolutionary American history in 1948.

1775 he became a volunteer but respected adviser on American affairs to the North ministry. Concerned not with reconciliation but with crushing the rebels, Oswald urged the separation of the southern colonies from the "mob of Northern Yeomen," the "despicable Rabble of Rioters," and the "Confederacy of Smugglers." Any means available to the mother country was justified: intrigue (1775), military punishment (1779), or even alliance with Russia (1781). The South was especially vital, he reasoned, because of its trade that Britain had dominated before the war and had to have again, and because it provided necessary supplies for the sugar islands. In doctrinaire language, the Acts of Trade and Navigation were called "most sacred laws." Finally, a territorial base in the South was necessary if Britain was to reestablish and guard a truncated yet closed and self-sufficient empire. Oswald did not write on the subject, but had he done so he might well have supported the Order in Council of July 1783.[20]

Shelburne doubtless knew nothing of Oswald's dealings

[20] See the "Plan Submitted (to the earl of Dartmouth) for Breaking Up the American Confederacy by Detaching One of the Southern Provinces," Stevens, ed., *Facsimiles*, 24: no. 2032, which contains the phrase quoted here. The "Memorandum with Respect to South Carolina," also addressed to Dartmouth, Lord North's secretary of state for the colonies, can be found ibid., no. 2034. The "General Observations, Relative to the Present State of the War" (1779), the "Supplement to the Papers of August 1779," and the "Plan for an Alliance with Russia in Order to Carry on the American War" (Feb. 1781) are in the Shelburne Papers, Clements Library. Oswald revised the February plan in April because Russia was said to be about to mediate the war. The proposal called for several thousand Russian troops to replace British garrisons in occupied American cities to allow operations in the Gulf of Mexico, and for a possible Russian conquest of California. R. A. Humphreys expresses doubt that Oswald thought the British ministry would accept the plan, but writes that it remains "a curious commentary" on his state of mind in the summer of 1782 ("Richard Oswald's Plan for an English and Russian Attack on Spanish America, 1781–1782," *Hispanic-American Historical Review* 18 [1938]: 95–101). Oswald's preoccupation with regaining a position of strength in the Gulf was more important than Humphreys appreciates, since it led Oswald directly into his discussions with Jay about the reconquest of Spanish-occupied West Florida. See below.

with the North ministry—otherwise, he would not have sent him to Paris to speak with Franklin—and the old man was always careful to preserve his anonymity.[21] One of the most surprising papers could not have escaped Shelburne's attention, however, because Oswald addressed it to him from Paris in July 1782, at almost precisely the same time—a little afterwards, in fact—that Benjamin Franklin was presenting his "Necessary" and "Advisable" articles as the terms of peace. It assumed that the war was not ending, but continuing.[22] The Americans "are, or ought to be" subject to the British government, Oswald said. To prevent future disturbances, the British constitutional model should be imposed: a viceroy or lord lieutenant with a privy council of six or eight to preside over the entire continent. A long list of reforms followed: oaths taken from the populace to observe "true and full obedience" to Parliament; forfeiture of charters; appointive councils; judges named by the crown; strict regulation of jury eligibility; a board of commissioners of the customs; admiralty courts; restricted access to the fisheries; discouragement of town meetings; supervision of colleges, especially Harvard with its "government of fanatics or independents" that needed "some episcopal gentlemen of learning" in its administration; disfranchisement for all who had served in Congress, other public office, or the rebel military; and the promulgation of the Acts of Trade as a single code. Possibly

[21] Oswald to the earl of Dartmouth, Feb. 2 and 21, 1775, Stevens, ed., *Facsimiles*, 24:nos. 2031 and 2033; Robinson, ed., *Memorandum*, p. 50.

[22] Oswald to Shelburne, July 12, 1782, F.O. 97/15, fol. 35, P.R.O. Franklin's "Necessary" and "Advisable" articles were given to Oswald two days earlier. The paper itself exists in two draft forms in C.O. 5/8, fols. 288–307, P.R.O. It is docketed "Plantations General/Propositions for Settling North America." Caleb Whitefoord, Oswald's hardworking and long-suffering secretary in Paris, complained that "Mr. Oswald being of a very active and speculative Mind, was much employed on drawing up Schemes and Plans either in behalf of the loyalists, and the Mother Country, or for annoying our Enemies. Some of those Plans were very long." Since the nature of these plans made secrecy mandatory and Oswald required multiple copies, Whitefoord, denied secretarial assistance for reasons of security, often had to write from 7 A.M. to 11 P.M. (W. A. S. Hewins, ed., *The Whitefoord Papers* [Oxford, 1898], p. 194).

some difficulties might arise in establishing his reforms, Oswald conceded, but he believed there would never be a better opportunity to settle "a regular constitution for his Majesty's American colonies." In retrospect, the conclusion contained highest irony; but the paper, which would have done credit to an undersecretary in the office of Lord George Germain before Saratoga, was deadly serious when it was written. Where was Oswald the free trader? The putty in the American commissioners' hands? As Britain's envoy engaged Benjamin Franklin in sweet talk about reconciliation, who was seeking to dupe whom?

The correct answer to the question about Oswald's objectives in the negotiations is that he wanted what Lord Shelburne wanted, except for a memorable parting of the ways in October 1782. Reduced to their essentials, these were: first, to break the Franco-American axis; next, to reestablish British-American peace and amity; and, finally, to win anew the economic dominance interrupted by the war. Shelburne considered the Scot qualified for the mission because of his experience, particularly in trade, his friendship with Laurens, and his age and personality, which promised good relations with Franklin. In addition, he stood apart from the political establishment which Shelburne disliked and distrusted and which returned the sentiments in full measure. It may be inferred that the earl saw in the elderly, modest, and diplomatically inexperienced merchant a rubber stamp who would function precisely as he was instructed. If so, on one occasion Oswald surprised him unpleasantly. Shelburne never had reason to doubt his friend's personal loyalty, however, and in the first stage of the negotiation, from April to July, the two men formed as deadly a set of political infighters as could be found on the London scene. Their principal victims were Charles James Fox and Thomas Grenville.

Rivals from the very inception of the Rockingham ministry, Foreign Secretary Fox claimed the making of peace pertained to his office while Home Secretary Shelburne insisted that pending the recognition of American independence the "colonies" remained within his own jurisdiction. Rockingham naturally sided with Fox. On two separate occasions the marquess suggested candidates for the Paris mission that

Shelburne, not surprisingly, found unacceptable.[23] The earl moved quickly to cover his flank by naming Oswald. A small victory—a minister was scarcely to be overruled in his own office—it was nonetheless vital, and the more significant because George III, suspicious of Rockingham and detesting Fox, gave it his support.[24] To assert his own claim to primacy in the negotiation, Fox immediately named Grenville to go to Paris for consultations not only with Oswald and the comte de Vergennes, the French foreign minister, but also with Franklin. Grenville's instructions, written by the foreign secretary and approved by the cabinet, were to probe for a separate peace with America if France showed herself unreasonable. On May 18 Grenville was voted full powers. While no specific reference to America stood in the commission, it was clear to all the world that Fox's man, his majesty's minister plenipotentiary and envoy extraordinary, was in command of British operations in Paris. Shelburne himself seemed to give up the game and to acquiesce in his own eclipse.[25] In reality, he was desperately maneuvering to prevent Oswald's outright recall and to preserve a link with Franklin not under the eye of his ministerial rival.

In Paris, Grenville met Franklin on several occasions. During one of these, the Doctor appeared to indulge in ambiguities designed to elicit favorable terms. Grenville believed he was to understand that with independence in hand, America would consider her alliance with France at an end. Next day

[23] These were William Hodgson, the London merchant who had already been in touch with Franklin about prisoners of war, and Henry Seymour, who possessed impeccable Old Whig credentials and was in Paris at the time on private business (see the marquess of Rockingham to Shelburne, Mar. 29 and Apr. 13, 1782, Bowood Papers).

[24] George III to Shelburne, Apr. 5, 1782, Mackintosh Collection, XXXVII, Add. Mss. 34523, fol. 365, British Museum; Russell, ed., *Memoirs and Correspondence of Fox*, 1:346.

[25] Charles James Fox to Thomas Grenville, Mar. 30, 1782, F.O. 27/2, fols. 42–46, P.R.O., printed in Russell, ed., *Memoirs and Correspondence of Fox*, 4:174–77. Also see the cabinet minute, May 21, 1782, Russell, ed., *Memoirs and Correspondence of Fox*, 4:191–92, Shelburne to Oswald, May 21, 1782, F.O. 97/157, fols. 6–7, and to Grenville, May 25, 1782, F.O. 27/2, fol. 107, P.R.O.

Franklin seemed to confirm the impression to Oswald, who departed hastily for London to report to the ministry.[26] On May 23 the cabinet, buoyed by Admiral Rodney's victory over the French in West Indian waters, considered the news from Paris. Influenced by Fox, who accepted Franklin at his reported word, the ministers voted fresh instructions for Grenville. Fox's envoy was to propose "the independence of America in the first instance, instead of making it a condition of a general treaty." In preparing to make his case to Franklin—that is, to convince him that an independent America was not obliged to support unreasonable French demands on Britain—Grenville was told to communicate with Oswald freely and openly about his mission, which was "connected more and more every day with the business of America." Condescension could scarcely be more marked.

Shelburne must have been aghast. His own role in the negotiation was diminished to the vanishing point. More important in national terms, he was convinced that Fox's snap judgment, based on a serious underestimation of American bitterness toward Britain, threatened to discard the country's prime bargaining counter and to strengthen the ability of a triumphant United States to support her ally.[27] Personal interest and high policy thus combined to produce for Shelburne a moment of great crisis, and he had few resources with which to meet it. His sole ministerial ally was Lord Ashburton. The king was with him. Oswald had succeeded in winning the confidence of the American commissioners in Paris. Further, perhaps for one of the few times in his life,

---

[26] Harlow, *Founding of the Second British Empire*, 1:253.

[27] See Oswald to Shelburne, July 8, 1782, F.O. 97/157, fol. 17, P.R.O.: "I could not see there would be much field for negotiation between Great Britain and the Commissioners of the Colonies after their Independence has been granted." Harlow is critical of Fox and uses the words "snap judgment" (*Founding of the Second British Empire*, 1:253–55 and n. 54). Also see Fox to Grenville, May 21, 1782, Richard Grenville, duke of Buckingham and Chandos, *Memoirs of the Court and Cabinets of George the Third*, 4 vols. (London, 1853–55), 1:28. Franklin must have smiled at Fox's naive message that "he and I are still of the same country."

Shelburne was moving in harmony with public opinion.[28] Finally, he seized the initiative with a boldness born of desperation and embarked with Oswald upon an extraordinary, clandestine, and constitutionally reprehensible maneuver to destroy Fox's cabinet motion of May 23 and to take control of the American negotiations.

On May 31 Oswald, fresh from London, delivered packets to Grenville, including Fox's instructions of May 26, based on the provision for "independence in the first instance" adopted by the cabinet three days earlier. As a courtesy he called also at Passy with letters for Franklin. The exact sequence of subsequent events is unclear, but Oswald spoke with both Franklin and John Jay, the latter having arrived from Madrid, and made a declaration so bold that it must have been concocted with Shelburne during the recent visit to London. He was willing to remain in Paris to serve the cause of peace, "if," Jay reported to John Adams at The Hague, "we think he may be useful, and is equally willing to be excused, if we judge there is no occasion for him." Grenville, Jay continued, "seems to think the whole negotiation committed to him, and to have no idea of Mr. Oswald's being concerned about it." Shelburne's man was suggesting nothing less than removing the nomination of the British negotiator from the London cabinet and lodging it firmly with the American commissioners.[29]

---

[28] Thomas Orde to Shelburne, Sept. 26, 1782, Bowood Papers. Orde, Shelburne's secretary of the Treasury and the future Lord Bolton, captured the public mood when he told his first lord that American independence was acceptable to the country "*as the price of peace*," that is, as part of a bargain for "a good, of which we stood in need." To embrace "a voluntary, unconditional and possibly *inconsequential* deriliction" was unendurable and self-inflicted humiliation. Even after the preliminaries were signed in November, the king continued to castigate Fox and Grenville for "the Strange, undigested opening of the negotiations" and blamed them for the disadvantageous terms of the treaty (George III to Shelburne, Dec. 22, 1782, Mackintosh Coll., XXXVII, Add. Mss. 34523, fols. 365–72, italics in original).

[29] John Jay to John Adams, [early July?] 1782, Jay, *Peace Negotiations*, p. 104.

Whether Franklin responded at once or allowed a day or two to pass for consultation with Jay cannot be established. It is certain, however, that he soon reached a momentous decision: American interests would be best served by dealing directly with the British, and with Richard Oswald instead of Thomas Grenville. In a second meeting, on June 3, Franklin declared himself. He hoped Oswald might be chosen to negotiate with the commissioners. "I told him," the Scot recorded in his diary with a delicacy purely decorative, "that if it was to trench on the character of Mr. Grenville's station, it would be the last thing I should incline to. That I believed him very capable and prudent, and had no doubt of his acquiring himself a reputation." (Two could play at condescension.) "As to my stay here," he continued,

> it was on account of various circumstances not the most agreeable. And with respect to my private affairs, they were in such situation that I should not suffer by my attendance. At least, I should make no account of these matters if I thought that upon so critical an occasion I would be of any service to my country, etc.
>
> The doctor replied, that he thought the Commission for the Colonies would be better in my hands than in Mr. Grenville's. That I understood more of Colony business than he did, and he himself had a longer acquaintance with me than Mr. Grenville, and could not say but he esteemed me; and therefore not only thought the Colony Commission should be left in my hands, but he wished it might be so.
>
> I replied, that his wishing it was enough to determine, if I found it was a task I could go through with.[30]

When Grenville called on Franklin on June 1 in highest expectation that the offer of "independence in the first instance" would be enthusiastically, even gratefully received, he was baffled to find the Doctor dour and unresponsive.[31] Without knowing that a deal was in process of being struck behind his back, the agitated and angry young man sought

---

[30] Oswald's minute of conversation with Franklin, May 31, 1782, printed in Lewis, *Administrations of Great Britain*, pp. 82–84.

[31] Grenville to Fox, June 4, 1782, Jay, *Peace Negotiations*, p. 105.

out Oswald. The Scot minced few words. Shelburne intended to make him commissioner to negotiate with the Americans (a point that Oswald had not disclosed to Franklin). He himself had already discussed the prospective appointment with Franklin, who seemed not only perfectly agreeable but also delighted at an arrangement he had "very much wished." Oswald added that he himself desired only to serve the cause of peace and very much regretted any difference at home between the two secretaries of state. When, finally, a shaken Grenville found voice to take up the last point, he was told bluntly that it was "owing to the Rockingham party being too ready to give up everything."[32] The blow to the young man's self-esteem was savage, and further mortification was at hand. Lafayette mocked him on a public occasion when he laughingly told him *that he had just left Lord Shelburne's ambassador at* [Franklin's residence in] *Passy.* Even though he did not suspect that Oswald had actually taken the initiative with the American, Grenville concluded that the "intended appointment has effectually stopped Franklin's mouth to me." Indeed, the bitter cup was not yet full. The Scot, apparently inadvertently, revealed to him the existence of Franklin's confidential memorandum calling for the cession of Canada and Nova Scotia. Carried to London from Oswald's first meeting with the Doctor in April, it had been rejected out of hand by then Home Secretary Shelburne, but, honoring Franklin's insistence that the communication was private and informal, Shelburne had unwisely decided not to inform the cabinet. Oswald's two revelations proved to both Fox and Grenville that they and, indeed, the ministry as a whole were abused by a double-dealing colleague and his minion. Their conclusion was sound but, fortunately for Shelburne and his envoy, their information was imperfect.

Grenville deserves sympathy. Diminished in the eyes of the French, the Americans, and the entire *corps diplomatique* in Paris just as he thought to take in hand his country's most important negotiation since 1763, he found himself checked and humiliated. Viewing his mission as "irretrievably in-

---

[32] Oswald to Shelburne, June 4, 1782, Buckingham and Chandos, *Court and Cabinets*, 1:35–38.

jured," he requested his own recall and suggested that Fox replace him with a nobleman of superior rank to take control of the shattered negotiation.[33] It is difficult to find sympathy for Fox, however. Pressing Grenville for additional proof of Shelburne's duplicity and intending to make Franklin's memorandum a resigning matter, his enemy's or his own, he embarked upon a course of action that showed him at his most impetuous and at his worst. He may have wished to remove the ambiguity from his minute of May 23 that allowed Shelburne to maintain that independence was still the price of a preliminary, if not a general, peace. Perhaps he hoped to reinstate Grenville in the negotiation with Franklin. He may have intended a display of overwhelming power within the cabinet to secure the succession to the mortally striken Rockingham. Whatever his line of reasoning, he was utterly determined to force Shelburne's opposition into the open, beat him in face-to-face confrontation, and drive him from the government. His hatred clouded his judgment. On June 30 he raised as a cabinet question "the policy of not reserving the independence of America as a matter of treaty and the price of peace but to grant it at once unconditionally." A mere reaffirmation and minor clarification of the earlier motion would be a pro forma exercise, Fox must have thought, a setting of the stage for the bloodletting to follow. No record of the June 30 meeting survives, but its results were reported laconically to Grenville by Richard Brinsley Sheridan, boon companion to Charles James Fox: "He was beat."[34] The blood on the floor was not Lord Shelburne's.

The cabinet's reversal came at a time of great confusion in the political world. The minute of May 23 had already

[33] As Grenville's temper cooled over the next fortnight, he moderated his original charge to a certain degree: Shelburne had told Oswald, he reported to Fox, that "he supposed he would not object to a commission if it should be necessary; and that since his (Oswald's) last return to Paris, Mr. Oswald has told me he found it very much Franklin's wish likewise." Grenville was, of course, quoting Oswald, and he knew nothing of Oswald's approach to Franklin (Grenville to Fox, June 16, 1782, Russell, ed., *Memoirs and Correspondence of Fox*, 1:375–82).

[34] Richard Brinsley Sheridan to Grenville, July 4, 1782, Buckingham and Chandos, *Court and Cabinets*, 1:53–54.

caused a public outcry, particularly among the loyalist exiles in the kingdom.[35] Rockingham, known to be dying while the cabinet was meeting, died the next day. Shelburne was recognized as the king's confidant. Obviously, sincere doubters and trimmers used the opportunity gratuitously provided by Fox to think again. Within days Rockingham and Fox were gone, and the earl presided over his own ministry. The Paris peace negotiations were at last united as Fox and Grenville had long hoped; but the controlling hands belonged to their enemies, the earl of Shelburne and Richard Oswald.

In achieving their decisive victory, Shelburne and Oswald had more than a common share of luck. Who could have predicted Fox's strange misjudgment in the cabinet? The clandestine approach to the Americans, so redolent of diplomacy in the reign of Charles II, was rich in potential disaster. Franklin might have declined to be drawn and preferred accepting independence "in the first instance" from Grenville. Nor would it have been the first time he had informed the French and the public of such a British maneuver. Shelburne's and Oswald's existence as public men was very much at the hazard. Luck is an insufficient explanation for their triumph, however. Shelburne outfought and defeated Fox, who had superior resources. Oswald won the confidence of the commissioners and used his standing to undermine Grenville. In the process Shelburne and Oswald cut very different figures from Harlow's politically inept free trade visionary and Lecky's elderly and incompetent dupe.

Oswald was formally commissioned to treat with representatives of the "Colonies and Plantations" on July 25. For the next six weeks he acted as his country's sole representative in the American negotiations. Fitzherbert dealt with the French and, ultimately, the Spanish. The two men met frequently to compare notes and exchange information. Neither was subordinate to the other; each was minister

---

[35] Orde to Shelburne, Sept. 26, 1782, Bowood Papers. Much bitterness among the loyalists was caused by Carleton and Digby, the British commanders in America, who read Shelburne's secret dispatches of June 5 and July 8, 1782, as instructions to announce Britain's intention to recognize American independence "in the first instance" (C.O. 5/178, fols. 219–30 and 232–37, P.R.O.).

plenipotentiary and envoy extraordinary, Fitzherbert report-
ing to Foreign Secretary Lord Grantham, Oswald to Home
Secretary Thomas Townshend. These formal channels of
communication notwithstanding, it was clear to all the world
that Britain's diplomat *en chef* was Shelburne, first lord of the
Treasury.

Oswald's instructions empowered him to accept independence, if the Americans declined any form of union or
league with Britain, as the first article of a treaty. The new
status was to be absolute, however. No national substitu-
tion—that is, France—was to be allowed in another dependent relationship. Further, common naturalization and a
generous territorial settlement were to be proposed, but the
Americans were to be pressed to make restitution or indemnification for loyalists' losses and to acknowledge prewar
debts of several million pounds sterling owed by Americans
to many hundreds of British creditors.[36] Before he could
bring these matters to a discussion, however, Oswald had to
face an angry John Jay who took exception to the phrase
"Colonies and Plantations" in the British commission. Without a specific reference to the "United States," the New
Yorker threatened that America would support French
claims around the world, guarantee the peace, and arbitrate
the future quarrels of Europe. Convinced that American
power was growing so rapidly that Jay's threats were not
empty rhodomontade, a worried Oswald recommended to
London that independence be granted at once "absolutely
and unconditionally," else "all farther correspondence with
the Commissioners must cease, as well as Mr. Fitzherbert's
negotiations" with France.[37]

Criticism rumbled through the cabinet at this lapse into
Foxite heresy. Lord Ashburton told Shelburne that he and

---

[36] Oswald's commission and instructions are printed in Russell, ed.,
Memoirs and Correspondence of Fox, 4:262–65. Also see Fitzmaurice, *Life of
Shelburne*, 2:170.

[37] Oswald to Thomas Townshend, Aug. 17, 18, 1782, F.O. 97/157, fols.
56, 91, P.R.O. The scene with Jay is described in Oswald's minutes for Aug.
7 and 8, 1782, quoted in Harlow, *Founding of the Second British Empire*,
1:276 and n. 105.

Chancellor Thurlow were "much dissatisfied" and that Oswald "seems to have mistaken strangely the course he ought to have taken."[38] The envoy should have followed the line laid down in his instructions. Shelburne, aware that Vergennes was opening the possibility of a Franco-British settlement at American expense, might have been tempted to call Jay's bluff. If so, he quickly put the idea aside. At the cabinet meeting on the evening of August 29, the earl stood by Oswald, opting for conciliation of America and a future entente. His colleagues put grumbling aside and accepted supplemental instructions for the envoy. If the Americans continued adamant in refusing to treat without prior acknowledgment of independence, Oswald was to promise a special act of Parliament granting the new status absolutely and irrevocably. In return, the Americans were to limit their further demands to possession of the backcountry, the Canadian boundary before the Quebec Act, and access to the fisheries on the Newfoundland Banks and in adjacent waters. The earlier instructions on prewar debts and loyalist indemnification were not repeated, but the ministers had not revoked them either. Subsequent events made it perfectly clear that they considered them still binding and expected Oswald to make a fight for them.[39] Plainly, too, Oswald be-

[38] Lord Ashburton to Shelburne, Aug. 29, 1782, Shelburne Papers, Clements Library, Corr., A, fol. 18, quoted in Harlow, *Founding of the Second British Empire*, 1:274.

[39] Oswald's instructions of Sept. 1, 1782, approved by the cabinet on August 29, were signed by Townshend and written by Shelburne (F.O. 27/2, fol. 108, P.R.O., and Harlow, *Founding of the Second British Empire*, 1:275). Harlow misses the continuing importance of the July instructions. He seems correct, however, when he states that the September 1 instructions as they stood were "beyond the limit of practical politics" and that a treaty in such terms would have brought down the ministry and the accession to power of a new and reactionary government. The argument here, however, is that Shelburne and his colleagues did not envisage a treaty in those terms and were horrified when Oswald sent home Jay's projet. See below.
Harlow also states that Shelburne was aware at this time of Jay's "firm and unambiguous offer" to trade recognition of independence for an end to cooperation with the House of Bourbon and to give at least tacit consent and encouragement to a British attack on the Spaniards occupying British West Florida. News of Jay's shift from threat to cajolery was not sent to

lieved the new instructions superseded the old, or at the least placed them within the scope of his discretionary powers. Fitzherbert and Strachey, the professionals, would never have made such a mistake.

The special act of Parliament proved unnecessary. Deeply worried by Gérard de Rayneval's mission to London and angered by an intercepted dispatch from Marbois, French minister in Philadelphia, to Vergennes denying any obligation to support American claims on the fisheries, Jay induced his colleagues to accept a compromise suggested by Oswald. Independence was to stand as the first article of the treaty on condition that the Scot's commission was amended to describe the Americans as the representatives of the "Thirteen United States of America." At the cabinet meeting of September 19 Shelburne again supported Oswald, and again he persuaded reluctant colleagues to acquiesce. Nothing, however, could disguise the growing uneasiness in cabinet and closet about a proceeding that many thought illegal.[40]

The new commission arrived in Paris on September 27. Ten days later Oswald accepted and transmitted to London Jay's projet of a preliminary treaty that contained not a word about loyalists, debts, and other points set out in his original instructions. The explanation came in a flurry of dispatches.[41] He had decided not to mention any form of union with Britain or to stipulate that American independence was to be absolute because the new nation would soon be beyond any possible control by an outside power. Although he had earlier believed that the cession of the backcountry should be used as a quid pro quo for loyalist relief,[42] he had not pressed the point because the Americans found the idea so repug-

---

London, however, until Oswald's dispatch of October 7, six weeks after the cabinet meeting of August 29 and a month after Rayneval's secret mission to London that so alarmed Jay and his colleagues (*Founding of the Second British Empire*, 1:283).

[40] The cabinet's decision occasioned Shelburne's letter to Oswald quoted in the first paragraph of this paper.

[41] To Townshend, Oct. 3, 5, 1782, F.O. 97/157, fols. 247–50, 289–92, P.R.O.; Oct. 7, 11, 1782, F.O. 7/157, fols. 150–51, 158–63, P.R.O.

[42] See his minutes of Aug. 29, 1782, F.O. 97/157, fols. 123a–24, P.R.O.

nant that it would have endangered the whole treaty. The vast area should be given to America as a mark of goodwill. Afterwards Britain might make a "plea" in behalf of the loyalists with reasonable expectations that a gratified America would grant it. He had long thought the Americans deserved readmittance to the Newfoundland fisheries on the old footing,[43] and to impose any restriction touching onshore curing, drying, or anything else, would create a perpetual American grievance. Finally, he had declined to argue about the prewar debts. He had acted throughout, he said, to avoid any suggestion of British ill-will and to secure the speediest possible return of "former Correspondence and Friendship."

Has Oswald the dupe finally emerged? Furious ministers in London believed so, and historians have extended the condemnations of October 1782 to the Oswald mission as a whole. The charge is faulty, not because Oswald was innocent but because his indiscretion was of a different order from that of the dupe.

Years before, Oswald had argued to the North ministry that a British lodgement in the American South would bring a renewal of the former mother country's commercial domination and secure supplies for the West Indies. Suddenly, in late September or early October, John Jay made a proposition that must have seemed beyond wildest dreams. It was nothing less than that Britain, with American connivance, should retake West Florida from the occupying Spanish. While his own motive was to remove a potential Spanish threat to the American backcountry, the New Yorker painted a magnificent picture for Oswald's delighted gaze. Possession of the province would give Britain command of the mouth of the Mississippi and its navigation and would furnish "an Entrepot of the Trade of the great backcountry of all the provinces of the 13 states, that would naturally go to the Southward, and in the same Manner as the other part to the Northward would center and issue from Quebec." With the postwar renewal of the Atlantic trade "there would be

---

[43] Oswald to Shelburne, July 10, 1782, F.O. 97/157, fol. 21b, P.R.O., expresses wonder that Franklin had thought it necessary to raise the subject at all.

reason to hope that in a mercantile View, We should not lose much by the Change that has happened." Indeed, Jay had told him "that We should lose nothing and should be saved the Expence & trouble of governing them. These are his Words. And as an Encouragement to the Undertaking has agreed to give us in the Treaty a full Freedom of Navigation on the Mississippi." Because the plan conferred an obligation on the Americans, Britain could count on the untroubled evacuation of her troops and weaponry from Charleston, New York, and Penobscot for a southern campaign. In Oswald's judgment, Jay was presenting a godsend that promised commercial benefits beyond avarice, secure supplies for the West Indies, and the reemergence of British-American cooperation against at least one of the Bourbon powers, itself a mighty step toward reconciliation.[44]

It was a beautiful plan and Oswald's excitement was altogether understandable, but it lay far beyond the realm of political reality. The envoy cannot be faulted for failing to perceive the fact from Paris, but in behaving as he did, he erred grievously. He should have told Jay that while he personally found the scheme enormously interesting, he lacked instructions and required direction from London after a full cabinet deliberation about a matter of such importance and

[44] He gives details of Jay's proposal in his Oct. 7, 1782, dispatch. Harlow states without obvious foundation that in speaking to Oswald about West Florida, Jay was "giving expression to a conception of future British imperial policy in North America that was characteristic of the new school of economists" (Adam Smith, Josiah Tucker, and Richard Price) which, of course, Shelburne, Oswald, and Vaughan purportedly shared (*Founding of the Second British Empire*, 1:303–8). The present argument is that Oswald's chief concern was something else altogether, namely, the restoration of the mercantile system to protect and supply the West Indies and to make Britain dominant again in an important part of the American trade. Harlow finds it fortunate that the Jay-Oswald plan was not implemented because its success would have made a future British-American clash in the trans-Mississippi territory inevitable. To say that because Shelburne's central aim was "an economic union as the corollary of a just and generous political settlement" there was "little point in maintaining a corridor into the Mississippi basin under British sovereignty" is a piling of hypothesis upon hypothesis. The same line might be argued about Canada, and it overlooks the invigorating effect on British-American reconciliation a cooperative enterprise against the Spanish in Florida would have had.

delicacy. Instead, Oswald rushed precipitately into a tacit
understanding with Jay that threatened to bind his government to a policy not of its own choice and to bring Oswald
himself into grave danger of open disavowal. Oswald thus
proved himself very much the amateur diplomat, but not the
dupe, and Shelburne himself must also share the blame since
he should have followed his original plan to give Oswald an
experienced colleague capable of preventing just such a mis-
step.

Under heavy pressure from loyalists, creditors, and an
aroused public opinion in their support, the London cabinet
exploded in anger. Jay's draft was brusquely rejected. A series of conditions was laid down. Commercial negotiations,
the only area in which Oswald might claim expert compe-
tence, were set aside pending the conclusion of peace. The
prewar debts were to be paid. The Nova Scotia boundary
required adjustment to the southwest at the expense of
Maine. If the Americans refused justice to loyalists, the king's
title to the backcountry was to be asserted and bartered to
raise a relief fund. To avoid "the numberless disputes, which
occurred perpetually before the present war," American fishermen were not to dry catches on the Newfoundland shores.
Shelburne administered a direct and cutting rebuke for "the
principle which you seem to have adopted of going before
the American Commissioners in every point of favour and
confidence." The harsh words must have stung, but harsher
actions followed. Henry Strachey was to go to Paris, ostensibly to assist with boundary questions, but in reality to prose-
cute British objectives across the board with greater
effectiveness. Oswald was to seek advice from Fitzherbert as
well. In a separate dispatch, Secretary Townshend twice ordered him to sign no treaty without prior approval of
Strachey and Fitzherbert.[45] For less reason, Thomas Gren-

[45] Shelburne to Oswald, Oct. 20, 1782, Fitzmaurice, *Life of Shelburne*,
2:193–94, and Oct. 23, 1782, F.O. 97/157, fol. 167b, P.R.O.; Townshend
to Oswald, Nov. 11, 1782, F.O. 27/2, fols. 410–13, P.R.O. Earlier Townshend's criticism of Oswald was less direct than Shelburne's but equally
biting. See his instructions to Strachey, Oct. 21, 1782, quoted in Sanders,
Strachey Family, p. 68: "I would not wish to have anything harsh said from
me to Mr. Oswald, but I think it necessary that he should know that he has

ville had demanded his own recall. Instead, Oswald remained in place, accepted Strachey and his own subordination with grace, and worked harmoniously and to good effect to achieve peace. His behavior tells much about his character, patriotism, and dedication to duty. It is no small encomium to say that without him there would have been no treaty in November 1782.

The burden of the last fierce weeks of the negotiation fell primarily upon Henry Strachey. His tenacity in contesting the points Oswald had put aside won the Scot's sincere praise and a backhanded compliment from John Adams. Argumentation, no matter how skillful, could never have brought peace, however. Twice Oswald intervened to save the treaty by persuading his colleague to moderate his position. The newcomer, believing that firmness would force an American retreat, clearly underestimated the commissioners' opposition to loyalist restitution and indemnification. Oswald knew that they were immovable, and said so. At the grand climacteric on November 25, after angry and emotional American threats to present claims for war damages, Oswald engineered a compromise that became the fifth article of the treaty: Congress was to recommend appropriate relief to the several states. The sixth article granted general amnesty. Strachey agreed because he assumed the congressional action would be received by the several states as the equivalent of a royal message to Parliament. In this, sadly for the reputation of the United States, he was to be proved wrong, but by the time the error was discovered, the treaty had been in operation many months.[46]

---

been in my opinion, a great deal too easy upon these subjects, so as to appear to all here to have been quite in the hands of Mr. Franklin and Mr. Jay."

In explaining the hardening of the British position, Harlow attaches considerable significance to the Spanish failure at Gibraltar, news of which reached London on September 30. This may have been a contributing factor, but existing pressures from loyalists and creditors were so great the ministry was bound to respond as it did.

[46] As late as November 8 Strachey was advising London that if loyalist restitution or indemnification were made sine qua non, the Americans would accept rather than break off the negotiation (F.O. 97/157, fol. 193,

Oswald's second major intervention concerned the American demand to cure and dry fish on the shores of the northern fisheries. The principal difficulty arose from Shelburne's inexplicable determination to impose a prohibition.[47] Oswald could not accept his chief's view that bickering fishermen were bound to constitute a standing threat to peace. To refuse the right to cure and dry, he argued, would bring an immediate "splitting" with America. While the exclusion might benefit a relatively small number of British fishermen, the nation as a whole would bear the costs of a rupture in the negotiations. Further, Oswald continued, the measure was certain to require vast sums and the use of force, whereas Britain's true interest was peace and reconciliation. Finally, he argued, by giving way on the minor point, the country gained a quid pro quo for the prewar debts.[48] After days of battle, with Oswald manfully supporting Strachey against Adams, Strachey accepted Oswald's recommendation that they use their limited discretionary powers to permit Americans to dry and cure fish on the shores of unsettled bays, harbors, and creeks of Nova Scotia, the Magdalen Islands, and Labrador. Fitzherbert approved. Honest John Adams, who had no thought of cheating anyone, bound his debtor countrymen to pay their British creditors. Strachey himself wrote home that without the concession made in the third article of the treaty, there would have been no agreement. Oswald had long known it.[49]

P.R.O.; a second copy is in C.O. 5/8, P.R.O.). Oswald's formal requisition calling for loyalist relief and general amnesty was presented to the American commissioners on November 4; their obdurate reply is dated November 7 (C.O. 5/8, fols. 317,319, P.R.O.).

About the compromise Strachey wrote in the November dispatch cited above, "My idea was and is that the Resolution of Congress to the different States concerning the Restitution of Property will be equivalent to a message from the King to Parliament and that it is not probable any refusal will be given except to a very few who are difficulties."

[47] Shelburne to Oswald, Nov. 23, 1782, F.O. 97/157, fol. 226, P.R.O.

[48] Oswald to Townshend, Nov. 30, 1782, F.O. 27/2, fols. 444–45, P.R.O.

[49] Henry Strachey to Evan Nepean, Nov. 29, 1782, Oswald to Townshend, Nov. 30, 1782, F.O. 97/157, fols. 221b, 241, P.R.O. See also

From the moment Oswald's enthusiastic report reached London, the Jay-Oswald proposition for West Florida was viewed with skepticism by the ministry. Bedeviled by loyalists, debts, boundaries, and fisheries, Secretary Townshend suspected that his man in Paris was (in his judgment, again) playing into American hands. While he distrusted the commissioners and feared French naval potential in the Gulf of Mexico, he was willing to keep the door slightly ajar. Oswald was told he might gauge the American disposition to guarantee untroubled evacuation of British forces for an attack on West Florida. Despite Jay's strong support for the project, the response was mildly discouraging. A signed treaty of peace was guarantee enough, Oswald was told.[50] In fact, British policy had already taken another direction. Foreign Secretary Grantham told Fitzherbert that while West Florida was certainly of value, it was better to treat it within the context of his negotiations with Spain.[51] Eventually, it became a useful counter to win concessions in other quarters of the globe. Why, then, did the British government accept the Preliminary Treaty's concluding secret article incorporating in effect the Jay-Oswald plan for West Florida? It was a token of respect for John Jay and for Richard Oswald's advice that cooperation would forward the cause of reconciliation.[52]

No reading of the evidence can ever justify calling the

Strachey to Oswald, Dec. 10, 1782, C.O. 5/8, fols. 389–90, P.R.O., in which Strachey tells his colleague that Shelburne and Townshend were "perfectly satisfied with our conduct" and asks for the paper Oswald had prepared on the fisheries since he anticipated strong parliamentary opposition. Oswald complied in a response to Strachey (Jan. 8, 1783, F.O. 97/157, fol. 252, P.R.O.). His lengthy paper is also dated January 8 (C.O. 5/8, fols. 394–400, P.R.O.). The original was sent to Shelburne and a copy to Townshend (see Oswald to Townshend, Jan. 26, 1783, C.O. 5/8, fol. 395, P.R.O., and the copy, F.O. 95/511, fol. 7, P.R.O.).

[50] Townshend to Oswald, Oct. 26, 1782, F.O. 97/157, fol. 166, and F.O. 27/2, fols. 360–61, P.R.O.; Oswald to Townshend, Nov. 5, 1782, F.O. 27/2, fols. 374–75, P.R.O.

[51] Lord Grantham to Alleyne Fitzherbert, Nov. 9, 1782, F.O. 27/2, fol. 376, P.R.O.

[52] Oswald to Strachey, Dec. 12, 1782, F.O. 95/511, fol. 240, and F.O. 97/157, fol. 245, P.R.O., a copy for Shelburne.

peace preliminaries the "Oswald Treaty." By attempting to commit his country to the West Florida plan, he showed a disregard for his instructions and ignorance of basic diplomatic procedures. Shelburne's stern treatment was deserved. When Strachey praised the treaty as "much beyond the most sanguine expectations," however, he was not indulging in warm self-congratulation.[53] He was implicitly if not explicitly paying tribute to Richard Oswald. Strachey, Fitzherbert, who approved the treaty, and Hartley, who tried and failed to better it, repeatedly tested and validated the old Scot's judgment. So, one may reason, did North and Fox, leaders of the coalition ministry after Shelburne's fall, who accepted the preliminaries as the definitive settlement. Further, British domestic politics certainly made the loyalist and debt provisions necessary, but given the vexed course of their ultimate settlement, it may fairly be asked if they did not occasion more trouble than they were worth.

Richard Oswald died in 1784, without making an apologia of his own. The old man must have been gratified by Shelburne's graceful tribute in the speech to the Lords in February 1783 but distressed by the rancor and vituperation that swirled around the treaty, by the wild charges that he and Strachey had put their names to a craven surrender and that he himself had acted more in American than in British interests, by the collapse of his hopes for West Florida and a revived mercantile system for the benefit of the sugar islands, and by the parliamentary condemnation of the agreement he had done so much to make. Still, he could have said, he had achieved the greatest objectives: he alone among the British negotiators had won the confidence of the American commissioners, a sine qua non for any successful negotiation. Peace was a reality. Reconciliation was at least beginning. America was detached from France in all but name, the end of a five-year national nightmare in Britain. Trade was

<hr>

[53] To Nepean, Nov. 29, 1782, F.O. 97/157, fol. 221b, P.R.O. Also see Strachey to Townshend, Nov. 28, 1782, F.O. 97/157, fol. 218, P.R.O., to Nepean, Nov. 30, 1782, C.O. 5/8, fol. 373, P.R.O., to Oswald, Dec. 10, 1782, C.O. 5/8, fols. 389–90, P.R.O. Oswald's encomium on Strachey is in his letter to Townshend, Nov. 30, 1782, F.O. 97/157, fol. 223, P.R.O.

quickly reviving and increasing, the July 1783 Order not withstanding. The constitutional ties between the two countries were dissolved, but a new British-American community of interests was reasserting itself through a thousand different channels. While he had stumbled badly over the diplomatic modalities in the West Florida business, he had taken the long view, and his priorities were right even though established at the expense of fishing monopoly, prewar debts, and justice for dispossessed and abused loyalists.

JONATHAN R. DULL

Vergennes, Rayneval, and the Diplomacy of Trust

ON THE NIGHT of August 15, 1782, Admiral de Grasse returned to Paris.[1] It was a far from triumphant return for the
victor of Yorktown because, for the last four months, he had
been a prisoner of war in England. His captors had treated
him, if not royally, at least nobly—and properly so. The ties
of aristocracy had to be preserved, even between enemies;
during the same week the British commander at Gibraltar
was being offered ice cream and fresh vegetables by the commander of the Spanish forces preparing to attack him.[2] De
Grasse, moreover, had fought courageously if not successfully at the Battle of the Saintes (named not for the combatants but for the Caribbean islands off which they fought).
The admiral's services to France did not end, however, on
that terrible day at sea in April 1782. Upon his return from
captivity he wrote Charles Gravier, comte de Vergennes, the
French foreign minister. The day before departing London
de Grasse had spoken privately with Lord Shelburne, head
of the British cabinet, who had communicated his intentions
about peace and had charged the French admiral to relay

[1] *Courier de l'Europe*, Aug. 30, 1782. De Grasse's rank was lieutenant général des armées navales.

[2] The duc de Crillon to General Eliott, Aug. 19, 1782, Archives du Ministère des Affaires Etrangères, Paris, Correspondance Politique (hereafter
cited as AAE, CP), Espagne, 608:224–25. As another example, Admiral
Rodney, de Grasse's captor, had been permitted to leave France at the outbreak of war when a French marshal loaned him the money to pay his
Paris gambling debts (Piers Mackesy, *The War for America, 1775–1783*
[Cambridge, Mass., 1964], pp. 319–20).

them to Vergennes.[3] Accordingly, de Grasse now sent Vergennes a résumé of this conversation with Shelburne.

The memorandum was delivered by de Grasse's nephew, a fellow prisoner of war who had accompanied his uncle back to France. The conversation that it described appeared so singular to Vergennes that, as he told one of his ambassadors, had he not known the admiral's character he would have regarded it as a piece of fiction.[4] According to de Grasse, Shelburne was willing to satisfy virtually all the desires not only of France, but of France's allies, Spain, the United States, and the Netherlands. Supposedly he offered unconditional independence for the United States, the restitution to France of the captured island of St. Lucia, and the abrogation of treaty articles restricting French fortification of Dunkirk. For France there also would be a fishery at Newfoundland, a sufficient establishment for slaving and commerce in Africa, and a return to the position in India she had held in 1763 or 1748. France's ally Spain would receive a choice of Minorca or Gibraltar, provided the British retained a post in the Mediterranean. Finally, Britain would agree to make no further conquests from the Netherlands and would accept the principles of the League of Armed Neutrality.[5]

While Vergennes could not deny de Grasse's veracity, he was dubious about the sincerity of Shelburne's offer, particularly given Shelburne's reputation for duplicity.[6] Unsure of the British minister's motives, Vergennes elected to play for time. He asked de Grasse to write Shelburne to thank him for the truly distinguished treatment he had received in England and to say that, although the proposals seemed capable of leading to peace, Louis XVI must first consult with his ally, Charles III of Spain. Meanwhile Vergennes solicited the agreement of the Spanish court for the sending of a repre-

[3] Admiral de Grasse to the comte de Vergennes, Aug. 17, 1782, AAE, CP, Angleterre, 538:56.

[4] "Un roman fait à plaisir" (Vergennes to the comte de Montmorin-Saint-Hérem, Aug. 18, 1782, AAE, CP, Espagne, 608:210–11).

[5] "Projet des préliminaires," AAE, CP, Angleterre, 538:54, 55.

[6] Vergennes to Montmorin, Aug. 17, 1782, AAE, CP, Espagne, 608:203–4.

sentative to sound out Shelburne; the Spaniards were expected to reply by early September.[7] Shelburne's initiative may have appeared suspicious, but it presented the only opportunity of breaking the deadlock affecting all the peace negotiations. Until the Spaniards carried out their impending assault on Gibraltar, France could not bargain seriously with Alleyne Fitzherbert, the British representative at Versailles; to keep the talks alive, she had elected to concentrate on the relatively simple issue of Newfoundland.[8] The other parties in the peace negotiations were no further advanced; distrust was seemingly universal. The American discussions with Britain were suspended at John Jay's insistence because the British negotiator was not empowered to deal with the United States by name.[9] George III strongly doubted Vergennes's intentions and felt that Benjamin Franklin was only playing with Britain.[10] Jay mistrusted Vergennes almost as much as did the British monarch. Jay had been meeting with the Spanish ambassador at Versailles, the conde de Aranda, in hope of finding common ground

[7] Vergennes to Montmorin, Aug. 18, 1782, AAE, CP, Espagne, 608:210–11. George III regarded the delay as further evidence of French duplicity (George III to the earl of Shelburne, Aug. 25, 1782, *Lord Shelburne, Bowood Circle and the American Revolution: Letters to Lord Shelburne, 1776–1789* [Oxford, 1976], pp. 16–17).

[8] Vergennes to Montmorin, Aug. 10, 1782, AAE, CP, Espagne, 608:173. See the French memoir on the subject in AAE, CP, Angleterre, 538:36–49. The British, however, refused to negotiate separately on this issue (Vergennes to Montmorin, Sept. 14, 1782, AAE, CP, Espagne, 603:380).

[9] For conflicting appraisals of Jay's policy compare Jonathan R. Dull, *Franklin the Diplomat: The French Mission*, American Philosophical Society *Transactions* 72 (1982):58–59, with Richard B. Morris, *The Peacemakers: The Great Powers and American Independence* (New York, 1965), pp. 301–10.

[10] George III to Baron Grantham, Aug. 11, 1782, and to Shelburne, Aug. 12, 1782, Sir John Fortescue, ed., *The Correspondence of King George the Third from 1760 to December 1783*, 6 vols. (London, 1927–28), 6:99–101. Shelburne's trust in Franklin had been shaken by Franklin's revealing to Vergennes what Shelburne had considered confidential assurances; Fitzherbert also warned that Franklin was not to be trusted (Vincent T. Harlow, *The Founding of the Second British Empire, 1763–1793*, 2 vols. [London, 1952–64], 1:271–72, 325n).

for negotiations with the British; French attempts to help had only convinced him that they were pro-Spanish.[11] For his part Vergennes feared the British and Americans would make peace behind his back.[12] The remaining belligerents were not even ready to talk. The Spanish ambassador was still awaiting instructions from his court on the terms to be presented to Britain,[13] and negotiations between Britain and her fourth adversary, the Netherlands, were no further along; on August 15 Matthijs Lestevenon van Berkenrode, the elderly Dutch minister at Versailles, was told he would be sent a colleague to assist him.[14] Finally, no one really trusted the Austrians and Russians, who had volunteered to mediate an end to the war.[15]

With five combatants involved and two mediators awaiting

[11] Samuel Flagg Bemis, "The Rayneval Memoranda of 1782 on Western Boundaries and Some Comments on the French Historian Doniol," American Antiquarian Society *Proceedings*, n.s. 47 (1937):15–92.

[12] See in particular Vergennes to the chevalier de La Luzerne, Mar. 23, 1782, AAE, CP, Etats-Unis, 20:463–68. For Vergennes's distrust of Shelburne see Vergennes to Montmorin, July 13, 20, 28, and Aug. 17, 1782, AAE, CP, Espagne, 608: 48–49, 78, 127, 203–4.

[13] Vergennes to Montmorin, Aug. 10, 1782, AAE, CP, Espagne, 608:174.

[14] The prince of Orange to Matthijs van Berkenrode, Aug. 15, 1782, F. J. L. Krämer, ed., *Archives, ou correspondance inédite de la maison d'Orange-Nassau, cinquième série*, 3 vols. (Leiden, 1910–15), 3:130–31. Matthijs Lestevenon van Berkenrode (1719–97) had represented the Netherlands at Versailles for more than thirty years (*Reportium der diplomatischen Vertreter aller Länder seit dem Westfälischen Freiden [1648]*, 3 vols. [Oldenburg and elsewhere, 1936–65], 2:244; *Biographisch Woordenboek der Nederlanden*, 7 vols. [Haarlem, 1852], 4:112). For a brief sketch of his new colleague Gerard Brantsen (1734–1809) see the *Nieuw Nederlandsch Biografisch Woordenboek*, 10 vols. (Leiden, 1911–37), 7:195. Vergennes felt that Brantsen was anti-French and had unsuccessfully opposed his appointment (Orville T. Murphy, *Charles Gravier, Comte de Vergennes: French Diplomacy in the Age of Revolution, 1719–1787* [Albany, N.Y., 1982], p. 326).

[15] It is untrue that France viewed the mediation sympathetically. See Vergennes to Montmorin, May 31, 1782, AAE, CP, Espagne, 607:224. In 1781 France had accepted mediation out of necessity (Jonathan R. Dull, *The French Navy and American Independence: A Study of Arms and Diplomacy, 1774–1787* [Princeton, 1975], pp. 211–15).

their chance, the negotiations resembled a circus of many rings. In this circus, though, all the performers had tight-ropes to walk. Vergennes had to mediate between the competing aims of America and Spain. Franklin and Jay had to encourage the British into offering concessions in the hope of gaining a separate peace while simultaneously convincing the French that America would never make one. Spain had to balance her hope of territorial gains against her well-justified fears of an expansionist America. The Dutch found some of their overseas possessions occupied by their ally—the French—and others by their enemy—the British; lacking military strength themselves, the Dutch had to fear both. Shelburne had to choose between concessions to America and concessions to France and her European allies in the face of a British public increasingly reluctant to make any concessions at all.

With so complex a set of interlocking negotiations it is tempting to treat the subject as a simple struggle for advantage, albeit one in which one of the participants consistently acted somewhat more admirably. Unfortunately, French, American, and British historians are at odds as to which was the honorable participant. There is an alternate way of viewing the negotiations, however, a way that reduces the danger of national bias. We can examine them as a struggle not only between competing states but also between trust and mistrust. All of the belligerents had ample reason to desire peace. To achieve it, they had to run risks, formulate strategy, and fight battles that were as consequential, if not so bloody, as those on the battlefield. To fight for peace, they had to decide that serious negotiations and substantial compromises were more profitable or less risky than the continuation of war. This decision, however, first demanded a given level of trust between enemies and in some cases among allies; it was the establishment of this trust that laid the foundation for peace.

Before discussing Vergennes and his French colleagues, let us look for a moment at the earl of Shelburne, who chose to direct personally the major part of the British negotiations. It was Shelburne who held the keys to a successful resolution of all the peace talks. Even though he had no allies to consult, he was perhaps the most politically exposed of all the peace-makers. Admittedly, he was not the only negotiator faced with political constraints. Jay and Franklin differed on dip-lomatic tactics, and Congress left them limited scope for ma-neuver, particularly on the issue of the loyalists. Vergennes faced within the royal council of state (the French cabinet) the opposition of the marquis de Castries, the French naval minister, who was a tenacious opponent of any settlement that did not improve the French position in India.[16] Aranda, who conducted Spanish negotiations from his ambassadorial post at Versailles, twice would have to disobey the orders of his superior, Spanish Foreign Minister the conde de Flori-dablanca.[17] The Dutch negotiators never did receive autho-rization to make the concessions Vergennes finally had to make for them. Nevertheless, it was Shelburne's willingness to risk repudiation that made peace possible. He had to ne-gotiate in the face of the realization that a major concession might undermine his tenuous majority in Parliament.[18] Moreover, while in both Spain and France opposition to peace was halfhearted or demoralized and lacked wide-spread public support, a powerful war party existed in Brit-ain. Viscount Keppel, the first lord of the Admiralty, and his fellow hawks in the cabinet had a strong rationale for con-tinuing the war, at least against France and Spain: a resur-gent British navy had the Spanish Empire and the French West Indies for the picking.[19] This argument was in all prob-ability correct,[20] and it held enormous appeal both to the merchant community and to the landed constituency that

[16] For Castries's view of the negotiations see volume 1 of his journal (1780–83), Bibliothèque du Ministère de la Marine, Paris, manuscript 182 (hereafter cited as "Journal du maréchal de Castries").

[17] See below. Aranda's mission to France is discussed in Richard Ko-netzke, *Die Politik des Grafen Aranda: Ein Beitrag zur Geschichte des spanisch-englischen Weltgegensatzes im 18. Jahrhundert* (Berlin, 1929).

[18] For Shelburne's political position consult John Norris, *Shelburne and Reform* (New York, 1963), pp. 240–41.

[19] Mackesy, *War for America*, p. 509.

[20] Dull, *French Navy and American Independence*, pp. 299–302, 333–34.

elected most members of the House of Commons. In taking
from France and Spain recompense for the loss of America,
Britain would serve revenge, profit, and strategic interest.
Shelburne had to face this opposition without a secure power
base in Parliament and, in the end, his administration perished. It is a measure of Shelburne's courage that he ran the
risk. It is a measure of his skill that he was able to secure
George III's sacrifice both of America, which the king considered his birthright, and of the opportunity to take revenge on France and Spain. Finally, it is a measure of his
vision that he sought through a moderate peace not only to
restore British trade and prosperity but also to reestablish
amicable relations with America and France.[21]

In Shelburne's search for peace the most serious obstacle
was France. The Americans probably could be bought out of
the war by concessions on peace terms and, thanks to his influence with the king, Shelburne had the power to make such
concessions. Moreover, Jay's fears of an Anglo-French agreement could be serviceable in bargaining down the Americans.[22] The Dutch were helpless, and without the French
navy the Spaniards would be almost as much so. Thus far,
however, the French had shown no willingness to compromise.[23] Neither the king nor Parliament was anxious to volunteer concessions to the perfidious French, who had aided
Britain's American subjects in their rebellion. The French
therefore had to be either frightened or lured into seriously

[21] This interpretation of Shelburne is largely based on Harlow, *Founding
of the Second British Empire*, 1:223–407. For a critique of Harlow see Charles
R. Ritcheson, "The Earl of Shelburne and Peace with America, 1782–
1783: Vision and Reality," *International History Review* 5 (1983): 322–45.

[22] Harlow, *Founding of the Second British Empire*, 1:285. For another critique of Jay's diplomacy see James H. Hutson, *John Adams and the Diplomacy
of the American Revolution* (Lexington, Ky., 1980), pp. 124–25.

[23] Vergennes admitted that the British ministry had reason to be frightened by the sweeping nature of the French demands. Once serious negotiations began, he intended to moderate them (Vergennes to Montmorin,
Aug. 10, 1782, AAE, CP, Espagne, 608:172). These French demands are
listed in AAE, CP, Angleterre, 537:197–98.

negotiating and into forcing the Spaniards and Dutch to follow. Shelburne chose the second course and picked de Grasse
to carry the bait.[24]

To understand why Vergennes accepted that bait, it is first
necessary to understand Britain's place in the pattern of
French foreign relations. All too often historians have
treated eighteenth-century France and Britain as inevitable
opponents in the battle for empire. In spite of persistent rivalry in some parts of the world, such as India and the West
Indies, the reality was far more complex. From 1716 until
the end of the 1720s the two countries were close allies (and
for another dozen years nominal ones). Only with the outbreak of the war between Spain and Britain, and then the
French invasion of Austria, did Anglo-French relations totally disintegrate. Their treaty of alliance formally ended in
1744, and during the next twenty years the British and
French fought two wars, contending for overseas dominance
and a strengthened position in the European balance of
power. The result of this contest was by no means an unmit-
igated triumph for Great Britain. True, she drove the French
from North America and dramatically improved her position
in India. The French, however, preserved their possessions
in the Caribbean and saw their colonial trade revive after the
end of the Seven Years' War. More critically, Britain's overseas
ascendancy after 1763 was accompanied by her isolation in
Europe. Her alliance with Prussia was shattered and she was
unsuccessful in forming one with Russia. Although the two
countries reached agreement in 1766 on a new commercial
treaty, they failed to negotiate a political alliance. Britain remained dependent on her own strength to discourage
French and Spanish attempts to retrieve their losses.

This Franco-Spanish policy was largely the work of the duc
de Choiseul, who directed French foreign affairs from 1758

[24] This, of course, is to accept de Grasse's account of his conversation
with Shelburne. Shelburne's report of the meeting was far different. He
told the king, "I assur'd him of Your Majesty's disposition to Peace, and of
the Sincerity of your Ministers without entering into particulars—that the
great point to be obtained was mutual Confidence" (Fortescue, ed., *Correspondence of George the Third*, 6:99).

to 1770. It failed because France and Spain lacked the resources to challenge British naval dominance. During the 1770 Falkland Island crisis Choiseul was dismissed, in demonstration of Louis XV's desire to avoid a new war. Choiseul's Continental strategy proved equally unsuccessful. France's brief alliance with Russia ended with the death of Empress Elizabeth in January 1762. After a few months of the inept rule of her successor, Peter III, his wife, Catherine, seized power and became empress. Choiseul's policy became not only strongly anti-Russian but also personally hostile to the new empress. France's ally Austria refused meaningful help against Russian expansionism, however, and Choiseul was reduced to stimulating anti-Russian resistance among the Swedes, Poles, and Turks. This course proved dangerous; by the end of Choiseul's administration the Poles were involved in a hopeless rebellion against a Russian occupying army, the Turks were losing a war against the Russians, and the Swedes were seemingly on the verge of civil war.

After Choiseul's dismissal, Louis XV hesitated for several months before choosing the duc d'Aiguillon as Choiseul's successor. The new foreign minister reversed his predecessor's British policy, seeking a rapprochement with Britain and an alliance against the Russians. Although British public opinion remained virulently anti-French, d'Aiguillon's approach evoked the interest of George III and of one of his secretaries of state, Lord Rochford. During the earlier stages of the Russo-Turkish war Britain had provided aid to the Russian navy, but in 1772 her Russian policy was thrown into question. In that year Prussia and Austria joined Russia in partitioning Poland, so as to avoid the choice between a general war and an intolerable strengthening of Russia. Peace was not guaranteed, however, for Russia now threatened both a renewal of its war against the Turks and a war against Sweden, whose king had overthrown the Swedish constitution in the fear party strife would lead her to Poland's fate.

It was now Russia rather than France that endangered the European balance of power. George III and Rochford realized this, but, cowed by the almost universal Francophobia in their country, they passed up the opportunity to improve relations. Moreover, by intimidating the French into canceling plans for fitting a naval squadron against the Russians, they publicly humiliated the French monarch. Ironically, this humiliation occurred only a month before Parliament passed the Tea Act and laid the groundwork for its own crisis. By discrediting d'Aiguillon, the British government in its blindness virtually precluded the possibility of French benevolent neutrality when colonial unrest led to the American Revolution.[25]

In 1774, the following year, Louis XV died and d'Aiguillon was replaced by Vergennes. The new foreign minister had been in Constantinople when war broke out between the Turks and Russians and in Stockholm when Gustavus III overthrew the Swedish constitution. Vergennes had aided in

[25] Two useful summaries of eighteenth-century British foreign policy are Paul Langford, *The Eighteenth Century: 1688–1815* (London, 1976), and David Bayne Horn, *Great Britain and Europe in the Eighteenth Century* (Oxford, 1967). Good introductions to post–1763 British diplomacy are Michael Roberts, *Splendid Isolation, 1763–1780* (Reading, England, 1969), and Frank Spencer's historical introduction to his edition of *The Fourth Earl of Sandwich: Diplomatic Correspondence, 1763–1765* (Manchester, England, 1961), pp. 1–66. Two perceptive articles on Anglo-Russian relations are Michael Roberts, "Macartney in Russia," *English Historical Review*, supplement 7 (1974), and H. M. Scott, "Great Britain, Poland and the Russian Alliance, 1763–1767," *Historical Journal* 19 (1976): 53–74. There are a huge number of books and articles on Choiseul. Recent work helpful for understanding his diplomacy includes two fine articles—H. M. Scott, "The Importance of Bourbon Naval Reconstruction to the Strategy of Choiseul after the Seven Years' War," *International History Review* 1 (1979): 17–35, and Geoffrey W. Rice, "Great Britain, the Manila Ransom, and the First Falkland Islands Dispute with Spain, 1766," *International History Review* 2 (1980): 386–409—a magnificent book—Michael Roberts, *British Diplomacy and Swedish Politics, 1758–1773* (Minneapolis, 1980)—and the first volume of a massive (although rather jejune and adulatory) biography—Rohan Butler, *Choiseul*, vol. 1, *Father and Son, 1719–1754* (Oxford, 1980). The unsuccessful Anglo-French rapprochement is handled superbly by Michael Roberts, "Great Britain and the Swedish Revolution, 1772–73," *Historical Journal* 7 (1964): 1–46. D'Aiguillon's ministry has not received the attention it merits; a detailed although hardly objective study is in Lucien Laugier, *Un ministère réformateur sous Louis XV: Le triumvirat (1770–1774)* (Paris, 1975), pp. 346–502. For the selection of d'Aiguillon see also Didier Ozanam and Michel Antoine, eds., *Correspondance secrète du comte de Broglie avec Louis XV (1756–1774)*, 2 vols. (Paris, 1959–61), 1:xci–xcii. For the impact on Vergennes of the humiliation of 1773 see Murphy, *Charles Gravier, Comte de Vergennes*, p. 217.

both these anti-Russian developments. Although he was cho-
sen as French foreign minister for his moderation, his subsequent policy resembled in many ways that of Choiseul.
Both ministers sought to weaken Great Britain, to counter
Russian expansionism, to preserve the French alliance with
Austria so as to preclude an Austro-British rapprochement,
and to cooperate in private with Prussia to maintain the balance of power in Germany. Vergennes finally accomplished
Choiseul's dream of using an American rebellion to weaken
Britain. Indeed, Vergennes, by bringing France herself into
the war, acted more aggressively than Choiseul had ever
done—Choiseul having specialized in finding others to fight
France's battles for her. Like Choiseul, Vergennes was greatly
concerned by the weakness of the French position in eastern
Europe. Russian exhaustion after the Turkish war of 1768–
74 gave France the respite needed to improve her position
with respect to Britain. Vergennes's strategy appears to have
been to weaken Britain to the extent that she would cease to
be a threat to French interests on the Continent (or even, at
best, so she would cooperate with France in restraining the
eastern powers). Viewed from a European perspective, the
American war was as much a part of the long history of
the Eastern Question as it was a part of the history of Anglo-
French colonial rivalry. The French strategy backfired, however. Rather than achieving freedom of maneuver in eastern
Europe, French hands were tied when the Russian threat revived in 1782. Vergennes correctly suspected that the Russians and Austrians had secretly agreed to expand against
the Turks as soon as the opportunity arose. A revolt against
the khan of the Crimea, a Russian puppet ruler, seemed to
offer the chance they had been waiting for. With the Russians
preparing for war and the Turks in peril, Vergennes was desperate to end French involvement in the American war.[26]

[26] The crisis over the Crimea is described briefly in Isabel de Madariaga,
*Britain, Russia and the Armed Neutrality of 1780: Sir James Harris's Mission to
St. Petersburg during the American Revolution* (New Haven, 1962), pp. 409–
12, 420–21, 428–31; for a fuller discussion see Robert Salomon, *La politique orientale de Vergennes (1780–1784)* (Paris, 1935), and Allan W. Fisher,
The Russian Annexation of the Crimea, 1772–1783 (Cambridge, 1970), pp.
124–30. Austria offered Egypt to France if she would participate in the

There were other reasons for France to desire a quick end to the hostilities with Britain. Should the American war continue, the French West Indies might come into risk. The Battle of the Saintes, at which de Grasse had been captured, was not in itself decisive, and France could replace the ships captured in the Caribbean. De Grasse's defeat, however, was symptomatic of a gradual disintegration of the French war effort. The French navy, like the Spanish, seemingly had lost its capacity to overcome adversity—as Vergennes put it, "Our navies are badly constituted. Spirit is not as it should be; laxity and discouragement take the place of emulation." If the impending Spanish attack on Gibraltar failed, only an enormously risky joint expedition against Jamaica could attain the victory needed to obtain Spain's war objectives. But the Jamaica undertaking seemed more likely to lead to the indefinite continuation of the war. France could count on funds to fight that war for only one more year.[27]

France could not make peace without Spanish concurrence, but it was not only Spanish demands that threatened to prolong the fighting. Franklin and Jay demanded for the United States fishing rights off Newfoundland, the entire trans-Appalachian West up to the Mississippi, and the right to navigation of that river. Vergennes was horrified by the possibility that peace might be held up by such extravagant claims.[28] He pointed out with perfect logic that the Americans had not earned them by conquest and could hardly

dismemberment of the Ottoman Empire (Murphy, *Charles Gravier, Comte de Vergennes*, pp. 318–19). Two recent authorities believe, however, that this offer was made in the expectation that it would be rejected since Joseph II of Austria did not wish the Ottoman Empire to be partitioned (Karl A. Roider, Jr., *Austria's Eastern Question, 1700–1790* [Princeton, 1982], pp. 162–64; Isabel de Madariaga, *Russia in the Age of Catherine the Great* [New Haven, 1981], pp. 387–88).

[27] Vergennes to Montmorin, Oct. 13, Nov. 1 and 12, 1782, AAE, CP, Espagne, 609:83–84, 159–60, and 211–12. Quotation is from the first reference (my translation).

[28] Vergennes's concern that the Americans might impede negotiations is discussed in Vergennes to La Luzerne, June 28, 1782, AAE, CP, Etats-Unis, 21:341.

claim them as British subjects.[29] Nonetheless, Vergennes could do little more than appeal for moderation. France still needed the Continental army to pin down British troops that would otherwise be sent to the West Indies, just as she still needed the help of the Spanish and Dutch navies to counter a British navy that greatly outnumbered her own.[30]

Shelburne's proposals not only met France's own limited war aims but, more importantly, promised a basis for negotiations with France's allies. First, however, Shelburne's sincerity had to be tested. Upon receiving Charles III's agreement to go ahead, Vergennes explained he would send his personal representative "not at all to negotiate formally but solely to reconnoiter [Shelburne's] true dispositions."[31] Vergennes chose to send to London one of his two under-secretaries, Joseph Mathias Gérard de Rayneval.[32]

Rayneval, like Fitzherbert, the British negotiator at Versailles, was still a relatively young man. Born in Alsace in 1736, he defended a thesis in law at the University of Strasbourg at the age of twenty-one and later wrote a book on

---

[29] Bemis, "Rayneval Memoranda," pp. 18–21, 42–79, prints the French memoranda on the American claims.

[30] Available ships of the line of each of the combatants are listed in Dull, *French Navy and American Independence*, pp. 373–76. For Vergennes's appreciation of the usefulness of even the Dutch navy's efforts, see Vergennes to Montmorin, Mar. 16, 1782, AAE, CP, Espagne, 606:314.

[31] Vergennes to Montmorin, Sept. 7, 1782, AAE, CP, Espagne, 608:316–17 (my translation). The Spanish response arrived on September 1, but Louis was at Compiègne and it was not until the fifth that he formally authorized the mission to England. Negotiations with Fitzherbert had been temporarily suspended because of the death on August 20 of Prince Alfred, the youngest son of George III.

[32] I have taken liberties with the title of Rayneval's position. In fact the first sous-secrétaire d'état was Rayneval's son, François Maximilien (1778–1858), who received the title in 1820 (Frédéric Masson, *Le Département des Affaires Etrangerès pendant la Révolution, 1787–1804* [Paris, 1877], p. 23). Before 1776 Rayneval's position was that of a premier commis, or first secretary. In that year Rayneval and his brother were given the honorary titles of secretary to the conseil d'état (Henri Doniol, *Politiques d'autrefois: Le comte de Vergennes et P. M. Hennin* [Paris, 1898], p. 55).

Germanic law.[33] He might have had a career as a legalist and scholar,[34] instead, he chose to follow his older brother Conrad Alexandre Gérard into the French diplomatic service. Upon receiving his law degree, Joseph joined Conrad at the French mission to the Elector Palatine, serving initially as secretary-interpreter. For the next seventeen years the younger brother emulated the elder. During this time Joseph served as interpreter at Mannheim, secretary at Dresden, chargé d'affaires at Ratisbon, and consul general at Danzig, a particularly important post during the Polish partition crisis. Finally, in January 1774 the two brothers were reunited at Versailles where they served as the foreign ministry's two undersecretaries for political affairs.[35] Joseph's bureau was responsible for handling the correspondence with Spain and Great Britain, among other states; Conrad eventually dealt with the commissioners from the Continental Congress.[36]

[33] *Institutions au droit public d'Allemagne* (Strasbourg, 1771). Vergennes's initial training also had been in law (at Dijon).

[34] Along with two other employees of the French foreign ministry Rayneval translated into French Anton Friedrich Büsching's work on geography, *Neue Erdbeschreibung*. The translation was published in fourteen volumes between 1768 and 1779.

[35] Conrad had been an undersecretary since 1766. For the careers of the two brothers consult Masson, *Département des Affaires Etrangères*, pp. 21–23, Jean-Pierre Samoyault, *Les bureaux du secrétariat d'état des affaires étrangères sous Louis XV* (Paris, 1971), pp. 288–90, Camille Piccioni, *Les premiers commis des affaires étrangères au XVIIe et au XVIIIe siècle* (Paris, 1928), pp. 246–50, A. Salomon, "Les Alsaciens employés au ministère des affaires étrangères à Versailles au XVIIe et au XVIIIe siècles," *Revue d'Histoire Diplomatique* 45 (1931): 449–72, John J. Meng, ed., *Despatches and Instructions of Conrad Alexandre Gérard, 1778–1780* (Baltimore, 1939), pp. 35–52, and Ruth Strong Hudson, "The Strasbourg School of Law and Its Role in the French Intervention in the American Revolution," Ph.D. diss., Western Reserve University, 1947. For their ancestry see Salomon, "Les Alsaciens," pp. 450–51, and Meng, ed., *Despatches of Gérard*, p. 35.

[36] Joseph's bureau also was responsible for correspondence with the Italian states, Portugal, Denmark, the Netherlands, and Sweden, Conrad's bureau for Austria, Russia, Prussia, Poland, Turkey, and the German and Swiss states (*Almanach Royal* for 1777, p. 218). The division of responsibilities between the two bureaus was roughly equivalent to that between the northern and southern departments of the British Foreign Office, each until 1782 with its own secretary of state.

Thus, both brothers were closely involved in the diplomacy of the American war. In 1776 Joseph drafted the document Vergennes presented to the council of state during the debate over secret aid to the American colonists; in the spring of 1777 he prepared a campaign plan very similar to that used in America the following year by the French fleet.[37] Conrad directed the negotiations that led to the Franco-American treaty of alliance, and on the conclusion of that alliance he was selected as the first French minister to the United States. When he left for Philadelphia in the spring of 1778, his brother took over his post at the foreign ministry, and, for the next fourteen years, Joseph Mathias Gérard, now ennobled as Gérard de Rayneval, handled the diplomatic correspondence with both the United States and Britain.[38]

What kind of man was Rayneval? Thomas Jefferson compared him unfavorably to his fellow undersecretary Pierre-Michel Hennin (who is perhaps best known for his extensive correspondence with Voltaire).[39] The American minister called Rayneval more cunning than wise and accused him of duplicity.[40] Other contemporary opinions of him were more favorable. Shelburne, who quickly learned to trust and respect him, called him "a Well-Instructed, Inoffensive Man of

[37] These documents are discussed in Dull, *French Navy and American Independence*, pp. 36–38, 44, 84–85. Rayneval's draft of the former is reproduced in Benjamin Franklin Stevens, comp., *B. F. Stevens's Facsimiles of Manuscripts in European Archives Relating to America, 1773–1783*, 25 vols. (London, 1889–98), 13: no. 1310.

[38] For the division of responsibilities at the time of the peace negotiations see the *Almanach Royal* for 1782, p. 244.

[39] Theodore Besterman, ed., *The Complete Works of Voltaire: Correspondence and Related Documents*, 51 vols. (Toronto, 1968–77). Hennin's diplomatic career is discussed in Doniol, *Politiques d'autrefois*, pp. 15–36.

[40] Julian P. Boyd et al., eds., *The Papers of Thomas Jefferson*, 21 vols. to date (Princeton, 1950–), 11:96. I suspect that part of Jefferson's hostility to Rayneval may have been caused by Vergennes, who liked to deliver good news personally and to send Rayneval with the bad. For an example of this see Marie Donaghay, "Calonne and the Anglo-French Commercial Treaty of 1786," *Journal of Modern History* (on-demand supplement) 50 (1978): D 1167.

Business."[41] Fitzherbert described him as a man of moderation.[42] Scholars also have held differing views of him. Some American historians have accused him of being anti-American: first, because in 1781 he drafted a memorandum setting forth the conditions for a compromise peace that would have surrendered Georgia and South Carolina to Britain, and second, because of his supposed pro-Spanish bias as a participant in the Aranda-Jay discussions of August 1782.[43] These criticisms, however, greatly overestimate Rayneval's influence, and they are mistaken about French policy as well. Rayneval's 1781 memorandum, with its insistence on American possession of New York, indicates the depth of the French commitment to the essentials of American independence, even in the darkest days of the war.[44] His role in the 1782 discussions seems clearly the result of French concern to eliminate in advance any roadblocks to peace, however much Rayneval may have bruised American feelings.[45] At

[41] Shelburne to George III, Sept. 13, 1782, Fortescue, ed., *Correspondence of George the Third*, 6:125.

[42] Harlow, *Founding of the Second British Empire*, 1:329.

[43] Morris, *Peacemakers*, pp. 179–81; Samuel Flagg Bemis, *The Diplomacy of the American Revolution*, rev. ed. (Bloomington, Ind., 1957), pp. 181–82; Bemis, "Rayneval Memoranda."

[44] Dull, *French Navy and American Independence*, pp. 213–14. The document is in AAE, CP, Etats-Unis, 15:269–78, and Angleterre, supplement 19:216–23. That it may have been dictated by Vergennes is suggested by Henri Doniol, ed., *Histoire de la participation de la France à l'établissement des Etats-Unis d'Amérique*, 5 vols. and supplement (Paris, 1886–99), 4:553n.

[45] Although the French intervention in the discussions was requested by Aranda, France had little reason to favor Spanish claims. Instead it appears that Vergennes's preference was for trans-Appalachia to remain British so that, like a British Canada, it would increase American dependence on France. (See the hints in Vergennes to Montmorin, Oct. 6, 1782, AAE, CP, Espagne, 609:53–54.) British possession of the disputed area also would have served French interests by facilitating a territorial exchange between Britain and Spain. This possibility was not broached, however, until Shelburne's discussions with Rayneval (AAE, CP, Angleterre, 538:174–75). Spain killed the idea by refusing to part with West Florida and New Orleans, which Shelburne had suggested might be part of an exchange for Gibraltar. Deprived of an outlet to the sea, the American West held little appeal to Shelburne, particularly since apparently he saw

any rate, that participation ended on September 6, when Rayneval told Jay he would be absent for a few days and Jay should deal henceforth with Hennin.[46] On the preceding day Louis XVI had approved the mission to England. Vergennes's choice of whom to send was obvious: besides enjoying the foreign minister's full confidence, Rayneval was conversant with both the Newfoundland negotiations and the western lands question.[47] His instructions were clear: his task was to ascertain the accuracy of the memorandum de Grasse had made of Shelburne's proposals. If Shelburne disavowed them, Rayneval was to return immediately to France; if he acknowledged them, Rayneval could discuss them unofficially. It was expected this would take no more than eight to ten days.[48]

Britain and the United States as so economically interdependent that American settlement of the area ultimately would profit Britain (Harlow, *Founding of the Second British Empire*, 1:299). France had other reasons to prefer having a decision on the area left to discussion between Britain and America. British concessions on territorial boundaries might be used to offset American concessions, particularly on the issue of the loyalists. As late as November 15 France still feared a deadlock in the American-British negotiations (see Rayneval's instructions of that date in AAE, CP, Angleterre, 538:395–99). Rayneval even went so far as to hint that France was unsympathetic to American claims beyond that of independence, although Shelburne prudently refrained from accepting French help in moderating American demands (Harlow, *Founding of the Second British Empire*, 1:280, 284, 301). American historians have tended to view France's policy as duplicitous. I cannot see how the French unwillingness to continue the war for American territorial objectives was more reprehensible than Jay's frantic signals to the British that America was anxious to abandon the French alliance.

[46] Gérard de Rayneval to John Jay, Sept. 6, 1782, AAE, CP, Etats-Unis, 22:197–98.

[47] A copy of Rayneval's memoranda on Newfoundland is given in AAE, CP, Angleterre, 538:36–49. Richard Oswald, the British envoy dealing with the Americans, described Rayneval's spoken English as bad, yet "full better" than Oswald's own bad French (Richard Oswald, Journal, Apr. 18, 1782, Public Record Office).

[48] Rayneval's instructions may be found in AAE, CP, Angleterre, 538:117–18 and 122–23. They are printed in Doniol, ed., *Participation de la France*, 5:105–6, and in Paul Vaucher, ed., *Recueil des instructions données*

Under these conditions began Rayneval's mission. On it hung the future of the peace negotiations. Rayneval later admitted that had he foreseen the delicacy of his task he would not have had the courage to accept it. He claimed his only reassurance was that he had adhered to Vergennes's instructions.[49] There is no reason to doubt the first part of Rayneval's statement. For eight years he had not left the side of the wise and experienced Vergennes. His prior services at Danzig and a few minor German courts were hardly preparation for the responsibility facing him when he reached England, for, as it happened, his first task was to violate totally Vergennes's instructions.

Immediately after he registered in a London hotel under an assumed name, Rayneval was summoned to Bowood, Shelburne's estate ninety-five miles southwest of the city.[50] On September 13 the two men held their first meeting. Shelburne began by praising Vergennes and by speaking of his own and his king's sincere desire for peace, but he denied the accuracy of de Grasse's memorandum. In spite of his orders, Rayneval remained to listen when Shelburne volunteered to discuss the proposals in the memorandum. By the afternoon discussions had become sufficiently detailed for maps to be brought out.[51] Rayneval's flexibility had preserved

---

aux ambassadeurs et ministres de France depuis les traités de Westphalie jusqu'à la Révolution française, vol. 25, pt. 2, *Angleterre (III)* (Paris, 1965), pp. 505–7. (Further volumes in this series will be cited as *Recueil des instructions*.) That the future of the negotiations rested on Rayneval's mission is clear from Vergennes to Montmorin, Sept. 14, 1782, AAE, CP, Espagne, 608:380.

[49] Rayneval to Vergennes, Sept. 18, 1782, AAE, CP, Angleterre, 538:203–4, 205–6.

[50] Harlow, *Founding of the Second British Empire*, 1:329. The estimate of Bowood's distance from London is Rayneval's. The buildings in which they met have been torn down or altered, but the lovely grounds in which they walked remain largely as they were.

[51] Rayneval's record of the meetings is given in AAE, CP, Angleterre, supplement 19:268–302 (a rough draft) and 538:146–92, and has been published in Henri Doniol, ed., "Conférences de M. de Rayneval avec les ministres anglais," *Revue d'histoire diplomatique* 6 (1892): 62–89, and in Doniol, ed., *Participation de la France*, 5:603–26. Also see Rayneval to Vergennes, Sept. 15, 1782, AAE, CP, Angleterre, 538:193–94.

the chance for a solution to the deadlocked negotiations. Furthermore, as the two men came to trust each other, they established a bridge between Vergennes and George III, each highly suspicious of the other's sincerity.[52] Perhaps the most astonishing aspect of the day's negotiations was their demonstration that Shelburne had found the key to French diplomacy. After expressing his belief that Britain and France would need no mediators, he spoke further of his feelings about Franco-British relations. He argued that if Britain and France could reconcile they would become the arbiters of the public tranquility of Europe. He then claimed that in 1768, when he had resigned as secretary of state, he had wished to concert with France a firm and decisive language toward Russia and Prussia, so as to prevent what had happened to Poland.[53] It is difficult to imagine anything more calculated to appeal to Rayneval, who not only had witnessed the partition at first hand but was even suspected by Frederick II of Prussia of translating a satire against Poland's occupiers.[54] Similarly, it is difficult to imagine anything more tantalizing to Vergennes, who had been so intimately connected with France's futile attempt to preserve Poland's freedom and who now was trying desperately to prevent the Turks suffering the same fate as the Poles.[55] In spite of his doubts about Shelburne's sincerity, Vergennes soon urged upon Spain a quick peace to be followed by a British, French, and Spanish entente to save the Turks.[56] Rayneval remained

[52] For the gradual winning of George III's trust see Fortescue, ed., *Correspondence of George the Third*, 6:125–26, 142, 159, 167.

[53] For Rayneval's record of the meeting of September 13 see AAE, CP, Angleterre, 538:160–61, and Doniol, ed., "Conférences de Rayneval," pp. 70–71.

[54] David Bayne Horn, *British Public Opinion and the First Partition of Poland* (Edinburgh, 1945), p. 29; Hennin also was a witness of the partition.

[55] Vergennes had suspected for months the existence of the secret Austro-Russian alliance and feared the Turks would lose not only the Crimea but also Wallachia and Moldavia (Vergennes to Montmorin, Nov. 6 and Dec. 20, 1781, AAE, CP, Espagne, 605:293, 523–24).

[56] Vergennes to Montmorin, Sept. 28, Oct. 2 and 6, 1782, ibid., 608:488–89, 609:16, 57–58. Spain showed no interest in the situation in

in England for another week of discussions with Shelburne and Shelburne's foreign minister, Baron Grantham. His return to France marked a fundamental dividing point in the negotiations.

This is most clearly seen in France's willingness to make concessions. Vergennes's major concern now became the winning of sufficient British concessions to Spain to persuade the latter to make peace. One almost feels in reading Vergennes's correspondence that he was negotiating as much with the Spaniards as with the British. In the process of winning British concessions for the Spanish, he was forced to conduct a steady retreat from France's own demands. Naval Minister Castries, outraged at the abandoning of France's attempt to restore her position in India, had to watch her abandon as well her conquests in the West Indies. Sarcastically, he

---

eastern Europe (Montmorin to Vergennes, Oct. 10, 1782, ibid., 609:72–73) although in mid–1783 she did promise France support against Russia (Murphy, *Charles Gravier, Comte de Vergennes*, p. 341). Vergennes, of course, may have been exaggerating his optimism about rapprochement with Britain in order to speed Spain toward peace. I am even less inclined to take Shelburne's recollections at face value. Shelburne's department had not been directly concerned with developments in eastern Europe, and in 1768 his advocacy of a firm anti-French policy over the Corsican issue had contributed to his forced resignation (Nicholas Tracy, "The Administration of the Duke of Grafton and the French Invasion of Corsica," *Eighteenth Century Studies* 8 [1974–75]: 169–82. Moreover, his handling of foreign affairs was marked, according to the Prussian minister in London, by "une confusion et une nonchalance qui désolent tous ceux ont affaire avec lui" (Graf Joachim Karl Maltzan to Frederick II, July 31, 1767, quoted in Roberts, *Splendid Isolation*, p. 6n). In 1780 Shelburne argued in the House of Lords that after the fall of Choiseul, Britain had passed up a favorable opportunity for alliance with France (*The Parliamentary Register . . . Fourteenth Parliament*, 17 vols. [London, 1775–80], 15:343). Only in 1787 did he claim in another speech to the House of Lords that in 1769 he had considered an Anglo-French rapprochement out of concern for Poland (*The Parliamentary History of England from the Earliest Period to the Year 1803*, 36 vols. [London, 1806–20], 26:554–66). The possibility of Shelburne's involvement in trying to rescue Poland cannot fully be dismissed, however. In 1771 he did meet secretly with d'Aiguillon (Roberts, "Great Britain and the Swedish Revolution," p. 17n; L. G. Wickham Legg, ed., *British Diplomatic Instructions, 1689–1789: France, 1745–1789*, Royal Historical Society *Publications*, 3d ser. 49 [1934]: 122–23).

advised Louis XVI to hold no more meetings of the committee to discuss peace terms, since every session cost France
another colony.[57]

Shelburne's position was equally complex. His immediate
problem now was the American negotiations. If the Americans refused reasonable terms, all Britain's other negotiations were pointless; if, however, the Americans accepted
peace, even under the convenient fiction that it was conditional upon all parties reaching agreement, Shelburne's
hands would be freed to force Spain and France to terms—
either at the negotiating table or on the battlefield. Shelburne did not wish the continuation of war and hoped not
only for peace but also for reconciliation with his country's
enemies. At least, however, with the Americans removed
from the hostilities he would have little fear of losing the
war.[58] Shelburne held a second advantage over Vergennes.
While Vergennes had to reconcile two conflicting parties, the
Spaniards and the British, Shelburne could play off his opponents against each other. By using the French negotiations
as a threat, he could drive the Americans to terms; by using
an Anglo-American peace (or even their alliance) as a threat,
he could drive the French and Spaniards to terms. Let us see
how Shelburne and Vergennes resolved their respective
problems.

The first breakthrough came in Shelburne's negotiations
with the Americans. Jay had insisted that his British counterparts specifically recognize American independence. News of
the Shelburne-Rayneval discussions so frightened him that
he accepted a formula that alluded to America as if independent while leaving George III free to disavow having made
such a recognition. Once this had been accomplished, Shel

[57] "Journal du maréchal de Castries," f. 147.

[58] Shelburne did manage to convince the king that the British war effort
was in poor condition (Fortescue, ed., *Correspondence of George the Third*,
6:128), but I find it difficult to believe Shelburne was being candid. Viscount Keppel, the first lord of the Admiralty, and Admiral Hood, the brilliant local theater commander, shared Vergennes's expectations that 1783
would bring British victories (Mackesy, *War for America*, p. 509).

burne's representative in Paris began serious talks with the Americans.[59] Jay's fears of a secret Franco-British agreement were groundless; Shelburne had no desire to resume warfare in North America. In his negotiations with the American peace commissioners, he abandoned ground much as Vergennes did with him.[60] Through October the two parties exchanged proposals; by the end of the month a team of negotiators on each side was at work in Paris. Details of these talks were kept as secret from the French as the Rayneval discussions had been from the Americans.[61] News of the meetings hardly could be kept hidden, however, and it may not be wholly coincidence that in early November the Spaniards began to soften their terms. Their attack on Gibraltar had failed and now a British fleet had resupplied the garrison. Should the Americans drop out of the war and the military initiative pass to the British, the Spanish Empire would be in peril.

The new Spanish position, however welcome to Vergennes, demanded further sacrifices from France. Spain offered to give France the Spanish colony of Santo Domingo (now the Dominican Republic), a huge and strategically valuable possession, but as yet economically undeveloped. In return, Spain wished to receive Gibraltar from Britain. It would be left to France to offer Britain compensation for Gibraltar—Aranda's suggestion, which shocked Vergennes, was the island of Corsica. Should France be unwilling to ac-

---

[59] Harlow, *Founding of the Second British Empire*, 1:285–86.

[60] The most thorough discussions of the subsequent negotiations can be found ibid., pp. 287–311, and in Morris, *Peacemakers*, pp. 343–85. Militarily, the Americans presented a far less inviting target than did the Spaniards and Dutch. It is possible, of course, that a series of victories against the other belligerents might have tempted the British into renewing offensive operations in North America, whatever Shelburne's wishes.

[61] Jay's diary for Oct. 24, 1782, in Richard B. Morris et al., eds., *John Jay*, vol. 2, *John Jay: The Winning of the Peace: Unpublished Papers, 1780–1784* (New York, 1980), pp. 449–50. Rayneval later told Shelburne that the Americans had been reserved because of France's unwillingness to support them in a variety of unreasonable demands (Shelburne to George III, Nov. 24, 1782, Fortescue, ed., *Correspondence of George the Third*, 6:161).

cept Santo Domingo, Spain was ready to cede it to Britain, whatever the consequences to the security of the French West Indies.[62]

Vergennes was left little choice but to accept the Spanish proposal. Britain's obtaining Santo Domingo would endanger the French West Indies, as would a continuation of the war. Unless, however, Vergennes could obtain Gibraltar from Britain or other concessions generous enough to satisfy Spain, the war would continue. Time was pressing both Shelburne and Vergennes. Parliament was scheduled to reconvene on November 26. Once it was in session, Shelburne's freedom of movement in the negotiations would be circumscribed.[63] Vergennes faced a more indefinite but ultimately more decisive deadline, as a huge French and Spanish fleet gathered at Cadiz to prepare for the transatlantic assault on Jamaica. Its commander, French Admiral d'Estaing, would stall its departure and try to impress the Spanish court with the dangers of the operation, but once it sailed the momentum of the war would be almost irresistible.[64] Aranda, an ambassador of enormous experience and a man of great character, could do nothing himself to speed the negotiations.[65] It was at his suggestion, however, that Vergennes sent Rayneval back to London, this time to deal openly.[66]

---

[62] The Spanish proposals are in AAE, CP, Espagne, 609:171–74. Also see the conde de Aranda to Vergennes, Nov. 7, 1782, Vergennes's report to Louis XVI, and Vergennes to Montmorin, Nov. 12, 1782, AAE, CP, Espagne, 609:175–78, 181–87, 207–12, 213–16.

[63] See Shelburne to Alleyne Fitzherbert, Oct. 1782, quoted in Norris, *Shelburne and Reform*, p. 256.

[64] Admiral d'Estaing departed for Spain on November 1 (Dull, *French Navy and American Independence*, pp. 317–19). For his delaying of the fleet's departure see p. 333n.

[65] Vergennes's opinion of Aranda is quoted ibid., p. 332. Aranda was a former president of the Council of Castile and a future chief minister of Spain. For his contributions to the enlightened domestic policy of Charles III, see Richard Herr, *The Eighteenth-Century Revolution in Spain* (Princeton, 1958), pp. 21–22, 29, 67, 75.

[66] Rayneval's instructions are in AAE, CP, Angleterre, 538:395–99, and are printed in Vaucher, ed., *Recueil des Instructions, Angleterre*, pp. 507–10,

By the time Rayneval began discussions on November 20, Shelburne was in a far stronger position than the French realized. His negotiators in Paris were in sight of a settlement with the Americans, and, in spite of Shelburne's protestations to the French, George III by now was eager to trade Gibraltar for gains in the West Indies.[67]

Rayneval calmly swallowed the bitter medicine administered by Shelburne.[68] Spain could have Gibraltar, but she would have to surrender her wartime conquests of Minorca and West Florida. In addition, Spain would have to cede Puerto Rico or France would have to surrender either Guadeloupe and Dominica or Martinique and St. Lucia. Rayneval dispatched the new terms by messenger and then, with great foresight, rushed back to Versailles to argue for their acceptance. He arrived just in time to assist Vergennes, who had to convince Aranda to accept the agreement on behalf of Spain. It appears unlikely that Aranda had the authority to do so; Floridablanca, his political superior (and also his political enemy), seems to have left on him the onus of surrendering the Spanish conquests. Nevertheless, Aranda reluctantly agreed to give up Minorca so as to prevent the rupture of negotiations. In addition, Vergennes agreed to cede Guadeloupe and Dominica. Immediately, Rayneval returned to London a third time, taking with him Vergennes's oldest son, who would serve both as Rayneval's secretary and as a personal pledge of Vergennes's good faith.[69] Seemingly,

---

and in Doniol, ed., *Participation de la France*, 5:212–15. For Aranda's suggestion of sending Rayneval back to England see AAE, CP, Espagne, 609:173.

[67] On the preceding day the cabinet had sent its final revisions of the proposed treaty to Paris by courier (Harlow, *Founding of the Second British Empire*, 1:294). For the king's position on Gibraltar see Fortescue, ed., *Correspondence of George the Third*, 5:125–26, 183–84.

[68] Rayneval's account of the meetings is in Rayneval to Vergennes, Nov. 21, 1782, AAE, CP, Angleterre, 539:3–7; supplement 19:311–15.

[69] Vergennes's sending of his son proved to be of great help in furthering trust of his motives, particularly with George III (Fortescue, ed., *Correspondence of George the Third*, 6:167, 168). Rayneval had warned Vergennes, however, that British trust did not extend to other members

only the issue of Florida remained as an obstacle to an agreement between Britain and the two Bourbon states.

It was not to be so simple. Shelburne had won for his king the offer of Guadeloupe, Dominica, and Minorca in exchange for Gibraltar. But this was not enough for the London merchants, who were outraged at the proposed British surrender of Gibraltar and at the prospective French acquisition of Santo Domingo from Spain.[70] Perhaps Shelburne could have postponed further the reopening of Parliament and ridden out the storm, but just as Rayneval was embarking at Calais for England the Americans and British signed a provisional agreement in Paris. For all practical purposes America was out of the war, and Britain was free to seize from Spain, France, and the Netherlands whatever compensation she wished for the loss of America. Courageously, Rayneval kept his composure on being told that France and Spain would have to offer more if they wanted to buy peace.[71] Spain would have to surrender Trinidad (or France, St. Lucia) and Spain could have only part of Florida.

Here then was the test of the trust established between Shelburne and Rayneval. Pride or anger could have led France to break off the negotiations, greed or revenge, the British. In either case the bloodshed would have continued. Shelburne and Rayneval trusted each other enough, however, to pursue the effort to escape the labyrinth. Their meeting continued and Shelburne offered an alternative. If Spain

---

of the French government, particularly Castries (Rayneval to Vergennes, Nov. 23, 1782, AAE, CP, Angleterre, 539:29).

[70] Rayneval to Vergennes, Dec. 4, 1782, AAE, CP, Angleterre, 539:135–43, 155–56; supplement 19:327–35, 341–42.

[71] Vergennes testified to Rayneval's courage, "I swear, sir, that my arms fell in reading your dispatch and after a few moments' reflection I have had to admire your sagacity in having conserved enough sangfroid to refrain from breaking off all negotiations in view of the new demands made to you" (Vergennes to Rayneval, Dec. 7, 1782, AAE, CP, Angleterre, 539:169–70 [my translation]). The strain of this time upon Vergennes was witnessed by the Russian ambassador (Ivan S. Bariatinskii to Ivan A. Osterman, Dec. 1/12, 1782, Nina N. Bashkina et al., eds., *The United States and Russia: The Beginning of Relations, 1765–1815* [Washington, D.C., 1980], pp. 169–70).

would end her attempt to gain Gibraltar, she could have both East and West Florida.[72] The door to peace remained open, if only a crack.

When Vergennes informed Aranda of the new offer, he learned that Floridablanca had authorized the ambassador to find out what advantages Spain could obtain from surrendering her claims to Gibraltar. Aranda, however, was authorized to surrender neither Minorca nor Florida.[73] Britain would have to improve her offer or the door to peace would slam shut. Now Shelburne and Grantham were faced with an agonizing decision. With firmness and skill Rayneval left them no doubt that unless Spain retained Minorca and Florida, France would not consent to peace. With great reluctance they agreed.[74] Now only Aranda's consent was needed. Technically, he lacked the authority to accept the terms. Thanks, however, to the efforts of d'Estaing and the comte de Montmorin, the French ambassador in Madrid, Charles III had accepted Aranda's prior breach of instructions; this news had arrived when Aranda learned of Shelburne's final offer. Aranda promptly accepted and sent his secretary to join Rayneval to negotiate final details.[75]

The agreement had been complex and the prospects of peace remained precarious. In the confusion of the negotia-

---

[72] Rayneval to Vergennes, Dec. 4, 1782, AAE, CP, Angleterre, 539:151–52. For Shelburne's increased trust of the French, see J. Leitch Wright, Jr., *Britain and the American Frontier, 1783–1815* (Athens, Ga., 1975), p. 5.

[73] Vergennes to Rayneval, Dec. 7, 1782, AAE, CP, Angleterre, 539:169–79; Vergennes to Montmorin, Dec. 9, 1782, and enclosure, AAE, CP, Espagne, 609:271, 353–56.

[74] Rayneval to Vergennes, Dec. 12, 1782, AAE, CP, Angleterre, 539:208–16; supplement 19:345–52. See also Legg, ed., *British Diplomatic Instructions*, pp. 202–5; Fortescue, ed., *Correspondence of George the Third*, 6:180–83. In exchange for East Florida, Spain surrendered the Bahamas, which she had recently captured.

[75] Montmorin to Vergennes, Dec. 1 and 7, 1782, AAE, CP, Espagne, 609:334, 342–45; Vergennes to Rayneval, Dec. 16, 1782, AAE, CP, Angleterre, 539:245–47; Vergennes to Montmorin, Dec. 17, 1782, AAE, CP, Espagne, 609:386–89. A critical element in Charles III's acceptance of Aranda's decision seems to have been his trust of Admiral d'Estaing.

tions, the status of Dominica, a West Indian island captured by France, had not been resolved—or rather, both Britain and France thought it had been assigned to them.[76] The issue was partly symbolic: would France be permitted to keep any of her conquests in the West Indies? Once again, peace depended on the trust established between the negotiators. A compromise was arranged so that France retained a lesser prize, the island of Tobago. On the issue of India it was Rayneval who conceded, telling Vergennes that if he were to be sacrificed for it, let his epitaph read, "Here lies one who preferred peace to renown and a few villages in Hindustan."[77] On a related issue, however, Shelburne had to make an equally painful concession. Not until October had the Dutch peace commissioner Gerard Brantsen arrived, and he had no power to make concessions.[78] Vergennes refused to delay the peace and negotiated on behalf of the Dutch. The British had captured from them the strategically vital port of Trincomali in Ceylon; Vergennes insisted on its return and gained it in exchange for a minor Dutch post on the Indian mainland.[79] He was aided by the news that a French expedi-

---

[76] Rayneval to Vergennes, Dec. 12 and 20, 1782, AAE, CP, Angleterre, 539:216, 265–70; Grantham to George III, Dec. 27, 1782, Fortescue, ed., *Correspondence of George the Third*, 6:196–97. For Dominica's importance see AAE, CP, Angleterre, 539:202, 271–72.

[77] Rayneval to Vergennes, Dec. 28, 1782, AAE, CP, Angleterre, 539:364 (my translation). Rayneval admited to Grantham that peace would not depend on a few villages more or less but on Louis XVI's discontent with George III's intransigence (Rayneval to Vergennes, Dec. 26, 1782, AAE, CP, Angleterre, 539:321–23). Given that France failed to improve her position in India or the Caribbean, her direct gains were very minor: the right to fortify Dunkirk, the recovery of Senegal, and the establishment of a more secure position in the Newfoundland fishery. She of course did gain her major war objective, the full independence of the United States.

[78] For Brantsen's difficulties see Lyman H. Butterfield, ed., *Diary and Autobiography of John Adams*, 4 vols. (Cambridge, Mass., 1961–66), 3:62, 86–88, 99–100.

[79] Vergennes told Rayneval that if Trincomali were surrendered, "everyone will throw rocks at us" (Dec. 22, 1782, AAE, CP, Angleterre, 539:282–83 [my translation]). In a personal letter to his colleague and

tionary force was en route to Ceylon, although it was not until March 1783 that news reached Europe that Trincomali had been recaptured.[80] These final issues resolved, a general armistice was signed on January 20, 1783, in time to prevent the sailing of the Jamaica expedition. The definitive treaties signed later basically ratified the preliminary agreement.[81]

What became of the protagonists of our story? Rayneval deserved an ambassador's post for his efforts. He did not receive one, supposedly because an exhausted Vergennes needed him at Versailles,[82] but more likely for the reason that his title of nobility was too recent. He bore the disappointment with character and, for another decade, continued to serve the foreign ministry with distinction.[83] He led the negotiations that produced the Anglo-French commercial

---

friend Hennin, Rayneval admitted that he would find the peace good even with the loss of Trincomali, but that this opinion undoubtedly was heresy (Rayneval to Pierre Michel Hennin, Dec. 29, 1782, Bernard Fäy, ed., "Correspondance Intime de Gérard de Rayneval avec Hennin," *Franco-American Review* 1 [1936–37]: 80).

[80] Vergennes to Rayneval, Jan. 10 and 15, 1783, AAE, CP, Angleterre, 540:137, 179–80; *Courier de l'Europe*, Mar. 21, 1783.

[81] Compare Doniol, ed., *Participation de la France*, 5 (supplement): 288–94, 340–51.

[82] Vergennes to Rayneval, Jan. 10 and 20, 1783, AAE, CP, Angleterre, 540:137b–37c, 236–40; Vergennes to Montmorin, Feb. 9, 1783, AAE, CP, Espagne, 610:223–24.

[83] In a personal letter to Vergennes, Rayneval had said that though he counted for little in the social order he counted for something when it was a question of honor (Rayneval to Vergennes, Jan. 1, 1783, AAE, CP, Angleterre, 540:36–37). When the comte de Moustier was named ambassador to the Court of St. James's, Rayneval professed to be anxious to return to his prior life of work and tranquility (Rayneval to Vergennes, Jan. 9 and 14, 1783, AAE, CP, Angleterre, 540:106–7, 155–56). His disappointment in not receiving the post himself is apparent in a letter he drafted but probably never sent which criticized the choice of Moustier (AAE, CP, Angleterre, supplement 19: 455–60). Before he left England in February, however, he was named as interim minister plenipotentiary and upon his return to France was given a gratification of 150,000 livres tournois (equivalent today to several hundred thousand dollars) (Masson, *Département des Affaires Etrangères*, p. 22).

treaty of 1786 and undertook a mission to the Netherlands during the diplomatic crisis of 1786–87.[84] He was removed from office in 1792 but survived the French Revolution, wrote extensively, and died in 1812 a member of the Legion of Honor and correspondent of the Institut de France.[85] There is a final irony to his story. The four-year-old son he left behind when he went to England in 1782 came to enjoy a spectacular diplomatic career and died a comte; the twenty-one-year-old son of Vergennes who accompanied Rayneval served only at a minor German post before ending his diplomatic career.[86]

Vergennes received as a reward for making the peace the position of head of the royal council of finances once held by the comte de Maurepas. Like the position of first lord of the Treasury, it made Vergennes de facto prime minister. He continued to direct French foreign policy. The hopes of British help in eastern Europe proved illusory, and although Britain withdrew temporarily from European affairs, this brought little respite to France's eastern allies. French attempts to save the Crimea from the Russians failed miserably, and only Austrian caution prevented a general dismemberment of the Ottoman Empire.[87] War was merely postponed

[84] Donaghay, "Calonne and the Anglo-French Commercial Treaty," pp. D 1157–84; Louis André and Emile Bourgeois, eds., *Recueil des instructions*, vol. 23, *Hollande (III)* (Paris, 1924), pp. 364–65; Murphy, *Charles Gravier, Comte de Vergennes*, pp. 432–46, 470–71.

[85] His final works were *Institutions du droit de la nature et des gens* (Paris, 1803) and *De la liberté des mers*, 2 vols. (Paris, 1811). During the American war he had written several pamphlets defending the French government's position (see Hudson, "Strasbourg School of Law," pp. 96–110; also see Masson, *Département des Affaires Etrangères*, pp. 22, 456–57).

[86] For François Maximilien Gérard de Rayneval see Masson, *Département des Affaires Etrangères*, p. 23. Vergennes's son Constantin (1761–1832) served as minister plenipotentiary at Coblenz from 1787 to 1791, became an émigré, and spent the remainder of his career in the military, becoming maréchal de camp in 1818. There is an excellent discussion of his character and education in Murphy, *Charles Gravier, Comte de Vergennes*, pp. 350–57.

[87] For the resolution of the Crimean crisis see M. S. Anderson, "The

a few years, however. When it broke out in 1787 France, bankrupt and on the verge of political breakdown, was too paralyzed to help the Turks. By then Vergennes, whose intervention in the American war had led the nation to bankruptcy, was no longer foreign minister. He had died in office in February 1787, just before the convocation of the Assembly of Notables, the first act in the great drama of the French Revolution.[88] Ironically, opposition to the Russians would eventually be offered, although ineffectively, by the government of Shelburne's protégé, William Pitt the Younger.

Shelburne's diplomatic future proved far shorter than did his French colleagues'. He was driven from office for yielding too much for peace, although his peace settlement stood.[89] Vergennes lamented his fall, and the two statesmen maintained their mutual respect.[90] Their vision of Anglo-French friendship was as premature as was Shelburne's of Anglo-American reconciliation, and yet those aspirations do honor to those who held them. Whatever their failings, Vergennes and Shelburne deserve praise, not only for their courage and statesmanship during the peace negotiations, but also for their ability to see that France and Britain shared a common-

Great Powers and the Russian Annexation of the Crimea, 1783–84," *Slavonic and East European Review* 37 (1958–59): 17–41. Anderson indicates that the Shelburne government's interest in concerting measures with France in eastern Europe was genuine, although limited by political constraints (a policy abandoned by Shelburne's successor, Fox).

[88] See also Jonathan R. Dull, "France and the American Revolution Seen as Tragedy," in Ronald Hoffman and Peter J. Albert, eds., *Diplomacy and Revolution: The Franco-American Alliance of 1778* (Charlottesville, Va., 1981), pp. 73–106.

[89] Norris, *Shelburne and Reform*, pp. 240–70, 295–307.

[90] For Vergennes's tribute to the patriotism of Shelburne and Grantham see Vergennes to Montmorin, Mar. 1, 1783, AAE, CP, Espagne, 610:280. For Shelburne's respect of Vergennes read his letter to Vergennes of May 19, 1783, Doniol, ed., *Participation de la France*, 5 (supplement): 314–15. See also Harlow, *Founding of the Second British Empire*, 1:445.

ality of interest.[91] Their service to peace and reconciliation merits our study and emulation.

[91] In his enthusiasm at the conclusion of peace even George III said that France and England were made to be friends (Rayneval to Vergennes, Jan. 24, 1783, AAE, CP, Angleterre, 540:249–50). He had used similar language in 1772 (Roberts, "Great Britain and the Swedish Revolution," p. 20). He, like Vergennes, saw better commercial relations as a way of achieving better diplomatic relations. In a sense the culmination of Vergennes's British policy was the Anglo-French commercial treaty of 1786. Vergennes, in his relief at the coming of peace, even went so far as to tell Rayneval that the prosperity of one nation redounded to the benefit of all (Vergennes to Rayneval, Feb. 1, 1783, AAE, CP, Angleterre, 540:318–22).

MARCUS CUNLIFFE

"They Will *All* Speak English"

Some Cultural

Consequences of

Independence

THE SCOTSMAN CALEB WHITEFOORD was secretary to the British negotiating team empowered to work out peace terms in Paris in 1782. When his side and the Americans signed and exchanged documents on November 30, they rode outside the city to dine in celebration of the occasion. In Whitefoord's recollection, a French guest at the dinner held forth on the "growing greatness of America," predicting that "the United States would form the greatest empire in the world." Whitefoord claims to have retorted: "Yes, sir, and they will *all* speak English; every one of 'em."[1]

This apparently chagrined response may seem an appropriate introduction for a discussion of the cultural, and more particularly *literary*, aftermath of the Peace of Paris. For in conventional literary histories of the United States, the early national period is supposedly full of British recrimination and condescension. The high (or low) point is often illustrated by the Rev. Sydney Smith's query in the *Edinburgh Review* of January 1820: "In the four quarters of the globe, who reads an American book?" Earlier in the same article, Smith had said:

[1] Richard B. Morris, *The Peacemakers: The Great Powers and American Independence* (New York, 1965), pp. 378–85.

132

The Americans are a brave, an industrious, and acute people; but they have hitherto given no indications of genius, and made no approaches to the heroic, either in morality or character. They are but a recent offset indeed from England; and should make it their chief boast for many generations to come that they are sprung from the same race with Bacon and Shakespeare and Newton. Considering their numbers . . . and the favourable circumstances in which they have been placed, they have yet done marvellously little to assert the honour of such a descent, or to show that their English blood has been exalted or refined by their republican training and institutions. Their Franklins and Washingtons . . . were born and bred subjects of the King of England. . . . And since the period of their separation, a far greater proportion of their statesmen and artists and political writers have been foreigners, than ever occurred before in the history of any civilised and educated people. During the thirty or forty years of their independence, they have done absolutely nothing for the Sciences, for the Arts, for Literature, or even for the statesmanlike studies of politics, or political economy.

After asking "who reads an American book?" Sydney Smith had continued, "Or goes to an American play? Or looks at an American picture or statue? What does the world yet owe to American physicians or surgeons? What new substances have their chemists discovered? Or what old ones have they analysed? What new constellations have been discovered by the telescopes of Americans? What have they done in the mathematics?" And so on through commerce and manufacture, to the ultimate Smithian stab. At the close of his summary of the bare "annals of this self-adulating race," he queried: "Finally, under which of the old tyrannical governments of Europe is every sixth man a slave, whom his fellow-creatures may buy and sell and torture?"[2]

[2] Review of Adam Seybert's *Statistical Annals of the United States of America, Edinburgh Review* 65 (1820): article 3. Such review articles were anonymous. In this case, however, the authorship is confirmed by republication (see *Essays by Sydney Smith [Reprinted from the Edinburgh Review]* [London, 1848], pp. 294–301). There is much useful information on publishing, authorship, and political coloration in David Paul Crook, *American Democracy in English Politics, 1815–1850* (Oxford, 1965). Two earlier studies by

Smith's severe interrogation, a famous item in the so-called War of the Quarterlies, seems of a piece with another notorious comment of the same era, from the London *Quarterly Review*, on "Republicanism, as it exists beyond the Atlantic, in all the glories of bundling, gouging, negro-driving, and dram-drinking; such poems as the Columbiad . . . and young ladies, who, when asked to dance, reply, 'I guess I have no occasion.'" The *Quarterly Review* said of Americans: "They have nothing original; all that is good or new is done by foreigners, and yet they boast eternally." Such pronouncements so infuriated the New York writer James Kirke Paulding that he produced several counterblasts, among them *John Bull in America, or the New Munchausen* (1825). *John Bull in America* parodied the gullible yet supercilious reactions of Tory travelers. Paulding's imaginary Briton follows the Smith line in asserting that since 1783 not one exceptional American has appeared. James Fenimore Cooper and Washington Irving "have, it is true, gained some little reputation; but I am credibly informed that the former of these gentlemen, has been once or twice in England, and that the latter never wrote English, until he had been long enough there to forget the jargon of his own country. So, after all, they furnish no exemption to my rule"—that post-Revolutionary America was a cultural desert (or as H. L. Mencken was to say much later of the American South, a "Sahara of the Bozart").[3]

This, then, is one common view: that literature and other forms of culture in the new nation were treated with igno-

William B. Cairns still retain a little value: *British Criticisms of American Writings, 1783–1815*, University of Wisconsin Studies in Language and Literature, no. 1 (Madison, 1918), and *British Criticisms of American Writings, 1815–1833*, University of Wisconsin Studies in Language and Literature, no. 14 (Madison, 1922).

[3] James Kirke Paulding, *John Bull in America* (1825; reprint ed., Upper Saddle River, N.J., 1970), pp. 164–65. The *Quarterly Review* piece (vol. 10 [1814]: 494–539) was a scathing gloss upon Charles Jared Ingersoll's *Inchiquin: The Jesuit's Letters* (1810). Paulding was particularly incensed by a comment in the same issue (p. 463) on his own work (see Cairns, *British Criticisms, 1815–1833*, pp. 33–34). Paulding was angered too by the *Quarterly*'s strictures on the United States contained in a review of William Faux's *Memorable Days in America* (1823) (vol. 29 [1823]).

rant hostility by the bulk of British observers. Paulding's riposte, in the shape of a dialogue between his "John Bull" and an educated American, scores heavily for the American side. The sociocultural difference between the two countries, in the words of Paulding's spokesman, is that "our world is not quite ripe, and yours a little decayed. We think our world is the better for blooming in all the freshness of youth; while you appear to be of opinion that your world, like a cheese, is the better for being a little rotten." Paulding's John-Bullish narrator records that the American "bowed and left me, before I had time to make a cutting reply."[4]

Another familiar claim is that, given the relatively small population and resources of the infant nation, its cultural achievement was in fact impressive. No political writings? What of the intense constitutional debates of the 1780s and their outcome in the ingenious, lucid, and persuasive *Federalist* papers of Alexander Hamilton, James Madison, and John Jay? "Who reads an American book?" What of the poetry of Philip Freneau, Joel Barlow, and Timothy Dwight? What of the description of America provided by the naturalist William Bartram, by the farmer-philosophe Crèvecoeur, and by Thomas Jefferson's *Notes on the State of Virginia*? Or, in fiction, of the psychological novels of Charles Brockden Brown? Again, Sydney Smith had asked, "Who looks at an American picture?" We can find positive answers in Kenneth Silverman's *Cultural History of the American Revolution.* The artist Benjamin West, resident in London from 1763 until his death in 1820, without disavowing his American origins, enjoyed high favor and even became president of the Royal Academy. The painter John Singleton Copley of Boston practiced his art in London for forty years after coming there in 1775. In December 1782 Copley was working on a portrait of the American merchant Elkanah Watson. After hearing of George III's speech acknowledging American independence, Copley added a Stars and Stripes flag to the background of Watson's portrait. "This was, I imagine," said Watson, "the first American flag hoisted in Old England." Gilbert Stuart, equally prominent as an American artist

---

[4] Paulding, *John Bull in America*, p. 196.

abroad, lived in England throughout the 1780s. Other
Americans known in the London art world of the epoch included John Trumbull and Robert Fulton.[5]

We may cite additional evidence of American promise.
The lexicographer Noah Webster, in the two decades after
1783, insisted on the need for and possibility of "a *national
language*, as well as a national government." In the same essay
(*Dissertations on the English Language*, 1789) he held out the
prospect that "within a century and a half, North America
will be peopled with a hundred millions of men, *all speaking
the same language.*" "They will *all* speak the same language,"
he went on, but their vocabulary, phrasing, and pronunciation would constitute *American* English, not English English,
and this standard *American* usage would be an essential element in unifying the new nation. In articles published in November 1783, Noah Webster sounded a note of patriotic
euphoria. America was "the last resort of liberty and religion
... where vice and despotism will be shrouded in despair,
and virtue and freedom triumph in the rewards of peace,
security and happiness." Religious toleration would help ensure for the United States a "greatness and lustre, before
which the glory of ancient Greece and Rome shall dwindle
... and the splendor of modern Europe shall fade into ob-
scurity."[6]

---

[5] Kenneth Silverman, *A Cultural History of the American Revolution: Paint-
ing, Music, Literature, and the Theatre ... 1763–1789* (New York, 1976), is
an excellent analysis. The Copley-Watson anecdote is cited in many books,
for example, James T. Flexner, *America's Old Masters: First Artists of the New
World* (New York, 1939), p. 156; also see Flexner's *John Singleton Copley*
(Boston, 1948). General considerations are presented in Lillian B. Miller,
*Patrons and Patriotism: The Encouragement of the Fine Arts in the United States,
1790–1860* (Chicago, 1966), pp. 1–23, in the early chapters of Neil Harris,
The Artist in American Society: The Formative Years, 1790–1860 (New York,
1966), and in J. Meredith Neil, *Toward a National Taste: America's Quest for
Aesthetic Independence* (Honolulu, 1975).

[6] The most detailed biography of Noah Webster is still that by Harry R.
Warfel, *Noah Webster: Schoolmaster to America* (New York, 1936), and Warfel
was the editor of *Letters of Noah Webster* (New York, 1953). Webster's *Dissertations on the English Language* (1789) were reprinted in facsimile and edited
by Warfel (Gainesville, Fla., 1951). Excerpts from his writings can be
found in such selections as Russel B. Nye and Norman S. Grabo, eds.,

Contemporaries of Webster, and subsequent commentators, have offered somewhat more cautious estimates, though usually dismissing British verdicts as ill-informed and resentful. These observers have put forward various explanations for the unexciting nature of American cultural accomplishments in the post-Revolutionary era. Moralists questioned whether a nation's true quality could or should be measured by its cultural products and pointed out that dazzling achievements in the fine arts tended to occur when a nation was past its prime and growing decadent. Writers such as the Massachusetts historian and blue stocking Mercy Otis Warren argued that perhaps the plainness and simplicity of "republican institutions" were incompatible with the sophisticated elegance of aristocratic societies.[7] Other commentators have maintained that no nation could expect to be preeminent in every art. Even the British had to look to Italy for lessons in opera or sculpture and to Germanic Europe for music or philosophy. It was thus unreasonable to expect that the young United States should immediately attain leadership in every field.

A third view held that a newly independent nation, occupied in settling and clearing its domain, could not give the highest priority to the fine arts. First things had to come first, and in the later 1780s problems of government filled the horizon. America, it was said, lacked the cultural resources—wealth, patronage, academies, galleries, libraries, printmaking, and engraving—available in Europe; and others felt that the absence of an effective international copyright agreement was a severe potential handicap to American authors. (Noah Webster and Thomas Paine, in the Revolutionary era, were among the keenest advocates of such protection, which was, however, not to be afforded to Americans until 1891.)[8]

American Thought and Writing, vol. 2, *The Revolution and the Early Republic* (Boston, 1965), pp. 281–88.

[7] William Raymond Smith, "Mercy Otis Warren's Radical View of the American Revolution," in Lawrence H. Leder, ed., *The Colonial Legacy*, vol. 2, *Some Eighteenth Century Commentators* (New York, 1971), pp. 219–25.

[8] There is an admirable condensed account of international copyright issues in Clarence Gohdes, *American Literature in Nineteenth-Century England*

A number of commentators have argued that things were
going well until the outbreak of the French Revolution
plunged the world into a quarter century of warfare and ideological controversy, which served, arguably, to disunite
America and to delay the emergence of independent national styles in literature and the arts. Another view maintained that, despite Noah Webster's early high hopes, the
American language was inevitably overshadowed by English
English. English books continued to dominate the American
market and to define American tastes. Not until the era of
Washington Irving and James Fenimore Cooper could the
United States provide an adequate livelihood for profes-
sional authors.

A final line of argument suggested that even if Crèvecoeur
or Barlow or Hugh Henry Brackenridge or Charles Brockden Brown were relatively unsuccessful in their own day, or
deficient in literary polish, their efforts could be seen as ini-
tiating an American *tradition* (for example, of psychological
introspection in Brown), even if later generations might not
always be aware that others had pioneered the modes they
themselves were attracted to.[9]

Such views could be thought compatible with the criticism
of national cultural pretensions delivered by certain Americans during the 1790s and the early nineteenth century. One
of the most withering analyses was that of the New Englander Fisher Ames. "What geniuses have arisen among
us?" he inquired:

(Carbondale, Ill., 1944), pp.16–18; also see Benjamin T. Spencer, *The
Quest for Nationality: An American Literary Campaign* (Syracuse, 1957), pp.
67–68, 143–46.

[9] Views of this sort, some of them originating as articles in the important periodical *Early American Literature*, can be found in Silverman, *Cultural History of the American Revolution*; Emory Elliott, *Revolutionary Writers:
Literature and Authority in the New Republic, 1725–1810* (New York, 1982),
which contains detailed discussion of Dwight, Barlow, Freneau, Brackenridge, and Brown; various essays in Everett Emerson, ed., *Major Writers of
Early American Literature* (Madison, 1972), and *American Literature, 1764–
1789: The Revolutionary Years* (Madison, 1977); and William L. Hedges,
"The Old World Yet: Writers and Writing in Post-Revolutionary America,"
Early American Literature 16 (1981):3–18.

This state of the case is no sooner made, than all the firefly tribe of our authors perceive their little lamps go out of themselves, like the flame of a candle when lowered into the mephitic vapor of a well. Excepting the writers of two able works on our politics, we have no authors. . . . There is no scarcity of spelling-book makers, and authors of twelve-cent pamphlets; and we have a distinguished few, a sort of literary nobility, whose works have grown to the dignity and size of an octavo volume. We have many writers who have read, and who have the sense to understand, what others have written. But a right perception of the genius of others is not genius; it is a sort of business talent. . . . Nobody will pretend that the Americans are a stupid race. . . . But has our country produced one great original work of genius?

Ames is an eloquent polemicist. But he wrote as a conservative, a Federalist, a detester of Thomas Jefferson and of what he took to be the decline of the United States into demagoguery and commercialism. His argument can therefore be read as a party harangue, the expression of a person convinced that "unmixed democracy" will subvert American liberty. And Ames concludes with the rather perverse notion that when democracy in America yields to despotism, *then* the new "emperor . . . will desire to see splendor in his courts" and there will be a flowering of the arts. "Nature, never prodigal of her gifts," will then at last produce "some men of genius" in the United States. Does Ames welcome that outcome, or not? Such jaundiced utterances could be dismissed as proofs that Federalists were fundamentally undemocratic (or unrepublican), and therefore apt—consciously or not—to repeat the cultural assumptions of the Old World.[10]

Two centuries later it may still be impossible to offer an entirely objective assessment of the state of American literary culture during the ten or twenty years that followed the Peace of Paris. Old patriotic sensibilities are not completely inert; raw nerves may still be touched. Moreover, new structuralist or other techniques of literary discourse may unin-

[10] Cited in Nye and Grabo, eds., *Revolution and Early Republic*, pp. 295, 302–4, from Fisher Ames's essay "The Future of American Literature," published in his *Works* (1809) but written somewhat earlier.

tentionally minister to the national pride by treating questions of mere literary merit as naively irrelevant; or historically disadvantaged groups may object that conventional modes of judgment are distorted. In such cases one encounters a dispute as to whether Americans were fundamentally the same as Europeans or importantly different; an assertion that Americans ought to be judged by special, perhaps self-established criteria, instead of by measures imposed by alien, uncongenial arbiters; a tendency to emphasize the hostility, incomprehension, and other handicaps that inhibit the flowering of a first-rate autonomous culture; and a contrary tendency, to claim that what was produced was first-rate, when seen in the proper light.

Despite such difficulties of fair interpretation, it ought to be possible to restate some of the realities of the post-1783 American literary scene. First, I would maintain that the *anti-Americanism* of Europeans, and more particularly that of the parent country, was *not of primary significance*. Certainly there were elements of British disapproval and schadenfreude. The tone of the quarterlies could be disdainful in the extreme, and their anonymous contributors seemed to profess omniscience, objectivity, and absolute insight. But this was the tone they took about everything and everybody, including one another.

The Tory *Quarterly Review*, established in 1809, was the avowed opponent of the Whig *Edinburgh Review* (1802). They differed in tone from such older periodicals as the *Gentleman's Magazine*, the *London Magazine*, and the *Monthly Review*—and from newer monthlies such as *Blackwood's Edinburgh Magazine* (1817). Gifford's *Quarterly Review* and Jeffreys's *Edinburgh Review* reserved their harshest criticisms for British authors. The poet John Keats was among the victims. According to Lord Byron (another target), Keats's early death was hastened by a brutal attack on his *Endymion*:

Who killed John Keats?
"I" says the Quarterly,
So cruel and Tartarly,
"Twas one of my feats."

These regally opinionated periodicals were also in their day extremely readable—in part, of course, because of their readiness to express ridicule and scorn. Their tomahawk tendencies made them much read and reprinted in the United States. But, to repeat, anti-Americanism was not a principal feature of editorial policy. True, most of the British commentators were poorly qualified to discuss American affairs. The poet William Cowper, for example, wrote occasionally about the United States with only the vaguest grasp of American geography or government. The same could be said of the *Quarterly Review*'s contributor Robert Southey (who was to be poet laureate from 1813 to 1843). As befitted a Tory publication, the *Quarterly* disapproved per se of republican and democratic societies. A *Quarterly* reviewer no doubt infuriated Paulding by dismissing one of his would-be humorous pieces as follows (January 1814):

> It was to be expected that in the process of time an American wag should make his appearance. In a nation derived from so many fathers it has justly been a matter of wonder that there should hitherto have existed so tame a uniformity, and that . . . such varied elements should produce the merest monotony of character that the world has yet seen. It is not our business to inquire into the cause of this phenomenon. . . . We will only observe that when the vulgar and illiterate lose the force of their animal spirits they become mere clods; and that the founders of American society brought to the composition of their nation few seeds of good taste, and no rudiments of liberal science.

The writer paused to suggest that eventually an American art and literature would emerge. Reverting to Paulding's *Lay of the Scottish Fiddle*, a jocose imitation of Sir Walter Scott, the reviewer said it was inevitable that American wit should first manifest itself in parody: "Childhood is every where a parodist. America is all a parody, a mimicry of her parents; it is, however, the mimicry of a child . . . abandoned to bad nurses and educated in low habits."[11]

[11] On British periodicals see Crook, *American Democracy*, and Cairns, *British Criticisms, 1783–1815* and *British Criticisms, 1815–1833*. The *Quar-*

PEACE AND THE PEACEMAKERS

It is also true that even in commentaries professing admiration for the United States, a tinge of amused condescension creeps in. Praise bestowed in one clause is usually balanced with disparagement. How are we, for example, to interpret these generalizations from an *Edinburgh Review* criticism (July 1803) of a British book of travels? The writer rebukes the author for expressing disdain for American publications, but does not muster more than two cheers for American culture (italics are mine): "Their party pamphlets, though *disgraced with much intemperance and scurrility*, are written with a keenness and spirit, that is not often to be found in the old world; and their orators, though occasionally *declamatory and turgid*, frequently possess a vehemence, correctness, and animation, that would command the admiration of any European audience."[12]

Nevertheless, anti-Americanism is not the key to such apparently unfavorable reactions. One elementary but important point is that some of the most frequently quoted British remarks, especially those from the *Quarterly*, were made dur-

---

terly Review's scolding of Paulding is quoted in Cairns, *British Criticisms, 1783–1815*, pp. 33–34. William Cowper's limitations of knowledge and sympathy are discussed in Pat Rogers, "On the Edge of the Abyss," *Times Literary Supplement*, Apr. 8, 1983. Cowper, who at one stage contributed an assessment of Barlow's *Vision of Columbus* to the *Analytical Review*, confessed in correspondence his indifference to public issues and foreign countries. According to Rogers, "Having regarded the American War at first with blithe confidence (there is no reference at all to the Declaration of Independence), he finds the news from Yorktown disconcerting, but chiefly because it means discarding two flag-waving poems 'that I was rather proud of.' He makes a vague reference . . . to the Peace of Versailles in 1783, without much sense of engagement. There is no allusion to the events in France of 1789. . . . As for *The Rights of Man*, 'I have not seen Payne's [*sic*] book, but refused to see it when it was offer'd me. No man shall convince me that I am improperly govern'd while I feel the contrary.'"

[12] *Edinburgh Review* 2 (1803): 448. The book in question was John Davis, *Travels . . . in the United States of America* (1803). The reviewer dismissed the author as "a pedagogue, who would be a wit and a fine gentleman" (p. 443), denying his claim to either condition, and noting with astonishment that Davis had managed to obtain a commendatory preface "from no less a person than the President of the United States" (Thomas Jefferson).

ing the War of 1812. There was an actual armed conflict as
well as a War of the Quarterlies. It would have been even
more remarkable if the combat had not colored the effusions
of journalists. On the other side of the story we should note
the many signs of willingness among Britons, especially
Whiggish ones, to welcome American publications. The New
World was looked to even with eagerness for tokens of inno-
vative literary genius. In this way, decades later, innovators
on the order of Whitman and Dreiser were to receive a more
enthusiastic welcome in certain British circles than in their
own land. Again, while American themes became part of the
repertoire of a sometimes xenophobic British pattern of humor, they took their place among a numerous company that
included illiterate yokels, pedantic Germans, nervous cur-
ates, nouveau-riche nabobs, fantasizing Irishmen, and fatu-
ous aristocrats. Sydney Smith, who had a brother in the
United States, was in the main pro-American and wrote little
or nothing about the country until 1815.

The large, uncomfortable fact is that the first generation
of American literati failed to produce masterpieces. This was
acknowledged, however sadly or reluctantly, by most of the
old chroniclers of American literary history.[13] The admission

[13] Edwin P. Whipple, *American Literature and Other Papers* (Boston, 1887),
contains a quite lively survey of writing between 1776 and 1876 (pp. 1–
138). Whipple seeks to praise at least some aspects of Brown and Brackenridge. Barlow, however, aroused him to mirthful scorn: "Joel Barlow is
fairly entitled to the praise of raising mediocrity to dimensions almost co-
lossal. Columbia is, thank Heaven, still alive; 'The Columbiad' is, thank
Heaven, hopelessly dead. . . . No critic within the last fifty years has read
more than a hundred lines of it, and even this effort of attention has been
a deadly fight with those merciful tendencies in the human organization
which softly wrap the overworked mind in the blessedness of sleep."

William P. Trent et al., eds., *The Cambridge History of American Literature*,
3 vols. (New York, 1917–21), 1:viii–ix, comments on the assumptions of
works such as Charles F. Richardson, *American Literature, 1607–1885*
(1887–89), and Barrett Wendell, *Literary History of America* (1900), which
take for granted that little if any significant literature appeared in America
before 1800, and indeed little before 1820. Such attitudes died hard. Russell Blankenship, *American Literature as an Expression of the National Mind*
(New York, 1931), while expressing a general pride in the nation's cultural
record, can muster little enthusiasm for most of the early products. Thus,
on the author of *The Columbiad* Blankenship comments, "The kindly thing

would have been less painful for American patriots if their preliminary claims had been more circumspect. Prophecies of future greatness made during and just after the Revolution were in general grandiose and unspecific. Some of them implied that American cultural greatness was not only guaranteed but imminent. "Columbia, Columbia," cried Timothy Dwight in 1777,

> to glory arise,
> The queen of the world, and child of the skies!
> Thy genius commands thee; with rapture behold,
> While ages on ages thy splendors unfold.

"We are called to sing a New Song," declared Nathaniel Appleton, "a Song that neither We nor our Fathers were ever able to sing before." In the words of John Trumbull:

> This land her Swift and Addison shall view,
> The former honors equalled by the new;
> Here shall some Shakespeare charm the rising age,
> And hold in magic chain the listening stage.

"Thy native land is big with mighty scenes," Mercy Otis Warren assured aspiring poets in 1782.[14]

Such rhetoric sometimes shaded into bombast. The praise

---

is to remember Barlow as a lover of freedom and to forget his heavy-handed toying with poetry" (p. 189). Percy H. Boynton's text *Literature and American Life* (Boston, 1936) says of Charles Brockden Brown, with some severity, that while he possessed "certain native gifts" he lacked self-discipline. Brown "oscillated between being a Poe and a [Harriet Beecher] Stowe, and his pendulum came to a dead stop in the middle" (pp. 202–3).

[14] The "Rising Glory" theme, as he dubs it, is discussed in Silverman, *Cultural History of the American Revolution*, pp. 228–35; also see his treatment of *translatio studii*—a venerable notion, adapted to American circumstances, of a westward global transit of the arts (pp. 9–11). Predictions of American greatness in the arts are described also in Michael Kraus, *The Atlantic Civilization: Eighteenth-Century Origins* (Ithaca, N.Y., 1949), pp. 216–307, and in Joseph J. Ellis, *After the Revolution: Profiles of Early American Culture* (New York, 1979), pp. 3–21. My quotations are borrowed from Nye and Grabo, eds., *Revolution and Early Republic*, pp. 366–67, and from Russel B. Nye, *American Literary History, 1607–1830* (New York, 1970), pp. 179–80, 186.

of republican institutions, the confidence that these would generate an exemplary new culture, went along with standard denunciation of the tyranny, despotism, and corruption supposed to typify Europe. In the process the faults of the mother country, "that detestable place" in Freneau's phrase, were exaggerated, and the extent of previous American association with England was correspondingly minimized. Such assertions, more extravagantly xenophobic than a Freneau or a Barlow probably realized, served to provoke British counterinvective. The persistence of slavery in America's "piebald polity," as the Anglo-Irish poet Tom Moore called it, made the United States vulnerable to charges of hypocrisy.

So did the curious record of the Americans on the matter of republicanism. With the Revolution came the proud boast that the colonies had always been republican. Why then had colonists, with hardly any exceptions, sung the praises of George III until the very eve of the Revolution? Why during the Revolution did the Americans show so little embarrassment in paying ceremonial tributes to the French monarchy of Louis XVI? Joel Barlow, a chaplain in the Continental army, joined with fellow officers in celebrating the birth of Louis XVI's heir, the dauphin. And in 1786 Barlow was at great pains to secure the patronage of Louis XVI for his would-be epic poem, *The Vision of Columbus*. The French monarch graciously accepted the dedication of the *Vision* and got sales off to a handsome start by purchasing twenty-five copies. (Barlow, incidentally, gleaned much of the background information in the *Vision* from the *History of America* by the Scottish historian William Robertson, who had never been across the Atlantic.) Barlow went to Paris and lived there through the dramas of the 1790s, a friend of Thomas Paine and author of the (by then) antimonarchical *Advice to the Privileged Orders*. But it could be said of Joel Barlow, unkindly, that he was himself a member of the privileged orders, practicing what we have learned to think of as radical chic. At any rate, former chaplain Barlow took advantage of his international connections, his cosmopolitan charm, financial shrewdness, and a measure of luck, to build up a sizable fortune. He has acquired a recent new renown through the anthologizing of the last poem he ever wrote, a grim depiction of the sufferings of Napoleon Bonaparte's army on the way back from Moscow. Had it taken Barlow so long to circle back to the antirevolutionary and anti-Napoleonic beliefs of his former associates, the conservatively minded Connecticut Wits? Understandably, his revised version of the *Vision*, now known as *The Columbiad* (1807), was no longer dedicated to Louis XVI, but to Barlow's friend Robert Fulton. It was also, however, a sumptuously bound and illustrated edition, selling at $20 a copy and looking gorgeous enough to adorn a royal library, if too magnificent for a republican one.[15]

Comparable complexities surround the stories of other figures in the early history of American literary nationalism. It is not easy to set the record straight. Pietistic literary historians have sometimes misleadingly portrayed arduous, frustrated pioneer efforts as clear-cut success stories—victories for the wholesome impulses of democratic patriotism. Richard Rollins and Joseph J. Ellis are, however, among the scholars who have recently explored the career of Noah Webster and shown that his career involved even more tergiversation than that of Joel Barlow.

Webster began, during the Revolutionary War, as an ardent nationalist, insistent that "America must be as independent in *literature* as she is in *politics*—as famous for *arts* as for *arms*." He was also tirelessly ambitious; "a person of my youth," he had added, "may have some influence in exciting a spirit of literary industry." This he had attempted by means

<hr/>

[15] Theodore A. Zunder, *The Early Days of Joel Barlow ... 1754 to 1787* (New Haven, 1934); James Woodress, *A Yankee's Odyssey: The Life of Joel Barlow* (Philadelphia, 1958); Elliott, *Revolutionary Writers*, pp. 92–127; Robert D. Arner, "The Connecticut Wits," in Emerson, ed., *American Literature, 1764–1789*, pp. 245–51. A. Owen Aldridge, *Early American Literature: A Comparatist Approach* (Princeton, 1982), pp. 187–88, suggests a source for Sydney Smith's mockery in a much-ridiculed debate of December 1796, when the House of Representatives produced the assertion that the United States was, as "a whole nation, the freest and most enlightened in the world." Smith's 1820 article referred to the American "orators and newspaper scribblers [who] endeavour to persuade their supporters that they are the greatest, the most refined, the most enlightened, and the most moral people upon Earth."

of his projected three-volume set of publications, heralded by the *Spelling Book.*[16]

Webster's aim was to establish a single American standard of pronunciation, spelling, and usage, purged of what he regarded as British linguistic corruptions and errors (such as the eighteenth-century habit of adding a superfluous *k* to *musick, Gothick* and other *-ic* endings). His schoolbooks would inculcate these "American" rules and provide American instead of British specimen instances. He insisted that the acceptance of a universal, rational system would serve to bind the former colonies into nationhood.

Some of his proposals were indeed sensible. Several of his spelling reforms were adopted, notably the change from *-re* to *-er* in words like *center* and the deletion of *u* from *colour, honour,* and the like. His small 1806 *Dictionary* was commendable as a one-man operation; the larger 1828 *Dictionary* was a quite heroic achievement, even if the immense *Webster's* of later decades was linked to the lexicographer in name only. He was right too to argue the importance for the United States of becoming, or remaining, a land of one common language.

In other respects Webster fails to fit the specification of far-sighted democratic innovator. By the 1790s he had begun to settle into a cranky Federalism, deploring what he took to be the follies and sins of such dangerous radicals as Jefferson and Paine. His dictionary definitions revealed increasing skepticism as to the desirability of *equality, democracy, republicanism,* and the like. One of the synonyms for *president* in Webster's 1828 dictionary—cynical, resigned, approving?—is *monarch.*

On the matter of language, Webster abandoned his early insistence that American English could or should differ radically from English English. He was gratified to discover, on a trip across the Atlantic in 1826, that "good usage in England accords almost wholly with the good usage in this country." His final view? "Our language is the *English*"; ex-

[16] Richard Rollins, *The Long Journey of Noah Webster* (Philadelphia, 1980); Ellis, *After the Revolution,* pp. 161–212.

cept for a "few peculiarities" in each, he declared it "desirable that the language of the United States and Great Britain should continue to be the same." What then of the Websterian dream of a distinct American culture founded upon a purified language? Had it ever been properly thought out, any more than the brainwave of Brissot de Warville, who jotted down in his journal the notion that Americans ought to start speaking a sort of franglais in order to break loose from the thrall of the mother tongue? Conceivably, Webster was doing actual harm by denying the existence and utility of regional dialects. If Americans paid attention to Webster, did they not risk denaturing their native speech?[17]

Another man of letters much cited in accounts of America's literary evolution is Michel Guillaume St. Jean de Crèvecoeur, commonly known as J. Hector St. John de Crèvecoeur, who published *Letters from an American Farmer* in 1782. He is known above all for the celebrated third chapter of the book, entitled "What Is an American?" Crèvecoeur is credited with being perhaps the first author to express the "American Dream," through his evocation of the American "new man," working as a yeoman farmer in an idyllic middle landscape. This picture is appealing and in some crucial sense true. But Crèvecoeur is a complicated case. He was in fact never an American citizen. Most of the *Letters* were written before the Revolution, when this French-born settler was a British citizen. The felicity he celebrates is that of British colonies under the protection of a benevolently remote yet powerful government. His "new man" is an Anglo-American, and certainly free in ways denied to Europe's landless poor. However, "new man" is also a rendering of *novus homo*, the self-

[17] Warfel, ed., *Letters of Webster*, p. 415. As for Brissot de Warville: "Americans must detest the English; they will try, if they can, to erase every trace of their origin. But since their language will always betray them, they must introduce innovations into their language as they do in their constitution. . . . What, then would stop them from adopting turns of phrase peculiar to the French language? Why would they make fun, as the English do, of Frenchmen who introduce gallicisms into their English? There is a double advantage . . . : Americans will be drawn closer to other nations and will be drawn farther away from the English. They will create a langauge of their own; there will exist an American language" (J. P. Brissot
148

made figure who is frequently mentioned in Roman history. John Adams was one of the Americans who spoke of *novi homines*, using the Latin tag as an evident commonplace of eighteenth-century reference. The degree of newness of Crèvecoeur's new man is no more clear-cut than his nationality.

Nor was Crèvecoeur's own allegiance free from ambiguity. He quit his farm in Orange County, New York, in 1780 and after some delay reached London aboard a British ship. The British authorities appear to have concluded that he was a loyalist (and that is how he is regarded by historians of loyalism). Certainly his wife's family and some of his friends were tinged with loyalism. The final part of *Letters from an American Farmer*, and the bulk of other material that remained unpublished until 1925 (*Sketches*), is at best lukewarm toward the American cause. Crèvecoeur returned to the United States in 1783, after a sojourn in Paris, but as French consul. He went back to France for several months in 1785 and left America for good in 1790. His volume of *Letters*, markedly more "patriotic" in the revised French editions of 1784 and 1787, when independence was an accomplished fact, enjoyed some popularity for a few years. But an American edition of 1793 was virtually ignored and, thereafter, *Letters from an American Farmer* remained out of print until 1904. For all that time the American Dream had to do without Crèvecoeur.[18]

There are other indications of a collapse of morale, from the élan of the 1770s to the worries of the 1780s, and the feuds and lamentations of the 1790s. Barlow's New England friends, the spry intellectuals of the war years, turned to the semidisenchanted light verse of the *Anarchiad* (1786–87).

de Warville, *New Travels in the United States, 1788*, ed. Durand Echeverria [Cambridge, Mass., 1964], p. 78).

[18] Marcus Cunliffe, "Crèvecoeur Revisited," *Journal of American Studies* 9 (1975): 129–44; Elayne Antler Rapping, "Theory and Experience in Crèvecoeur's America," *American Quarterly* 19 (1967): 707–18; James C. Mohr, "Calculated Disillusionment: Crèvecoeur's *Letters* Reconsidered," *South Atlantic Quarterly* 69 (1970): 354–63; A. W. Plumstead, "Hector St. John de Crèvecoeur," in Emerson, ed., *American Literature, 1764–1789*, pp. 213–31. It should be said that Plumstead and some other recent commentators do not perceive Crèvecoeur as a deviously unhappy figure, but rather as a pioneer of literary Americanism.

They had enthusiastically supported the American side in the War of Independence. By degrees these Connecticut, or Hartford, Wits became caustic. Indeed, "Christopher Caustic" was one of their pen names. "The Echo" (1805) sharply attacked Jefferson and his administration:

> Sometimes We talk in hypocritic strain,
> Sometimes we're hand in hand with atheist Paine,
> Sometimes Our style is mere bombastic sound,
> Sometimes 'tis mean and grovelling on the ground.[19]

Philip Freneau was a skillful versifier and pamphleteer with a more deeply revolutionary or at any rate anti-British impulse. "That rascal Freneau" served as a journalist for the Jeffersonians in the early 1790s. His animus against kings and aristocrats never abated. What did fade were his dreams that America might enable people of talent to live by the pen. In one of his personae Freneau as "the Late Mr. Robert Slender" offered wry advice to aspiring authors not to expect to find an audience for their literary wares. There were simply not enough Americans interested in such things.[20]

[19] "The Echo," no. 20, a collaborative work mainly written by Theodore Dwight and Richard Alsop, for *The American Mercury* (1791–1805). This, from the final section, was composed by Alsop. It is cited in Vernon L. Parrington's valuable edition *The Connecticut Wits* (1926; reprint ed., 1969), p. 509.

[20] Elliott, *Revolutionary Writers*, pp. 146–47; Lewis Leary, *That Rascal Freneau: A Study in Literary Failure* (New Brunswick, N.J., 1944) and "Philip Freneau: A Reassessment," in Leary, *Soundings: Some Early American Writers* (Athens, Ga., 1975), pp. 131–60; Philip M. Marsh, *Philip Freneau: Poet and Journalist* (Minneapolis, 1967). Also see some acute remarks by Lewis P. Simpson, "The Satiric Mode: The Early National Wits," in Louis D. Rubin, Jr., ed., *The Comic Imagination in American Literature* (New Brunswick, N.J., 1973), pp. 49–61. The most convenient excerpt from the views of "Slender" is to be found in Robert E. Spiller's fine compilation, *The American Literary Revolution, 1783–1837* (Garden City, N.Y., 1967), pp. 5–12. Slender makes a lighthearted complaint against condescending literati from Britain and Ireland who "boast that they have introduced the Muses among us since the conclusion of the late war. . . . They are, however, excuseable [*sic*] in treating the American authors as inferiors; a political and a literary independence . . . being two very different things—the first was

This was the discovery too of the novelist Charles Brockden Brown, often described as America's first professional author. He wrote six novels between 1798 and 1801. Twenty years later, in recommending Brown's fictions, James Kirke Paulding was obliged to confess that most Americans had probably never heard of them. The most Paulding could venture was a pious expectation that Brown's "future fame will furnish a bright contrast to the darkness in which he is now enveloped." In the years before his death in 1810, Charles Brockden Brown still did some writing but had to spend most of his time as a businessman.[21]

Freneau's Princeton classmate Hugh Henry Brackenridge had collaborated with him in a glowingly optimistic undergraduate poem, "The Rising Glory of America" (1772). After war service Brackenridge settled in frontier Pennsylvania to practice law, with strongly patriotic and democratic impulses. His major work was a long picaresque novel, *Modern Chivalry*, published in installments from 1792 to 1815. In the more perfunctory surveys of American literature *Modern Chivalry* is treated as rollicking backwoods comedy. There is indeed some humor of a semi-Jeffersonian sort, as in a mocking account of the self-importantly snobbish concerns of the Society of the Cincinnati. Brackenridge never became a high Tory. On the other hand, a principal theme is that men should remain in their proper stations, once these have been established. The two chief characters are Captain Farrago and his servant Teague O'Regan. Farrago's enterprises usually fail; he is a gentleman. The unschooled "bog-trotter" O'Regan succeeds in various adventures, such as being elected to the legislature. Despite his name, however, Farrago is no foolish Don Quixote or other absurd character; in the latter stages of the novel he has in fact become governor of

---

accomplished in about seven years, the latter will not be completely effected, perhaps, in as many centuries" (Spiller, *American Literary Revolution*, p. 8).

[21] Paulding's comments on Brown, cited in Spiller, *American Literary Revolution*, p. 386, were originally published in the second series of *Salmagundi* (1819–20).

his state. Nor is the illiterate, cloddish O'Regan presented as a shrewd peasant on the Sancho Panza pattern, still less a crafty manservant like Mozart's Figaro. O'Regan's Irish brogue is rendered half-phonetically, with every appearance of authorial disdain. *Modern Chivalry* is a peculiar back-to-front book, in its boisterous yet unjovial way arguably not less but more class-conscious than comparable European tales of the era.[22]

As a group, American writers were, like their artist colleagues, definite in their support for the Revolution. Crèvecoeur's complications of nationality and kinship made him somewhat unusual. So did the loyalist connections of Thomas Green Fessenden and of his friend Joseph Dennie, the editor of the Philadelphia *Port Folio*. It is nevertheless intriguing to consider how few of the new nation's literati bore any active combatant role. John Trumbull and Noah Webster were never in uniform. Brackenridge, Barlow, and Timothy Dwight secured relative comfort, privilege, and leisure in the commissioned rank of army chaplain. Of the three only Dwight had strong religious convictions, and his military service was quite brief. Chaplain Barlow devoted more time to writing poetry than to preaching or to pastoral duties. Brackenridge resigned from the Continental army in 1778 to launch a literary magazine. After the venture failed, Brackenridge did not reenter the military; shifting from theology to jurisprudence, he opened up a law practice in Pittsburgh in the spring of 1781, several months before the tide of war had swung decisively in favor of the United States.[23]

Philip Freneau's wartime record, given his fierce literary commitment to the patriot cause, is likewise equivocal. He spent the first years of the conflict in blissful tranquillity, living with a well-to-do planter in the Virgin Islands. During

[22] On Brackenridge and *Modern Chivalry* see Ellis, *After the Revolution*, pp. 92–110, Elliott, *Revolutionary Writers*, pp. 171–217, Gordon S. Wood, *The Creation of the American Republic, 1776–1787* (Chapel Hill, 1969), pp. 480–82, Simpson, "The Satiric Mode," pp. 58–61, and William F. Keller, *The Nation's Advocate: Henry Marie Brackenridge and Young America* (Pittsburgh, 1956), pp. 22–27, 45–47, 177–78.

[23] Biographical details culled from standard biographies. On Barlow's chaplaincy, for instance, see Zunder, *Early Days of Joel Barlow*, pp. 102–63.

the latter part of the war Freneau was still based in the Caribbean and still for the most part a gentleman of leisure, though involved in intermittent spells of privateering—a form of legalized piracy whose dangers were offset by the possibility of large profits. Freneau never forgave the British for intercepting one of his voyages and locking him up for several weeks in the unhealthy confines of a prison ship. But his fury at such treatment was, it seems, prompted by his captors' disbelief in his cover story (that he was *not* a privateer) and by their refusal to show him the courtesies appropriate to a gentlemanly product of the College of New Jersey.[24]

One could go on adding to the list of Americans with literary or intellectual ambitions who, though they may have been active after 1783, did not exactly flourish then, if *flourish* means "win fame and wealth." And there were others whose Americanness was somewhat uncertain. There is, for example, the Vermonter Ethan Allen, who fell under the shadowy accusation of having engaged in treasonable correspondence with the British enemy; or Tom Paine, absent in Europe from 1787 to 1802, once an American hero but then assailed as an atheist and iconoclast, a man supposedly without a country and without gratitude either to the United States or to George Washington. Again, John Paul Jones the naval officer was no man of letters. Some, though, might discern parallels with the career of Tom Paine. Both of them were British by birth and upbringing, of artisan stock. Both were intelligent, restless persons, whose dislike of authority was probably compounded by awareness that poor, obscure men could only hope to win recognition by ingratiating themselves with powerful patrons. Jones and Paine were drawn accordingly to the American side, but being prickly characters then began to suspect that their Revolutionary services had been undervalued. Both, as if by preference, subsequently lived in France. John Paul Jones estranged himself further by transferring to the Russian navy, having accepted a rear admiral's commission from Catherine the Great. Paine ("the American Voltaire") offended nearly all

---

[24] Marsh, *Philip Freneau*, pp. 67–72.

his onetime American associates by appearing to reject formal Christianity in his *Age of Reason* (1794–96) and then by attacking President Washington in a ferocious open letter. Brackenridge alluded to *The Age of Reason* as the work of "an uncommon, but *uninformed* man." Even if theologians were wrong, he asked, "why dissipate the vision? Does it not constitute a great portion of our happiness? Are those men supposed to have done nothing for the world who have raised fabrics of this kind to the imagination *even upon false grounds?*" James Kirke Paulding, in *A Sketch of Old England* (1822), was at pains to disavow admiration for Paine:

> I have no great regard to the memory of this person, although his early writings were serviceable to our cause in the time of the revolutionary war. All that he ever wrote in favour of freedom, is insufficient to atone for the indecent and arrogant manner in which he questions the authority of Holy Writ; nor can all the clearness of his reasonings in support of human liberty, counterbalance the injury he has inflicted upon it, by giving its enemies a plausible pretext for connecting the progress of political freedom with the spreading of religious indifference, if not absolute unbelief.[25]

The ambivalences in such biographies remind us that in Washington Irving's classic tale "Rip Van Winkle," the principal character sleeps right through the American Revolution. Returning to his native village after his twenty-year slumber, he is bewildered to find, for instance, that "the ruby face of King George" on the old inn sign has been "singularly metamorphosed." In the amended version, "the red coat was changed for one of blue and buff, a sword was held in the hand instead of a sceptre, the head was decorated in a cocked hat, and underneath was painted in large characters, GENERAL WASHINGTON." Irving himself in a figurative sense held dual nationality. He was an American, named in honor of the Union's great hero. His family, on the other hand, was strongly Scottish, still with close family ties to Britain. Irving's

[25] Brackenridge's comments on Paine occur in *Modern Chivalry*, ed. Claude M. Newlin (New York, 1937), book IV, p. 573. Paulding's strictures are in *A Sketch of Old England* (1822; reprint ed., London, 1822), pp. 83–84.

fame was to be international and would rest chiefly upon *The Sketch Book of Geoffrey Crayon, Gent.* (1820) and *Bracebridge Hall* (1822)—volumes initially published in London and predominantly "English" in treatment.[26]

Even where an American author had no external ties to the former mother country, his handling of Anglo-American relations was often puzzlingly double-edged. Thus, William Wirt of Maryland and Virginia was the son of a Swiss immigrant. He prospered as a lawyer and married into the Virginia gentry. In 1803 he had considerable success with a batch of essays collected under the title of *The Letters of the British Spy.* They purported to have been written by an English member of Parliament who viewed the United States in general and Virginia in particular with condescending disapproval. Wirt presented character sketches of James Monroe, John Marshall, and other prominent Virginians, and used the British persona as a way of criticizing aspects of Virginia society, such as the state's low educational standards. Wirt's approach is on the whole playful, imitating the geniality of Addison and the whimsicality of Laurence Sterne. He pretends to rebuke his supercilious narrator, and asterisked footnotes draw the reader's attention to the "author's" monarchist slurs upon American republicanism. It would appear that Wirt himself wished to see reforms in Virginia education but, if so, why risk weakening the impact of the criticism by attributing it to an unsympathetic British traveler? Perhaps readers of the *Letters* knew who was the real author. But then, why should they and Wirt conspire at so curious a simulation?[27]

[26] Stanley T. Williams, *The Life of Washington Irving*, 2 vols. (New York, 1935), is still the most amply detailed biography, but for the themes covered in this essay see especially William L. Hedges, *Washington Irving: An American Study, 1802–1832* (Baltimore, 1965).

[27] The best modern edition of *Letters of the British Spy* (Chapel Hill, 1970) carries an introduction by Richard Beale Davis. On Wirt himself, consult Jay B. Hubbell, *The South in American Literature, 1607–1900* (Durham, N.C., 1954), pp. 236–37, and William R. Taylor, *Cavalier and Yankee: The Old South and American National Character* (New York, 1961), pp. 70–80, 178–80.

Revolutions, it is said, devour their children. That drastic judgment may apply to the leading orators and intellectuals of the French Revolution. It would be too extreme a comment on the literati of Revolutionary America. None, not even avowed loyalists like the Boston poet-clergyman Mather Byles, perished on the scaffold. A handful subsequently hinted that independence had been a mistake. Such was the assertion made by Joseph Dennie in May 1800, in a letter to his parents. The "settled attachment to *Englishmen* and English principles" that he professed, and the contempt for America's "rascal populace," were, however, not proclaimed in print and may in their hyperbole represent a certain attitudinizing bravado.[28] Loyalists, high Federalists, and emphatic patriots all recognized that the Revolution was irreversible. Few if any genuinely hankered after a return to British suzerainty. Rip Van Winkle in Irving's tale appears happier under the American flag than he was before, once he recovers from the shock of his awakening. It is important not to exaggerate the malaise of American literature in the first decades after the Peace of Paris. One could, after all, produce any number of highly pessimistic verdicts on American culture, delivered during the latter part of the nineteenth century or indeed the twentieth century. It would obviously not follow from these that their authors regarded American independence as a disastrous error.

Nevertheless, to recapitulate and conclude, the early era of American independence was, culturally speaking, a letdown. Excessive expectations of literary as of other forms of "rising glory" were announced at the outset of the Revolution. The expected outpouring of literary genius failed to occur during

---

[28] Dennie's rambling letter is reproduced in Harold Milton Ellis, *Joseph Dennie and His Circle: A Study in American Literature from 1792 to 1812* (1915; reprint ed., New York, 1971), pp. 114–20. A private letter, similar in tone, was sent to Dennie's mother in April 1792 (see Lewis P. Simpson, *The Man of Letters in New England and the South* [Baton Rouge, 1973], pp. 54–55). Young Dennie, in his tory-curmudgeon role, announced that if only the Revolution had been avoided, "I might now . . . in a Literary Diplomatic, or lucrative Situation [have] been in the service of my rightful King." See the crisp assessment, "Literary Opinions of Joseph Dennie," in Leary, *Soundings*, pp. 253–70.

the next twenty or thirty years. British military, economic, and cultural power did not go into a decline, but on the contrary seemed more impressive than ever. West, Copley, and other American artists who had brought renown to their country by achieving fame in London tended to remain in Europe—as if to reinforce the depressing facts of life borne in upon their literary colleagues: that style, themes, milieu, and patronage were all still largely defined by the Old World.

American literature turned out, at least in the short run, to lack a distinctive vocabulary and idiom, or any markedly "democratic" ambience. Ironically, plain-folk imagery and attitudes were more evident in the literature of the supposedly aristocratic mother country. In Burns and Wordsworth, in the unheroic couplets of George Crabbe's *The Village* (1783), the painstaking accuracy of Robert Bloomfield's *The Farmer's Boy* (1800), or in the unabashed dialect of John Clare's *Poems Descriptive of Rural Life* (1820), Britain produced a literature that made contemporary American verse seem lifelessly genteel.

Why was this so? Several reasons have already been suggested, such as the absence of a sizable leisured native population; the time it would necessarily take to evolve distinctive, appropriate American modes; and the divisive, protracted tensions of the Revolutionary and Napoleonic wars. There were in fact some perfectly good reasons why the emergence of a major "American" literature proved slower and harder than had been forecast. But they sometimes sounded like excuses, or recriminations against Britain, rather than sober explanations. On the matter of language, for example, the United States faced problems of cultural identity that could not be resolved in a decade or even a half century. The mistake was to underestimate the size of the task—and to misstate it—as Noah Webster did in hypothesizing the existence of an American English that would constitute both the purest, most authentic form of the language to be found anywhere in the world *and* a dynamic American variant such as befitted a separate new nation.

A second formidable difficulty lay in the ideological assumptions of the new nation. Literary expression was shaped, and in several ways inhibited, by democratic-republican imperatives. The American patriotic creed didactically imposed upon authors the duty to indicate the superior virtue of mankind in the New World. Villainy was the attribute of foreign or nonwhite persons, or of Americans who had succumbed to insidious temptation (drugs, alcohol, seduction, religious heresy). In ideal American circumstance, divisions by class or creed did not exist. The operation of such roles forced early American imaginative literature into moralistic simplifications or into idiosyncratic, covert evasion (as with a novelist like Charles Brockden Brown). Europe and Europeans tended to be portrayed in censorious caricature.

The process was by no means entirely to be deplored. The United States was at least attempting to get to grips with some fundamental issues—of protest and restraint, novelty and tradition, nationhood and federalism, leadership and democracy. The challenge these presented during the 1780s (for example, over Shays's Rebellion) was intensified as a result of the French Revolution. Americans were entitled to take pride in the reflection that, if they had not finally resolved the crises of modernity, they had grappled more successfully with them than the ultras of either persuasion, conservative or radical, in Europe.

Nevertheless, a degree of disillusion marked the early history of literature in the United States. The ideological conflicts of the Revolutionary era turned a number of American authors toward social conservatism, so that their political opponents were prompted—somewhat unfairly—to portray them as sympathizers with monarchy and aristocracy. An awful question confronted Brackenridge and others. If the people were sovereign, and popular choice turned against the work of a particular author, should he accept the verdict as vox populi, vox dei? Political democracy must assume that people were collectively sensible and that majority decisions were decisive. But if so, given the poor sales of native American authors, few or none had any real function in the United States. Unwilling to accept such a deduction, men of letters looked for consoling explanations such as the argument that, in the absence of an international copyright agreement, unfair foreign competition was depriving them of a livelihood, or perhaps that things would improve in ten or twenty years with the growth of national wealth, numbers, and sophistication.

A horrid suspicion remained, forcing itself toward the surface in *Modern Chivalry* and other early works. If majority taste was fallible in literary or aesthetic matters, why should it be politically infallible? But if the mass of Americans were creatures of defective sense, why believe in republican or democratic principles—untried and, according to most political philosophers, unsound? Why have made a Revolution?

Such literary misgivings affected even the most emphatic spokesmen for American democracy. Philip Freneau more and more frequently expressed the view that solitude and public indifference were the lot of the American author. Democracy was all very well in the abstract, and greatly preferable (thought Freneau) to the snares and delusions of the old order. Yet he could not help looking back to a half-imaginary metropolitan golden era. In his wistful "Author's Soliloquy" he invoked:

> Thrice happy DRYDEN who could meet
> Some rival bard on every street:
> When all were bent on writing well,
> It was some credit to excel
> While those condemn'd to stand alone
> Can only by themselves be known.

Did the mainly conventional pathos of a Freneau poem of 1781 acquire a deeper meaning ten or twenty years afterward, when the image could be glossed as a pessimistic prophecy of conditions under independence?

> So nightly on some shallow tide,
> Oft have I seen a splendid show;
> Reflected stars on either side
> And glittering moons were seen below
> But when the tide had ebb'd away,
> The scene fantastic with it fled,
> A bank of mud around me lay,
> And sea-weed on the river's bed.[29]

---

[29] Quoted in Leary, *Soundings*, p. 143; also see Simpson, "The Satiric Mode," p. 58.

SAMUEL F. SCOTT

Military Nationalism in Europe in the Aftermath of the American Revolution

ANY ATTEMPT TO evaluate the impact of the American Revolution upon Europe is severely complicated by the fact that within only a half-dozen years after the peace treaty that secured American independence, revolution broke out in France. Thereafter, the two great revolutionary strands of the late eighteenth century became so intertwined as to frustrate efforts to separate and distinguish them completely. Historians have, therefore, tended to treat these two phenomena either as entirely discreet developments (with, perhaps, some passing references to possible links between the two) or within a more general context of a "democratic" revolutionary movement affecting the whole of "Atlantic" civilization.[1] Both approaches can be justified; neither is thoroughly satisfactory.

In an effort to identify the military influence of the American Revolution on Europe, this essay will be restricted to an investigation of the period from the close of the American war to the beginnings of the French Revolution. This approach, too, has its problems. It is a very short span of time for a complex phenomenon to be appreciated and to have its

[1] Traditionally, American and French historians have treated their respective revolutions as sui generis. The major proponents of the "Atlantic Revolution" have been Robert R. Palmer, *The Age of Democratic Revolution: A Political History of Europe and America, 1760–1800*, 2 vols. (Princeton, 1959, 1964), and Jacques Godechot, *La grande nation: L'expansion révolutionnaire de la France dans le monde, 1789–1799*, 2 vols. (Paris, 1956).

full effect, particularly in light of eighteenth-century communications and certain political, social, and cultural differences between the two continents. More troublesome than
the differences between Europe and America, however, are
the similarities; for as much as some might insist upon the
unique qualities of the American Revolution, it remains true
that many American practices and institutions, including the
military, resembled or reflected those of Europe. In addition,
European perceptions were often more significant than
American realities in determining the influence of the American Revolution. In spite of such difficulties, however, it is
important to examine European reactions to what was, at
least until 1789, the most momentous political development
of the age.

For Europe, the most obvious consequence of the 1783
Treaty of Paris was the establishment of a greater degree of
equilibrium among the great powers than had existed for the
past two decades; indeed, the balance of power in 1783 may
have been closer to realization than at any other time in the
century. With the loss of its North American colonies and the
cession of other possessions to France and Spain, Britain
seemed to have lost the colonial and commercial dominance
that it had enjoyed since 1763. France, on the other hand,
had avenged its humiliating defeat of that year and looked
forward to a considerable and profitable expansion of trade
with the new American republic.[2] Not only was the relationship between the two major colonial powers of Europe put
on a more equal footing by the peace settlement, but by the
early 1780s the Continental powers had managed to work
out a greater degree of parity among themselves than had
been the case in the past. In Prussia, which had barely escaped annihilation in the Seven Years' War, Frederick II devoted the next twenty years to consolidating and
strengthening his state. Austria—a convenient shorthand
term for the central European domains of the House of

---

[2] French expectations for American commerce were quickly frustrated;
even by the late 1780s England had managed to establish a greater volume
of trade with the United States than had existed before the Revolution.
For a brief summary of this situation, see Michel Devèze, *L'Europe et le
monde à la fin du XVIIIe siècle* (Paris, 1970), p. 353.

Habsburg—had become reconciled to the loss of Silesia, for which it had engaged in two long and costly wars in midcentury and was concentrating on internal recovery. Catherine II was directing the vast human and material resources of Russia against her weaker neighbors, Poland and the Ottoman Empire, rather than challenging the other major powers in eastern Europe. Besides avoiding confrontation, the eastern powers had been able to cooperate in the first dismemberment of Poland in 1772, to their mutual aggrandizement.[3]

Beyond this general effect of the American war, what influence did the American Revolution have upon the military establishments of the major powers, which together dominated Europe and much of the world outside Europe? In order to respond to this question, it is necessary to examine not only what appeared to be distinctive about the Revolution from a military standpoint but also the military institutions of the European powers, perceptions of the American Revolution in Europe, and how each of the great powers responded to American developments.

Three aspects of the war in particular have been commonly represented as military innovations: more open tactics, especially the use of sharpshooters and skirmishers; the employment of militia on a large scale to supplement, or even occasionally to replace, regular forces; and an officer corps in which ability, rather than birth, determined advancement. Yet, as we shall see, all of these innovations had parallels—often limited, to be sure—in Europe. The United States was, after all, an unmistakable, albeit distant, offshoot of European society. At the same time, America and Americans were known in Europe primarily through travel literature or the writings of political philosophers that often presented them in a romanticized or idealized form. For Europeans, then, America was sufficiently similar that they

[3] Olwen Hufton, *Europe: Privilege and Protest, 1730–1789* (Ithaca, 1980), pp. 126–39, provides a recent, succinct account of the balance of power at this period. The so-called War of Bavarian Succession (1778–79) between Prussia and Austria was essentially a show of force on the part of both powers, with no large-scale engagements and a quick return to the status quo.

might draw from the American Revolution military lessons applicable to their own armies. On the other hand, American conditions were different enough—or at least considered so—that military developments there might be ignored as irrelevant to European circumstances.

What determined whether American military examples would be accepted or rejected in Europe were the conditions in each country and what were conceived to be national interests. Briefly, the great powers of eastern Europe, Prussia, Austria, and Russia, were far removed from America in almost all respects and had no direct experience in the American war. Furthermore, all three were autocratic political systems and closed social hierarchies; to them even minor change in their armies posed a threat to the entire status quo. Authorities in Britain rejected the military lessons of their defeat until British troops were engaged in a comparable conflict more than two decades after the close of the American Revolution. Only in France was there any clear indication of military influence from the American war in the short period between 1783 and 1789. General intellectual ferment and a broad desire for military reform created an atmosphere in France that was conducive to change, and when revolution first began to develop there many military men who had participated in the American Revolution drew upon their experiences to offer models for change. In order to better appreciate how and why the great powers of Europe responded to the military developments of the American war, it is necessary to provide a description of the military establishment in each of them and a discussion of how national conditions affected their response.

The Prussian state, composed of scattered territories that stretched from the Rhineland to Polish (West) Prussia, had emerged from the international wars of midcentury—the War of Austrian Succession (1740–48) and the Seven Years' War (1756–63)—as the preeminent military power in Europe.[4] Because of his phenomenal success with limited re-

[4] There are a number of excellent, readily available works on the Prussian army of this period, notably Christopher Duffy, *The Army of Frederick the Great* (London, 1974), W. O. Shanahan, *Prussian Military Reforms,*

sources, Frederick the Great was recognized as a military genius and his army was accepted throughout Europe as *the* model of military organization. While he had experimented with militia and partisan "free battalions," Frederick himself had confidence only in the standing, or regular, army. In the 1780s it consisted of nearly 200,000 men and constituted the third largest force in Europe, although the state's total population (approximately 5,000,000) placed it behind a dozen other countries.

The Prussian officer corps was homogeneous. While admitting a basic equality among all officers, the army reserved the vast majority of officer positions for the nobility. Although a number of bourgeois had been commissioned during the crisis of the Seven Years' War, most of them were eliminated after 1763. By the 1780s, 90 percent of the officer corps was aristocratic, and the nonnobles were concentrated in the less prestigious branches—hussars, light infantry, artillery, and other technical branches. The ranks were filled by natives, who were liable to conscription, and foreign mercenaries. Since the 1730s the Prussian state had been divided into "cantons," each of which was responsible for furnishing a sufficient number of recruits to maintain a regiment at full strength. Every spring the authorities would draft enough young men to fill the unit. After receiving their basic training, of between one and two years, the soldiers could return home; in peacetime they were required to perform only about two months' service each year, during the spring review and summer exercises, although they remained liable to active duty for an indefinite period. In typical eighteenth-century fashion, exemptions were granted to numerous social classes and occupational groups, as well as to whole regions, in order to keep as many productive subjects as possible at home and on the job. Toward the same end, the state made every effort to enroll foreigners, particularly

1789–1813 (New York, 1945), and Peter Paret, *Yorck and the Era of Prussian Reform, 1807–1815* (Princeton, 1966). For a more general context, see Gordon A. Craig, *The Politics of the Prussian Army, 1640–1945* (Oxford, 1964), Karl Demeter, *The German Officer-Corps in Society and State, 1650–1945*, trans. A. Malcolm (New York, 1965), and Martin Kitchen, *A Military History of Germany, from the Eighteenth Century to the Present Day* (Bloomington, Ind., 1975). These form the basis of the following discussion.

other Germans from the numerous small states of the Holy Roman Empire; in the later part of the century foreigners made up between three-fifths and two-thirds of the Prussian army.[5]

In such a force, composed of natives subjected to an inequitable system of conscription and foreigners serving only for pay, desertion was a constant and serious problem. The rigorous system of Prussian discipline that attempted to control these troops was as much the product of the army's composition as it was the result of prevailing military principles. Similarly, the rigid linear tactics that characterized Frederick II's maneuvers were adopted not only for their tactical effect, but also as a means of greater disciplinary control. This system, which served so well in the wars of the midcentury, became frozen after 1763. Indeed, its worst features were exaggerated: able middle-class officers were purged and replaced by aristocrats—including foreigners—whose primary claim to command was their social status; light infantry, whose effectiveness largely depended upon their independence and initiative, were disdained because these same qualities ran counter to the very essence of the regime. In much the same spirit the Prussian state refused to develop the incipient patriotism that was expressed in certain localities such as Brandenburg and Pomerania. This was not due to Frederick's ignorance or lack of appreciation of "nationalism." In his early wars he had made an effort to develop devotion to the kingdom of Prussia among his officers. In 1746 he wrote of the value of citizen-soldiers and concluded: "With such troops one could defeat the world," but immediately qualified this conclusion, "were victories not as fatal to them as to their enemies." Frederick realized that he could not exploit the related concepts of nationalism and citizenship without revolutionizing the bases of his state; this he refused to do.[6]

---

[5] Interestingly, the efforts of Prussian recruiters in the middle and late 1770s were hampered in Germany by British competition for mercenaries to serve in the American Revolution.

[6] Robert R. Palmer, "Frederick the Great, Guibert, Bülow: From Dynastic to National War," in Edward Mead Earle, ed., *Makers of Modern Strategy: Military Thought from Machiavelli to Hitler* (Princeton, 1943), pp. 54–55. The quotation of Frederick II is on p. 55.

For two decades after Frederick's death in 1786 the Prussian army remained frozen in this mold. Neither the American nor the French revolution had any significant impact upon the Prussian military establishment. It would take the catastrophic defeat of 1806 to change the Frederician model.

The Austrian army in the late eighteenth century was an accurate reflection of the Habsburg state that it served: it was composed of a wide variety of multinational units and was governed by an almost equal variety of regulations.[7] On paper it amounted to roughly 300,000 men in the late 1780s, but its actual strength hovered around 200,000. Although some officers came from the middle class and a handful were promoted from the ranks, nobles predominated both in numbers and in the hierarchy of command. Foreigners passed readily into Austrian service from other European armies. As a whole, the officer corps was "aristocratic and international" in its composition; its cohesion rested upon a sense of personal loyalty to the ruling house and the professional commitment of its members.

The methods of recruiting soldiers ranged from conscription to voluntary enlistment. In the hereditary lands of the Habsburg rulers, Bohemia, and Galicia (after 1772), subjects were liable to conscription, although exemptions were numerous. Elsewhere, for example, in Hungary and the Tyrol, enlistments were voluntary, but force and subterfuge were employed to encourage recruitment. In addition, like other major powers, Austria recruited extensively in the German states of the Empire; up to one-third of the troops were foreign mercenaries. The most distinctive of the many military institutions of Austria was the *Militär-Grenze*, or the Military Border along the Turkish frontier. In theory, in this region all men between the ages of sixteen and sixty capable of bearing arms were to perform military service as light troops, that is, for scouting, raiding, and in the role of skirmishers; in

---

[7] Material on the Austrian army of the eighteenth century is much more difficult to find in English than are sources on its Prussian counterpart. The works of Gunther E. Rothenberg are essential in filling this gap. See "The Habsburg Army in the Napoleonic Wars," *Military Affairs* 37 (1973): 1–5, *The Military Border in Croatia, 1740–1881: A Study of an Imperial Institution* (Chicago, 1966), and *The Art of Warfare in the Age of Napoleon* (London, 1977), particularly pp. 19–21 and 166–68.

return for this they received allotments of land. These *Grenzer* constituted approximately one-fourth of the entire Habsburg army at the outbreak of the Seven Years' War, and their effectiveness so impressed friend and foe alike that there developed a general, but temporary, movement to copy these formations. However, despite their superiority to line troops in these functions and in difficult terrain, such units did not conform to the standards of an age that demanded tight control, complete subordination, and regular formations and tactics. From 1769 on, the organization, training, and employment of *Grenzer* were made to conform more and more closely to that of the line troops; simultaneously, the obligation to serve was broken down into categories so that fewer and fewer of those eligible in fact performed active duty. By the 1780s the Prussian model reigned supreme.

Except for Britain, protected by its decisive naval superiority, no other European power so consistently opposed the French in the Revolutionary and Napoleonic wars as did Austria. Until 1814 the only results of this persistence were repeated defeats, loss of influence, and humiliation. Yet the Habsburgs rejected any substantial change in their armed forces, refusing even to adopt the modifications introduced into the Prussian system after 1806. Neither the innovations of the American Revolution nor the immediate challenge of the French Revolution could deter Austria from traditional forms; the Austrian army remained an apparent anachronism, a multinational dynastic organization, well into the nineteenth century. The exceptionally diverse nature of its population and political institutions dictated such a position—and so too did the fact that in 1815 Austria sat with the victors.

On the opposite periphery of European civilization from the United States was the sprawling Russian Empire.[8] With

---

[8] The problem of finding sources on the Russian army in the eighteenth century is even greater than for the Habsburg army. A recent, thorough study of Russia in this period, Isabel de Madariaga, *Russia in the Age of Catherine the Great* (New Haven, 1981), contains a good deal of useful information on the army. Philip Longworth, *The Art of Victory: The Life and Achievements of Generalissimo Suvorov, 1729–1800* (London, 1965), is also helpful. The most comprehensive work is in Russian, L. G. Beskrovnyi, *Russkaya armiya i flot v XVIII veke* (Moscow, 1958).

the largest population of any state in Europe it could, potentially, field the most men. Russia's problem was mobilizing its resources, and the size of its army fluctuated considerably according to time and conditions. By the late eighteenth century it boasted a paper strength of around 400,000 in wartime. The officer corps was composed mostly of aristocrats and country gentry, few of whom had any extensive professional training or could handle the more sophisticated military functions of the technical branches or staff work. As in Austria, a substantial proportion of officers was foreign-born.

While the composition of the Russian officer corps paralleled that of other European armies, the recruitment policies of the government resulted in a distinctively national rank and file.[9] The peasants of each region were liable to a "recruit levy," by which the necessary numbers of new troops were conscripted into the army (essentially, for life) by the authorities. As elsewhere, certain regions such as Livonia, Belorussia, Little Russia, and some social and ethnic groups, were exempted from the recruit levy, and wealthy peasants and townsmen could purchase exemption by special payments. Nevertheless, there were almost no soldiers from outside the borders of the empire; the troops were drawn overwhelmingly from the population of Russian serfs and served under a disciplinary system that rivaled or surpassed that of Prussia in its brutality. Still, Russian troops, motivated by a sincere devotion to their monarch and the Orthodox faith, often displayed remarkable loyalty and tenacity.

Besides this premodern form of nationalism the Russian army of the late eighteenth century displayed other characteristics that set it apart from the forces of neighboring states. In the mid-1780s Gen. Grigori Potemkin introduced looser uniforms for greater ease of movement and comfort, made discipline and the general treatment of soldiers more humane, and emphasized the use of light infantry and cavalry (including the Cossacks). These reforms reflected the

---

[9] David Ogg has maintained: "Of all the armies of the period only that of Russia could, in any sense, be described as national" (*Europe of the Ancien Régime, 1715–1783* [New York, 1965], p. 154).

ideas of Gen. Alexander Suvorov, Russia's greatest military innovator of the period. Suvorov departed from most of his contemporaries and presaged coming methods of waging war in a number of respects. He advocated attacks in column with the bayonet, rather than reliance on linear tactics and firepower; he stressed the importance of independent action by skirmishers and sharpshooters; and he showed an almost unique concern for the welfare and dignity of the soldiers under his command.

These peculiar features of the Russian army were developed to deal with indigenous conditions and in no way reflected revolutionary influences, either American or French. The same Suvorov who encouraged a sense of self-worth and initiative among his men ruthlessly crushed Pugachev's rebellion and Polish independence and was as totally opposed to political or social revolution as was his sovereign, Catherine II. Furthermore, when Paul I succeeded to the throne in 1796, the new czar began to remodel the Russian army along Prussian lines.

In view of the enormous distance—political and social, as well as geographic—that separated the monarchies of eastern Europe from the United States, it should not be surprising that the military developments of the American Revolution had no significant impact there. But what of Britain? Most American institutions were, after all, derived from British examples and, in spite of independence, close ties between the two countries persisted. In addition, defeat is more frequently a teacher than victory. One might well expect the British military establishment to be profoundly affected by the experience of the American war.[10] Yet even the shock of

---

[10] There is an abundance of readily available studies of the British army in the late eighteenth century. Of special relevance to this essay is Piers Mackesy, "What the British Learned," in Ronald Hoffman and Peter J. Albert, eds., *Arms and Independence: The Military Character of the American Revolution* (Charlottesville, Va., 1984). Also pertinent are John Shy, *Toward Lexington: The Role of the British Army in the Coming of the American Revolution* (Princeton, 1965), and Richard Glover, *Peninsular Preparation: The Reform of the British Army, 1795–1809* (Cambridge, 1963). For the lot of the British soldier see Arthur N. Gilbert, "Why Men Deserted from the Eighteenth-Century British Army," *Armed Forces and Society* 6 (1980): 553–67.

American independence did not divert the British army from its traditional pattern and, with peace, it reverted to well-established practice. The regular army in peacetime consisted of slightly fewer than 20,000 men stationed at home, where their major function, outside of their normal routine, was mob and riot control.[11] A force of equal or somewhat larger size was scattered in numerous garrisons throughout the substantial remnants of Britain's colonial empire.

British officers continued to come almost exclusively from the upper classes of society, from either landed or, less often, commercial wealth. Most commissions and promotions came through purchase, up to the rank of lieutenant colonel, and postings were largely the result of "connections." The few officers promoted from the ranks were not accepted as genuine equals by their comrades and could expect only the most limited advancement, at best. Although some Swiss, German, and even French served as officers, by far the largest proportion of "foreigners" in the officer corps consisted of Scots (who constituted one-fifth to one-third of the total). After the Treaty of Paris, just as before 1775, the personnel and ethos of the British officer corps remained faithful to the ideal of the gentleman amateur.

The troops whom these officers commanded came from the opposite end of the social spectrum. Normally, enlistment was for life and, in theory, was voluntary. Recruits received a bounty for enrolling and were plied with drink and fanciful promises about the comforts and glories of military life. When all else failed, impressment was the solution. For those forced, misled, or desperate enough to volunteer sincerely, army life was a harsh experience. Discipline was as barbarous as on the Continent; flogging was a normal punishment and included up to, and occasionally beyond, a thousand lashes. Not surprisingly, desertion was common. Foreign mercenaries, notably Hessians and Hanoverians, did not form part of the standing army in Great Britain but were employed abroad during wartime. Militia units were called to

[11] Tony Hayter, *The Army and the Crowd in Mid-Georgian England* (Totowa, N.J., 1978), provides an excellent analysis of this function.

active service during crises, either as a home defense force or to deal with such domestic disturbances as the Gordon riots of June 1780. During the wars of the French Revolution and Napoleon, militiamen were incorporated into regular units.

After 1783 some British officers returned home impressed by their American experiences that tended to reinforce ideas that had been developing in Europe for a generation before the outbreak of the American Revolution. Since midcentury there had been growing interest in, and discussion of, the role of the *petite guerre*, the fast-paced, highly mobile war of hit-and-run that marked many of the engagements of the recent struggle. Intimately related to such warfare was the employment of light infantry who served as scouts, skirmishers, and sharpshooters in this type of fighting. Veterans of the American war appreciated the importance of the "little war" and the role of light infantry, although their model for the latter was the Hessian *Jäger* rather than the American rifleman. Such combat required troops who were not only self-reliant but also who were better trained and disciplined than line infantry. Beyond this, returning officers were convinced of the superiority of two ranks over the customary deployment in three, and of looser formations over those generally in use.

These ideas, however, had no immediate effect upon existing military doctrine in Britain. The American war was viewed as an aberration by the established authorities. The rough terrain and the virtual absence of cavalry in America made American practices inappropriate to combat in the open plains of central Europe, the traditional battleground of Continental wars. Instead, the British army moved increasingly in the direction of the Prussian system: rigid drill and discipline, Frederician tactics, emphasis on line infantry, deployment in three ranks, and tight formations. The British military establishment was not to be carried away by impressions gained in a colonial conflict; it would continue with conventional, tried and true methods. Not until the life-or-death struggle with Napoleon and British involvement in the Peninsular War would the lessons of the American Revolution be put into practice.

To all appearances, France's participation in the American

Revolution had exactly the opposite effects of Britain's defeat and humiliation. Twenty years before, in another Treaty of Paris, France had lost most of its colonial empire. French naval and military forces had been overwhelmed by the British fleet and the Prussian army. The most common term used in describing the French army during the period from the Seven Years' War to the American Revolution is *disarray*, as French military theorists argued about the directions that reform should take. From the outbreak of the American rebellion, France had supported the colonials, and it formally entered the war in 1778. France's entry forced Britain to expand its commitments beyond North America to the Caribbean, Europe, Africa, and India. Although the direct French contribution to the victory of the United States was restricted to one campaign, it was the most decisive action of the war—Yorktown. As a result of the subsequent peace, Britain lost the most important part of its overseas empire while France made colonial gains in the West Indies, Senegal, and India. Simultaneously the eastern European powers were concentrating their military efforts in their own part of the Continent. France had regained its rightful place in European power politics!

French success in the American war restored France's military prestige, but did not resolve all military issues in the country. After 1783 the French army consisted of less than 170,000 officers and men, although its population was the largest in Europe outside Russia.[12] As in other European armies the officer corps was overwhelmingly aristocratic; in fact, legislation in the early 1780s restricted direct commissions to nobles. By 1789 approximately nine-tenths of all French officers were noble, and commoners who held commissions had virtually no hope of advancement. Despite the apparent homogeneity, there were bitter divisions between court and country nobles since the former monopolized the high command—the ranks of colonel and above being re-

---

[12] For a summary description of the French army in the 1780s, see Samuel F. Scott, *The Response of the Royal Army to the French Revolution: The Role and Development of the Line Army, 1787–1793* (Oxford, 1978), pp. 4–45.

served exclusively for the upper aristocracy. Resentments festered among nobles and nonnobles alike.

The men who served in the ranks of the French army were recruited by voluntary enlistments (normally, for eight years) for a bonus. As elsewhere in Europe, fraud and violence were commonly used by recruiters. There were also a number of foreign mercenaries in French service, although the proportion of "foreign" units (nearly one-fifth of all regiments) was substantially more than the percentage of foreign soldiers (fewer than one in eight) because many French subjects from Alsace and Lorraine enlisted in foreign regiments. The native troops were drawn from all regions of the country, although men from the frontier provinces of the north and east were overrepresented. The soldiers were predominantly from the "popular classes" (artisans, small shopkeepers, urban and rural laborers), but consisted of men from every social status, even including nobles. While the conditions of army life were excessively harsh by today's standards, they were somewhat milder than in most contemporary armies and were further improved by disciplinary reforms in the late 1780s. Indeed, these changes were but a part of a much more general reform movement at that time; and this development poses the question of the influence of the American Revolution.

Because it was directly involved in the American war as an ally of the United States and because it became the scene of revolution itself such a short time after the Peace of Paris, France is the most likely country in Europe where one might find strong evidence for the influence of the American Revolution. Beyond any doubt, there were major ideological similarities (as well as differences) between the two revolutions.[13]

[13] Besides Palmer, *Age of Democratic Revolution*, and Godechot, *Grande nation*, there are numerous studies of this relationship. Among the most interesting are Bernard Fäy, *The Revolutionary Spirit in France and America: A Study of Moral and Intellectual Relations between France and the United States at the End of the Eighteenth Century*, trans. R. Guthrie (New York, 1927), Louis Gottschalk, *The Place of the American Revolution in the Causal Pattern of the French Revolution* (Easton, Pa., 1948), and Durand Echeverria, *Mirage in the West: A History of the French Image of American Society to 1815* (Princeton, 1957). More recent are Gérard Defamie, "Le mythe américain à la

More directly pertinent to the subject at hand, there were hundreds of French officers and thousands of French soldiers who had participated in the American war, many of them for two and a half years or more. Theirs was an experience much more immediate and personal than anything most Europeans could possibly claim. How were they affected by it? The reactions to the French Revolution by the military personnel who served in the United States have already been studied. For most of them, their service in America was an unusual tour of duty, but part of a century-long colonial struggle against a traditional enemy, Britain. A significant minority of the officers, of whom Lafayette is the best-known example, were prominent leaders in the early, more moderate phase of the French Revolution. As the political system in France became more democratic and republican, however, they abandoned or were forced to abandon the army and their country.[14] The men in the ranks had no influence whatsoever in changing the French army immediately following the American war. Only when revolution gripped their own country in 1789 were they in a position to effect change. Yet in spite of claims that the veteran soldiers of the American war brought back to France the seeds of revolution, the evidence indicates that they were not especially active either in the agrarian violence that swept parts of France in 1789 or in subsequent army mutinies.[15]

---

veille de la Révolution française," *L'Information Historique* 36 (1974): 59–64, and Claude Fohlen, "The Impact of the American Revolution on France," in *The Impact of the American Revolution Abroad* (Washington, D.C., 1976), pp. 21–38.

[14] The most comprehensive investigation of the French officers who fought in the American war is that of Gilbert Bodinier; see "Les officers du corps expéditionnaire de Rochambeau et la Révolution française," *Revue Historique des Armées* 3 (1976): 139–63, and "Etude du comportement des officiers qui ont combattu en Amérique, pendant la Révolution" (Paper delivered at the One-hundred-second Congrès National des Sociétés Savantes, Limoges, April 1977, a copy of which was kindly provided to me by the author).

[15] Forrest McDonald originally posed the hypothesis that the veterans played a pivotal role in antifeudal uprisings in his "Relation of the French

There were, however, a number of military innovations introduced in France at the end of the Old Regime and early in the Revolution that bear a strong resemblance to practices or institutions found earlier in the American Revolution. Developments in three areas in particular will be examined here: growing concern over the role of light infantry, changes in the organization and composition of the militia, and attempts to insure a more able, more professional officer corps. None of these issues originated in the aftermath of the American war; they all antedated the Treaty of Paris by a couple of decades. Yet they received more immediate attention and reached a certain level of resolution in the years between 1783 and 1789.

Discussion about the employment of light troops in the *petite guerre* (characterized by rapid and largely independent movement in missions, such as patrols, raids, reconnaissance, and screening) dated to the mid-eighteenth century when the comte de Saxe envisaged one-tenth of infantry forces being deployed as skirmishers.[16] Shortly before French entry into the American war, in 1776, new regulations reorganized the standard French infantry regiment so that one of its ten companies was composed of *chasseurs* (light troops), who enjoyed an elite status second only to that of the grenadier company.[17] Light troops continued to receive attention in the 1780s. Lauzun's Legion, which included infantry, mounted, and cannoneer units and which had served in America under the comte de Rochambeau from 1780 to 1783, was completely reorganized shortly after returning to France; most

---

Peasant Veterans of the American Revolution to the Fall of Feudalism in France, 1789–1792," *Agricultural History* 25 (1951): 151–61. For a reconsideration and partial refutation, see Samuel F. Scott, "The Soldiers of Rochambeau's Expeditionary Corps: From the American Revolution to the French Revolution," in *La révolution américaine et l'Europe* (Paris, 1979), pp. 565–78.

[16] Paret, *Yorck*, p. 41.

[17] On Saint-Germain's reorganization of 1776, see Capitaine Bacquet, *L'infanterie au XVIIIe siècle: L'organisation* (Paris, 1907), pp. 121–22. *Chasseur*, like the German term *Jäger*, literally means huntsman but came to be applied to light infantrymen.

PEACE AND THE PEACEMAKERS

of its officers and men were incorporated into a new light cavalry formation, the regiment of Lauzun Hussars.[18]

In October 1787 Louis XVI appointed a Council of War, composed of some of the most eminent military men in France, to discuss and determine army reforms. While the council dealt with a wide range of issues, including organization, tactics, discipline, pay, supply, and promotion, the structure and functions of light troops occupied an important place in its deliberations and decisions. Six existing *chasseur* regiments, consisting of both foot and mounted troops, were divided into separate infantry and cavalry units, while six regiments of dragoons were converted into mounted *chasseur* regiments. All twelve of the new *chasseur à cheval* regiments were organized along the same lines as the other light cavalry branch, the hussars.[19] Beyond that, while maintaining the *chasseur* companies in the regiments of line infantry, the council created twelve new battalions of light infantry or *chasseurs à pied*. Between the American Revolution and the French Revolution the proportion of light troops in the French regular army was increased to an unprecedented level. This growing emphasis on light units reflected a conviction, dating to Saxe and held by the comte de Guibert among others, that the French national "genius" was bold and aggressive, characteristics well suited to the *petite guerre*. On May 20, 1788, under the influence of the Council of War, a new Instruction was issued for the army that provided for more flexible, more mobile formations—just the kind of tactics that could best exploit the peculiar advantages of light infantry.[20]

To what extent can these changes be attributed to experi-

[18] Details on the reorganization can be found in the Archives de la Guerre (henceforth, A.G.), Vincennes, Etat-Major de l'Armée, Archives Historiques, carton Xc 83.

[19] Eduard Desbrière and Maurice Sautai, *La cavalerie de 1740 à 1789* (Paris, 1906), p. 93, and Henri Choppin, *Histoire générale des dragons depuis leur origine jusqu' à l'Empire* (Paris, 1879), p. 360.

[20] Robert S. Quimby, *The Background of Napoleonic Warfare: The Theory of Military Tactics in Eighteenth-Century France* (New York, 1957), pp. 302–4; J. Colin, *Les transformations de la guerre* (Paris, 1920), pp. 20–21; Eugène Carrias, *La pensée militaire française* (Paris, 1960), pp. 170–80.

ences from the American Revolution? Obviously, that conflict did not initiate the ideas behind the reforms. Some
historians argue that its impact was negligible.[21] This is
largely a reaction to those who have made exaggerated
claims for unique military contributions by the American
war. It is undeniable that the light infantry tactics used in this
struggle had been employed earlier in Europe and that the
Continental army used orthodox linear tactics whenever possible, especially in large-scale combats. It is equally undeniable that skirmishers used their greater mobility and
marksmanship successfully in the "little war." Furthermore,
that the significance of American warfare should be dwarfed
by the much more immediate and much more impressive
military accomplishments in the wars of the French Revolution is only to be expected. The truth of the matter is that
the American Revolution was fundamentally a European-
type conflict. It reinforced preexisting trends in Europe (as
Peter Paret admits) and it tended to confirm some military
theories, for example, those of Guibert about lines of skirmishers. It is as misleading to exclude American developments completely from their larger European context as it is
to insist upon their uniqueness. Finally, in dealing with the
influence of American warfare it is necessary to investigate
not only what actually occurred but also what image Europeans had of it. And in Europe there was considerable
enthusiasm—often based upon substantial misunderstanding—for the "natural" quality of the fighting and of the men
who did the fighting.

Probably no aspect of the American war was as miscon-
ceived as the role of the militia. From the beginning of the
American Revolution to the outbreak of the French Revolu-

[21] Peter Paret presents the strongest case for this position; besides *Yorck*,
pp. 39–43, see his article "Colonial Experience and European Military Reform at the End of the Eighteenth Century," *Bulletin of the Institute of Historical Research* 37 (1964): 47–59. Steven Ross concurs in *From Flintlock to
Rifle: Infantry Tactics, 1740–1866* (Cranbury, N.J., 1979), pp. 41–42. For a
modification of this view, see Jacques Godechot, "L'influence de la tactique
et de la stratégie de la guerre de l'indépendance américaine sur la tactique
et la stratégie française de l'armée de terre," *Revue internationale d'Histoire
Militaire*, no. 41 (1979): 141–47.

tion, interest about the United States grew in Europe, particularly in France. The number of books on the subject increased markedly during this period, as did the number of articles dealing with American affairs in French journals and newspapers (some of them subsidized by the French government). Many of these writings idealized the Americans as a natural, reasonable, egalitarian, and independent people, and the militiamen perfectly embodied these qualities. French newspapers helped to develop and spread the legend of the "invincibility" of American militia, especially after their victory at Saratoga, emphasizing the patriotism and spirit of these citizen-soldiers.[22]

Although this was partly the result of govenment propaganda aimed at gaining support for French aid to the Americans, it also conformed to a new and more favorable view of the soldier in society that was developing in France during the last decades of the eighteenth century. French literature presented the simple soldier in a more sympathetic and honorable light than had been the case earlier. This improved image was closely tied to Enlightenment ideas in support of a popular national army, ideas which had been expressed by philosophes such as Montesquieu, Mably, and Diderot and which are best summed up in the words of Rousseau: "Every citizen ought to be a soldier by choice, none should be one by profession."[23] Even military thinkers endorsed this concept. The comte de Guibert, perhaps the most influential military theorist of his day, extolled the virtues of a popular army and "a national militia" and claimed that any state possessing such a force would be immune from attack by its neighbors. He further maintained that the very concept of *patrie* was meaningless in a country defended by despised

[22] Fohlen, "Impact of American Revolution," pp. 28–30; Robert R. Palmer, "The Impact of the American Revolution Abroad," in *Impact of the American Revolution*, pp. 11–13; Defamie, "Mythe américain," p. 62; Godechot, "Influence de la tactique," p. 141.

[23] Charles Dejob, "Le soldat dans la littérature française au XVIIIe siècle," *Revue politique et littéraire, Revue Bleue*, 4th ser. 12 (1899): 449–58; Emile Léonard, *L'armée et ses problèmes au XVIIIe siècle* (Paris, 1958), pp. 148, 153–54, 263, 277–79; Palmer, "Frederick the Great, Guibert, Bülow," pp. 63–68.

and miserable mercenaries.[24] Although Guibert repudiated this position seven years later in 1779, when he realized its political and social implications, the concept of a national citizen army remained vigorous. Joseph Servan, who would later serve as minister of war during the French Revolution, anonymously published a book in Switzerland in 1780 entitled *Le soldat citoyen* (The Citizen Soldier). In it, he argued for a militia in which all citizens between the ages of eighteen and forty would be obliged to perform military service and urged that "the soldier should beyond any doubt, be regarded as a citizen; for he is the man of the nation, charged with the defense of our properties and our persons."[25]

Thus, "popular opinion" in France (essentially confined to the literate upper classes) was disposed to accept the glowing reports about the value and success of militiamen coming from North America. When French officers went to America and fought alongside native militia units, however, such romanticized views of the militia were modified or even reversed. American militiamen did, on occasion, display admirable bravery and remarkable patience, but they were inadequately trained, lacked any genuine discipline, and were too slow to assemble and too quick to disperse, and, in general, were thoroughly undependable. Many American officers, foremost among them being General Washington, had identical opinions regarding the usefulness of their own militia.[26]

In addition, the French had a militia system of their own,

[24] Comte Jacques Antoine Hippolyte de Guibert, *Essai général de tactique, précédé d'un discours sur l'état de la politique et de la science militaire en Europe; avec le plan d'un ouvrage intitulé: La France politique et militaire*, vol. 1 (London, 1772), especially "Discours préliminaire," pp. xvii–xviii, lvii, cx.

[25] *Le soldat citoyen, ou vues patriotiques sur la manière la plus avantageuse de pourvoir à la défense du royaume* ([Neufchâtel], 1780), pp. 74–75, 148–49.

[26] The best summary of French officers' evaluations of the American militia is Orville T. Murphy, "The French Professional Soldiers' Opinion of the American Militia in the War of the Revolution," *Military Affairs* 32 (1969): 191–98. For some examples of American officers' views on the same subject and in the same vein, see John Shy, *A People Numerous and Armed: Reflections on the Military Struggle for American Independence* (New York, 1976), pp. 161, 173, 217.

PEACE AND THE PEACEMAKERS

which by the late 1780s was almost universally condemned. This was a force of part-time soldiers called up in wartime either to be incorporated into regular units or to take over garrison duties and free the regulars for the front lines. In peacetime the militia gathered at irregular intervals for about two weeks of exercises. In the 1780s the Provincial Troops (as the militia was called) had a paper strength of approximately 75,000 men. In theory, unmarried men between the ages of eighteen and forty were eligible for this service; in fact, there were many exceptions, for example, clergy, nobles, government officials, members of the professions, merchants, manufacturers, and even the servants of clerics and noblemen. Furthermore, others used their influence or wealth to gain exemption, and since the government could not afford to mobilize all those who still remained eligible, those who did serve were selected by lot. Thus, the whole burden of militia duty fell largely upon the peasants. Because of the gross inequities of this system, no institution of the Old Regime was more generally condemned in the lists of complaints drawn up for the Estates General in 1789 than was the militia.[27]

There were, then, opposing views of militia in France during the 1780s. One view idealized the American militiaman as the embodiment of current enlightened principles; others were much more skeptical of the value of militia—the result of practical experience in the United States—and thoroughly condemned the clearly inequitable operation of the system in their own country. Interestingly, when revolution began and hundreds of communities throughout France spontaneously and enthusiastically formed National Guard units, these formations resembled the image of a popular militia, fostered by the philosophes and exemplified by the myth of the American militiaman. At first these units enrolled citizens from every walk of life (although the government later restricted membership to better-off "active" citizens) and within a year of their creation boasted enroll-

---

[27] Léon Hennet, *Les milices et les troupes provinciales* (Paris, 1884); Albert Duruy, *L'armée royale en 1789* (Paris, 1888), pp. 41–42; and Albert Soboul, *L'armée nationale sous la Révolution (1789–1794)* (Paris, 1945), pp. 24–25.

ments of over two and a half million men. Their primary functions were to maintain order and be available as a reserve force for the regular army.[28]

Beyond doubt, immediate circumstances, especially the desire for protection against government repression and the determination to prevent anarchy, played a critical role in the establishment of the National Guard. Yet the American example cannot be neglected. It was no coincidence that the first commander of the National Guard was Lafayette, who had become as much a hero in his own country as in the United States because of his contributions to the American Revolution. He and some of his comrades from the American war, such as the vicomte de Noailles, held up to the men of their new commands the example of the American militia and attempted to inculcate a similar spirit in them.[29] In the same vein, as the danger of foreign intervention in France increased, Camille Desmoulins, the Revolutionary journalist, in early 1790 warned hostile European powers to respect French sovereignty since the American Revolution had proved the superiority of citizen-soldiers over regular armies and foreign mercenaries.[30] Finally—without presuming to judge their motives—it is a fact that at least two dozen soldiers who had served in America under Rochambeau enlisted in the "paid" units of the Parisian National Guard at this time.[31]

It would be preposterous to maintain that without the example of the American militia Frenchmen would not have created their National Guard in 1789. To discount the Amer-

[28] See Godechot, *Grande nation*, 1:136–37; Albert Soboul, *Les soldats de l'an II* (Paris, 1959), pp. 44–52; Chamborant de Périssat, *L'armée de la Révolution, ses généraux et ses soldats, 1789–1871* (Paris, 1875), pp. 8–9; S. Vialla, *Marsielle révolutionnaire: L'armée-nation (1789–1793)* (Paris, 1910), pp. 8–103.

[29] Fäy, *Revolutionary Spirit*, pp. 269–76, provides much more detailed information on this point.

[30] Palmer, *Age of Democratic Revolution*, 1:502.

[31] This information can be found in A.G., 20 Yc 645, 646, and 647, Garde nationale [parisienne] soldée: 3e, 4e, 5e, Divisions. The estimate is due to the fact that only half of these "troop registers" have survived.

ican example is likewise untenable. No matter how erroneous the perception, American militiamen were utilized as models for this new establishment that presaged "the nation-in-arms." Again, one must bear in mind the context for this development. A crucial factor in explaining why an image of the American militia was more acceptable than pragmatic experience was that the Enlightenment, a transcontinental phenomenon that also had influenced the American periphery of European culture, prepared the informed French public for this kind of innovation.

In a similar fashion, the Enlightenment by its emphasis upon a more egalitarian, as well as more natural, society helped to create an atmosphere that would later help to implement the principle of "careers open to talent." In this instance, as in others, the American Revolution seemed to translate ideas into reality. French officers who served in America were impressed (sometimes unfavorably) with the ease with which American officers and enlisted men interacted. Even more striking was the impression that American society could produce competent officers who were not drawn from a native aristocracy of birth but rather from merchants, farmers, tradesmen, and manufacturers.[32]

In France at this time military men were ambivalent and divided over the relative importance of birth and of ability in the appointment and promotion of officers. Military service was, after all, the historic basis and traditional justification for noble privilege, and the anachronistic concept of the nobility as a warrior caste remained strong. On the other hand, the expanding size and increasing complexity of armies, together with the defeats suffered in the midcentury wars, clearly indicated the need for professionally trained officers. Consequently, in the latter half of the eighteenth century there was a trend to require professional ability from French

[32] Substantiation for these impressions can be found in Murphy, "Opinion of American Militia," p. 194, Godechot, "Influence de la tactique," p. 142, Bodinier, "Officers de Rochambeau," p. 157, Howard H. Peckham, *The War for Independence: A Military History* (Chicago, 1958), p. 206, and Durand Echeverria and Orville T. Murphy, trans. and eds., "The American Revolutionary Army: A French Estimate in 1777," *Military Affairs* 27 (1963): 158.

officers.[33] One form that this took was an expansion of educational facilities for officer aspirants. In 1751 the Ecole Militaire was founded in Paris, and a quarter of a century later twelve new military schools were established in the provinces. Technical schooling was provided for officers in the *armes savantes*, the Artillery and Engineers. Another step in the direction of a more professional officer corps was the suppression of the sale of military offices (the ranks of captain and colonel being venal). In 1776 the minister of war, the comte de Saint-Germain, announced that henceforth each time a company or a regiment changed hands the purchase price would be reduced by one-quarter, so that by the fourth turnover venality would be abolished. This measure not only tightened royal control over the appointment of officers, it also substantially reduced the importance of wealth for military advancement.[34]

It would appear that a logical conclusion of these policies would be to make proven ability the primary or sole criterion for a commission or promotion. While such a decision would have conformed to Enlightenment principles, it flew in the face of the growing "aristocratic reaction" in France. Without denying the importance of education and talent, nobles, especially the provincial "nobility of the sword," were determined to restrict the application of these criteria exclusively to their own caste. Under their pressure the so-called Ségur decree in May 1781 reserved direct commissions to nobles who could furnish proof of four generations of nobility. The

[33] An excellent summary of this development is André Corvisier, "Hiérarchie militaire et hiérarchie sociale à la veille de la Révolution," *Revue internationale d'Histoire Militaire*, no. 30 (1970): 77–91. Also see David D. Bien, "Military Education in Eighteenth-Century France: Technical and Non-Technical Determinants," in Monte C. Wright and Lawrence J. Paszek, eds., *Science, Technology and Warfare* (Washington, D.C., 1971), pp. 51–59, Pierre Chalmin, "La formation des officiers des armes savantes sous l'ancien régime," *Actes du soixante-seizième congrès des sociétés savantes* (Paris, 1951), pp. 165–82, and Roger Chartier, "Un recrutement scolaire au XVIIIe siècle: L'école royale du génie de Mézières," *Revue d'histoire moderne et contemporaine* 20 (1973): 353–75.

[34] Henri Choppin, *Les insurrections militaires en 1790* (Paris, 1903), pp. 34–35.

only concessions to ability without birth were that limited promotions from the ranks (roughly 10 percent of all officer positions) were continued and the requirement of four generations of nobility was waived for a handful of descendants of officers of exceptional merit, that is, generals, recipients of the Cross of Saint Louis, and some officers killed in action.[35] Thus, at the same time as French officers serving in America were discovering that commoners too could be fit for military command, their fellow officers in Europe were closing off most opportunities for a commission to nonnobles and the recently ennobled.

Discontent and division persisted in the French officer corps in the 1780s. In 1788 the Council of War upheld the court aristocracy's monopoly of the grades of colonel and higher, thereby outraging the petty nobility who agitated for equality of treatment for all nobles. Commoners had even greater reason to protest their nearly total exclusion from the officer corps.[36] Standards for commissions and promotions remained hotly debated but unresolved at the onset of the French Revolution.

When *cahiers de doléances*, or lists of grievances, were prepared for the meeting of the Estates General in the spring of 1789, a common demand was that all enjoy equal opportunity to enter and advance in the officer corps.[37] The National

[35] For a more thorough treatment, see David D. Bien, "La réaction aristocratique avant 1789: l'exemple de l'armée," *Annales, Economies, Sociétés, Civilisations* 29 (1974): 23–48, 505–34, and Georges Six, "Fallait-il quatre quartiers de noblesse pour être officier à la fin de l'ancien régime?" *Revue d'histoire moderne* 4 (1929): 47–56.

[36] So incensed was the provincial nobility that some of them forced Guibert, a dominant force in the council, to leave the nobles' assembly of Bourges during the elections for the Estates General; see Jean Egret, *La pré-révolution française (1787–1788)* (Paris, 1962), p. 93. For the reaction of commoners, see David D. Bien, "The Army in the French Enlightenment: Reform, Reaction and Revolution," *Past and Present*, no. 85 (1979): 88–89.

[37] Léonard, *Armée et ses problèmes*, p. 295; Ernest d'Hauterive, *L'armée sous la Révolution, 1789–1794* (Paris, 1894), p. 43; Jules Leverrier, *La naissance de l'armée nationale, 1789–1794* (Paris, 1939), p. 26. For specific examples of this demand, see Soboul, *L'armée nationale*, p. 34, François Furet and Denis Richet, *The French Revolution*, trans. Stephen Hardman (Lon-

Assembly recognized such claims early in the Revolution. The first article of the Declaration of the Rights of Man and Citizen, passed on August 26, 1789, pronounced: "Men are born and remain free and equal in rights." Article VI added: "All citizens . . . are equally admissible to all public dignities, offices and employments, according to their capacity, and with no other distinction than that of their virtues and talents."[38] The application of this principle in the army and developments in the Revolution itself would lead to a complete renovation of the French officer corps within the next five years.[39]

Many of the same general principles and ideals that provided the bases for the early legislation of the French Revolution can be found in comparable documents of the American Revolutionary period. Sorting out who borrowed what from whom is an extremely troublesome and possibly futile task, since both Americans and French drew upon essentially the same sources for their political philosophy. Beyond that, attributing intellectual influence is a tricky business under the best of circumstances. What is certain is that some French veterans of the American war played an important, even a leading, part in the opening phase of the French Revolution and that their work contributed to establishing the principle of equality of opportunity within the army, as within society as a whole.

Shortly before the Estates General began its sessions, a group of nobles known as the Committee of Thirty established themselves as a guiding influence in the liberal "patriot" party. Officers who had served in the American

---

don, 1970), p. 66, M. Chaulanges, A. G. Manry, and R. Sève, eds., *Textes Historiques, 1789–1799: L'époque de la Révolution* (Paris, 1970), p. 11, and Jeffry Kaplow, *Elbeuf during the Revolutionary Period: History and Social Structure* (Baltimore, 1964), p. 200.

[38] The Declaration is available in English in a number of sources; one of the handiest is Georges Lefebvre, *The Coming of the French Revolution*, trans. Robert R. Palmer (Princeton, 1947), pp. 189–91.

[39] For elucidation, see Samuel F. Scott, "'Careers Open to Talent' in the Armies of the Revolution: Myth and Reality," in Warren F. Spencer, ed., The Consortium on Revolutionary Europe *Proceedings*, 1982 (Athens, Ga., 1983), pp. 60–74.

Revolution—Lafayette, Noailles, and the brothers Alexandre and Charles Lameth among them—constituted a large and prominent element within this group.[40] When the Estates General opened in early May 1789 the most active members of the Second Estate (the nobility) were the liberal minority, in which could be found most of the American veterans who had been elected deputies, including a number of the same men as in the Committee of Thirty.[41] On a broader, less official level, many French members of the Order of the Cincinnati strongly supported the reform legislation of this period.[42] Not all American veterans responded in the same way to the events of 1789. Most officers, serving at their posts in subordinate capacities, reacted with passive interest. Some, for example, the count von Fersen and the marquis de La Rouerie (better known in the American war as Colonel Armand-Tuffin), vehemently opposed the new changes from the beginning. Among those veterans of the American Revolution who advocated more equitable reforms, it is impossible to dissociate their American experiences from conditions in France that led others, who had no such background, to endorse the same policies. Nonetheless, it remains true that many officers who had been exposed to the more democratic practices in the American army supported similar procedures in the French army at the outset of the French Revolution.[43] As for other military changes in the 1780s, it is as impossible to define exactly, as it is to deny the influence of, the American war in opening careers to talent.

[40] On this poorly known but influential organization, see Daniel L. Wick, "The Court Nobility and the French Revolution: The Example of the Society of Thirty," *Eighteenth-Century Studies* 13 (1980): 263–84.

[41] See the works of Bodinier cited above, "Officiers de Rochambeau," p. 147, and "Etude du comportement des officiers," as well as his "Les officiers de l'armée royale et la Révolution," in *Le métier militaire en France aux époques de grandes transformations sociales* (Vincennes, 1980), p. 60.

[42] Asa Bird Gardiner, *The Order of the Cincinnati in France* (Providence, 1905), pp. 45–48.

[43] Although it has no direct bearing on the question of influence, it is of interest that some 200 soldiers who had served in America under Rochambeau's orders would eventually benefit from the new policy by being promoted from the ranks after 1789.

The most obvious impact of the Treaty of Paris upon Europe generally was to establish a more even balance of power among the major states in the wake of Britain's loss. On a more specific level, the great powers reacted to the military lessons of the recent conflict in diverse ways, but essentially according to how national interests were perceived. In eastern Europe, where monarchy and aristocracy had allied to share political and social dominance, change was rejected. In Prussia and Austria the authorities refused to sacrifice the tight control over troops with no national loyalties that traditional tactics and formations provided; the employment of large numbers of skirmishers operating independently or the massive induction of militiamen who had not been subjected to rigorous training and discipline might well lead to the disintegration of their armies, the ultimate defense of the existing institutions. In Russia the ruler and the nobility could tolerate somewhat less rigid control of their troops because these were native serfs, inured to complete domination by their noble lords and motivated by strong religious and monarchical loyalties. Still, there was no thought of any significant change in what was the most oppressive military, political, and social system in Europe. In almost stereotypical fashion, Britain rejected any precipitate reaction to its defeat, despite the urging of some officers; the British army would come around to adopting changes only in the nick of time to fend off disaster at the hands of Napoleon.

Only the French military establishment responded positively to the military developments of the American war in the years between 1783 and 1789. The number and proportion of light troops—whose functions were comparable to those of American skirmishers—were substantially increased. At the outbreak of the French Revolution a new, popular form of militia was introduced, its inspiration at least partially due to the image of the American militia that had become established in France. At the same time, criteria for entrance into and advancement within the officer corps were made more egalitarian—and more similar to practices in the American army—thanks, in part, to the efforts of American veterans. Within a few years these changes would be vastly expanded: tens of thousands of *tirailleurs*, or sharpshooters, would fight as skirmishers in the armies of the Republic, the concept of a citizen army would be fully realized by the *levée en masse*, and men from every social class would find their military careers limited only by their ability and experience.

Why was France more receptive to American developments than the other major powers of Europe? To begin with, these innovations did not, in fact, represent drastic changes. French armies had employed light troops in the *petite guerre* since the middle of the eighteenth century. Militia forces had been mobilized, to varying degrees, in France's wars throughout the century. And the decades-long debate over qualifications for officers was reaching a climax in the 1780s. Furthermore, since the Seven Years' War, in no other country of Europe was there such lively discussion of and predisposition to military reform. As ministers of war, both the duc de Choiseul (1761–70) and Saint-Germain (1775–77) had made fundamental changes in almost all aspects of the army. The whole artillery system was revised in 1765, 1772, and 1774, when Gen. Jean-Baptiste Vaquette de Gribeauval's system was definitively adopted. The great controversy over whether *l'ordre mince* or *l'ordre profond* (line or column) should determine French tactics raged through the 1770s and well into the 1780s.[44] The Ségur decree of 1781 and the reforms of the Council of War in 1787–88, already discussed, are but other examples of the military ferment of the period.

It is within this framework that the role of the American Revolution can be best appreciated. Many French officers, who served alongside their American allies in the war, returned to France with favorable impressions of the country and its inhabitants. For some, their American experience reinforced their commitment to military developments already underway in Europe, such as increased emphasis on the use

[44] For further information on these controversies and reforms, see Léonard, *Armée et ses problèmes*, pp. 239–57, Quimby, *Background of Napoleonic Warfare*, pp. 108–218, L. Lèques, *Les administrations militaires depuis les temps anciens jusqu' à nos jours* (Tours, 1876), pp. 119–21, and Matti Lauerma, *L'artillerie de campagne française pendant les guerres de la Révolution* (Helsinki, 1956), p. 15.

of light infantry in the *petite guerre*. A few thought favorably of the potentialities of militia or were impressed by the quality of nonaristocratic officers. Even more important than the actual experiences or the personal impressions of the veterans were the favorable images of Americans and American institutions that had been created by French writers and publicists both before and following French participation in the war. When the first stirrings of revolution in France gave rise to expectations of basic change, American models, modified by French conditions, helped to direct early military reforms, reforms that would be carried further in the course of the second great revolution of the century.

BRADFORD PERKINS

The Peace of Paris
Patterns and Legacies

JOHN ADAMS, JOHN MARSHALL, John Quincy Adams, Woodrow Wilson, Henry Kissinger—these men are among the Americans who have negotiated for peace at Paris. Since the time of the elder Adams the United States has taken part in many peace negotiations, using that term to refer both to meetings that ended wars and those, like Paris in 1919, that fixed terms on a defeated enemy. Not one has taken place in Washington, even after the United States became a major power; two thirds were held in Paris—hence the roster of distinguished names.

One of these settlements, the two-hundred-page document fixing terms upon Germany in 1919 and creating the League of Nations, had immense importance. But so too did the treaty of 1783, the first in the series. In form it was only one among several treaties by which Britain terminated the war touched off by the American Revolution, only one part of a world settlement. As such, it could be brief, a mere three or four pages in the printed version. However, because it not only acknowledged the independence of the United States but placed it firmly on the road to empire in North America and, ultimately, to global leadership, this treaty of Paris challenges in world importance the settlement of 1919.

Preliminaries of peace between Britain and America were signed, of course, in 1782, and that really ended the War of the American Revolution as far as these two parties were concerned. However, because the alliance of 1778 pledged America not to make peace with Britain until France did so, the American preliminaries remained provisional, at least technically, until France settled with England in January 1783. After some further delay, but only minor changes in the terms, the definitive treaty of peace was signed on September 7, 1783.

Diplomatic historians, so critics allege, devote far more concern to controversies and the causes of war than to the structure of good relations or even to negotiations for peace. Such complaints sometimes come from those who seem to believe that the study of peace will make the world more peaceful, and a few set out on programs of "peace research" with a clearly didactic purpose. Still, the underlying allegation is not without merit. Controversies do tend to be more dramatic, and certainly the diplomatic records they generate are more extensive. Their attraction is obvious, even inevitable.

Many years ago the Carnegie Endowment for International Peace commissioned a multivolume series on Canadian-American relations, essentially to probe the reasons for the long reign of peace, broken after the American Revolution only by the War of 1812.[1] With few exceptions, authors in this series found themselves drawn to devote perhaps three-quarters of their pages to disputations rather than settlements, to divisive rather than soothing forces. One is really left to wonder what, aside from good fortune, prevented more than political clashes.

The same emphasis on discord is evident in the literature on Anglo-American relations in the early nineteenth century. For years, certainly since the appearance of Julius Pratt's *Expansionists of 1812* in 1925, a scholarly debate has raged over the origins of the War of 1812.[2] In the chapter on the years from 1801 to 1815 in the recent *Guide to American Foreign Relations since 1700*, over one hundred fifty entries call attention to writings bearing upon the coming of the war; a mere eight, including articles and parts of books, cite works on the treaty that ended it.[3] Except for a semischolarly treatment published in 1962, no extensive account of the Ghent nego-

[1] Carnegie Endowment for International Peace, *The Relations of Canada and the United States*, 24 vols. (Toronto, 1936–46).

[2] Julius W. Pratt, *Expansionists of 1812* (New York, 1925).

[3] Richard Dean Burns, ed., *Guide to American Foreign Relations since 1700* (Santa Barbara, 1983), pp. 169–92.

tiations appeared between Frank A. Updyke's *Diplomacy of the War of 1812* in 1915 and my own *Castlereagh and Adams* in 1964.[4]

A slightly more complicated comment, but one with the same thrust, may be made about studies of the Paris negotiations of 1919. In the last two decades much has been written about them, but certainly the most stimulating of these recent writings deal not with the German settlement and the framing of the League Covenant but rather with the contemporary challenge of radical socialism, especially bolshevism in Russia. A decade ago a Danish historian, Inga Floto, published a study of Col. Edward M. House's activities sufficiently broadly conceived to provide an overall picture of the peace negotiations. However, although it has been supplemented and corrected, the most satisfactory treatment of the peace conference continues to be Paul Birdsall's *Versailles Twenty Years After*, published in 1941.[5] In contrast, there have been substantial recent contributions to the historical debate over American entry into World War I, even if they lack the passion shown in the debate between "revisionists" and "traditionalists" over the same issue in the 1930s.

Given this pattern, it comes as no surprise that negotiation of the Peace of Paris of 1783 has received far less attention than the coming and the course of the Revolution. When one turns to the negotiations, principal reliance may be placed on only three books, the most recent nearly twenty years old. The first is Samuel Flagg Bemis's *The Diplomacy of the American Revolution*, published in 1935, a classic work that is, however, marred by excessive nationalism. The second is Vincent T. Harlow's *The Founding of the Second British Empire*, which concentrates almost exclusively, as the title suggests, on the formulation of British policy; the first volume of this work

[4] Fred L. Engleman, *The Peace of Christmas Eve* (New York, 1962); Frank A. Updyke, *The Diplomacy of the War of 1812* (Baltimore, 1915); Bradford Perkins, *Castlereagh and Adams* (Berkeley, 1964).

[5] Inga Floto, *Colonel House in Paris* (Copenhagen, 1973); Paul Birdsall, *Versailles Twenty Years After* (New York, 1941). For the radical challenge, see especially Arno J. Mayer, *Politics and Diplomacy of Peacemaking* (New York, 1967).

appeared in 1952. The third, *The Peacemakers*, by Richard B. Morris, came out in 1965. Morris's research is exhaustive; he integrates, as did Bemis to a degree, the Anglo-American aspects with those involving other powers; his book is both thoughtful and forceful. While Morris may not sufficiently depart from the nationalistic emphasis of Bemis, *The Peacemakers* towers over all other treatments of the negotiations.[6]

Professor Morris's present thoughts on the Peace of Paris are included in this volume. Other essays approach the negotiations from various angles, drawing in part upon the authors' previous researches. (Reference in particular is to Jonathan R. Dull, who has studied French policy as it relates to naval concerns more intensively than anyone else, and to James H. Hutson, whose contributions include an intensive critical study of John Adams as a diplomat).[7] What, then, can a diplomatic historian who has done serious research only on other areas hope to contribute? As with every interesting historical issue, there never will be, regarding these negotiations, a single, accepted truth, and their complexity, too, assures that there will continue to be differing interpretations. Approach from a distance, so to speak, may even encourage speculations.

This paper seeks not to trace the negotiations from first to last, but rather to explore two themes. First, how justified was the hypersuspiciousness of the Americans and how effective were the tactics engendered by this spirit? Second, how much credit is owing them for the territorial settlement? In other words, did the American negotiators successfully defend claims that might have been lost, or did they lose lands they might have won? The answers given to these questions may

[6] Samuel Flagg Bemis, *The Diplomacy of the American Revolution* (New York, 1935); Vincent T. Harlow, *The Founding of the Second British Empire, 1763–1793*, 2 vols. (London, 1952–64); Richard B. Morris, *The Peacemakers: The Great Powers and American Independence* (New York, 1965). Biographies are also helpful, especially Frank Monaghan, *John Jay: Defender of Liberty* . . . (1935; reprint ed., New York, 1972).

[7] Jonathan R. Dull, *The French Navy and American Independence: A Study of Arms and Diplomacy, 1774–1787* (Princeton, 1975); James H. Hutson, *John Adams and the Diplomacy of the American Revolution* (Lexington, Ky., 1980).

serve to demythologize the Americans, whose weaknesses and mistakes, although not entirely overlooked, have often been excused or explained away. The paper will close with comparisons between these negotiations and other settlements in which the United States has engaged.

The Franco-American alliance of 1778 pledged the parties, once France entered the war, not to make a separate peace with Britain. It also made the independence of the erstwhile colonies a sine qua non of peace. But the alliance said nothing about the territorial extent of the nation-to-be—whether, for example, it should be limited to the lands east of the Appalachians or should incorporate, perhaps, all of British North America. This silence is important. Since the end of the Seven Years' War in 1763, the British Empire had held title to the continent west to the Mississippi, north and south of the Great Lakes. Nevertheless, it was by no means clear—or at least not mutually accepted by Whitehall and the colonials—what were the proper boundaries of the colonies, of Canada, and of other British territory—not part of either—that the Americans might claim.

Most colonies had charters that supported claims far beyond the Alleghenies. However, by the Proclamation of 1763 the British government placed the western lands directly under crown administration. The future United States were not the only ones to suffer, for the Proclamation also placed under crown control and separated from Canada those lands north of the Great Lakes but west of the "Nipissing line," a line running up the Ottawa River to Lake Nipissing and beyond. Thus there was created a vast imperial holding astride the Lakes, a region separated both from Canada and the American colonies, all of which the latter might claim for themselves if they had the strength or the gall to do so.

In 1774, it is true, by the Quebec Act the British altered their policy and even extended the boundaries of Canada south to the Ohio River, but the Americans looked upon this, one of the Intolerable Acts, as totally beyond respect, and it contributed in a marginal way to the crisis that erupted into war a year later. The Americans had, of course, also protested against the Proclamation of 1763, but in fact it opened

a way for them in 1782. As a historian of Quebec has observed, "The Proclamation gave the Americans a solid
ground for the claim [to lands as far as the Nipissing line]
that their intense hatred of the Quebec Act drove them to
make."[8]

Historians of the peace settlement have often celebrated
the success of John Jay and Benjamin Franklin in gaining for
their country possession of the "Northwest," the lands between the Ohio river and the Great Lakes, and they have also
noted the failure to obtain all of Canada. But they have seldom made much of the negotiators' failure to obtain the
northern half of the imperial province delineated by the
Proclamation of 1763.

The Continental Congress first turned attention to terms
of peace in 1779. In instructions for John Adams, named
peace negotiator while Franklin continued as minister to
France, Congress directed Adams to seek, although it did not
make this a sine qua non, the Nipissing boundary and even,
if possible, all of Canada as well as Newfoundland. The instructions contained two other points that, indirectly connected later on to the boundary issue, became central
concerns in the negotiations. Adams was to require British
recognition of independence as a price of any negotiations at
all; in other words, no concessions in other areas, including
boundaries, were to be made to secure it. Finally, the instructions directed the negotiator to govern himself, not only by
his understanding of American interests and by the obligations of the French alliance, which prohibited a separate
peace, but also by "the advice of our allies."[9] How these three
guides might be reconciled was not made clear.

In 1781, for complicated reasons including the gloomy
state of the war, French pressure and bribery, and fear that
pursuit of an independent line might cost French support in
negotiations then looming, Congress approved new instructions. Adams had alienated the French foreign minister, the
comte de Vergennes, both by his truculent nationalism and

[8] Alfred Leroy Burt, *The Old Province of Quebec* (Toronto, 1933), p. 331.

[9] Edmund Cody Burnett, *The Continental Congress* (New York, 1941), p. 437.

his habitual abrasiveness; he was therefore submerged in a commission of five, the four new men being supposed to be less contentious and not anti-French.[10] More astonishingly, Congress ordered the commissioners not merely to seek French advice but to submit absolutely, the matter of independence apart, to French guidance: "You are . . . to undertake nothing in the negotiations for peace or truce without their knowledge and concurrence; and ultimately to govern yourselves by their advice and opinion."[11] "Never in history," Samuel Flagg Bemis expostulated, "has one people voted to put its entire destiny more absolutely, more trustfully, under the control of a foreign government."[12]

The instructions of 1781 were a disgrace, produced by the exigencies of war and, for many congressmen at least, more by fear of France's desertion than the trust of which Bemis wrote. Later, several efforts were made to repeal them; all failed, for even Yorktown did not make Congress confident enough to assert American freedom of action. Still, by referring the commissioners to the instructions of 1779 for a statement of American desires, those of 1781 showed where Congress's wishes lay—Nipissing or Canada—even when it lacked the self-confidence to proceed independently.

Toward the end of November 1781 word reached London that Lord Cornwallis had surrendered at Yorktown. This news, followed by unfavorable reports from other fronts, "broke the morale of the governing classes and paralyzed the national will to make war."[13] The government lost hope of victory but, partly because the king remained obdurate, failed to fix another course.

No sooner did Parliament convene, late in January 1782 after a month-long Christmas recess, than the position of the North ministry became impossible. Soon Gen. Henry Con-

[10] The five commissioners were Benjamin Franklin, John Jay, John Adams, Henry Laurens, and Thomas Jefferson. Jefferson never reached Paris.

[11] William C. Stinchcombe, *The American Revolution and the French Alliance* (Syracuse, 1969), p. 158.

[12] Bemis, *Diplomacy of the American Revolution*, p. 190.

[13] John Brooke, *King George III* (London, 1972), p. 219.

way presented in the Commons a resolution against "the further prosecution of offensive warfare on the Continent of North America."[14] The motion passed. Conway and his supporters repeatedly denied that they favored abject surrender to the Americans; what they desired, they said, was reconciliation with the colonies and a concentration of military resources against Britain's other enemies. Still, this was a distinction without a difference. As even George III recognized, in a military sense the game was up. By adroitness or chicane Britain might limit American boundaries, perhaps circumscribe independence itself. Parliament would not, however, tolerate a military effort to narrow either. Drawing the proper lesson, the North government resigned on March 20.

The war ministry was succeeded first by one headed, nominally at least, by the marquess of Rockingham, and this in turn was followed, after Rockingham's death early in July, by a ministry led by the earl of Shelburne. The complex political factors at work are unimportant for present purposes; the key points are two. First, over some opposition Shelburne was able, even while part of Rockingham's uneasy coalition, to gain effective control of negotiations with the Americans, and he retained this control after forming his own ministry. Secondly, and on the other hand, his political position was never assured, whether because of rivalries within the Rockingham government or because, having lost the backing of many of Rockingham's coadjutors, notably Charles James Fox, his own ministry's hold on the House of Commons was tenuous at best. Fortunately for the negotiations, the summertime recess of 1782 protected him from parliamentary attack. In any case, Shelburne was not only the most important figure on the British side but, after the death of Rockingham, the only one who counted.

Like most opponents of Lord North's ministry, Shelburne had spoken strongly in defense of the rights of the colonies. Even by 1782, however, he had not reconciled himself to independence. Failing, like many equally deluded countrymen, to understand the depth of American alienation, he

---

[14] Ian R. Christie, *The End of North's Ministry* (London, 1958), p. 319.

hoped by offering generous terms and a relaxation of London's control to reconsolidate the empire on a modified basis. In his own words, he sought "unequivocal terms of reunion and reconciliation, founded in a just attention to our mutual interests."[15]

From Franklin in particular Shelburne soon learned that his dream was a phantom. He then sought only to restore comity and to assure himself that, independent of Britain, the Americans did not intend to be satellites of France. But the initial quest for reconciliation fixed a tone on the discussions that Shelburne would have found it difficult to abandon, even had he so desired. In July, after the dream had faded, he explained his position: "I have never made a Secret of the deep Concern I feel in the Separation of Countries united by Blood, by Principles, [and by] Habits. . . . But . . . I have long since given it up *decidedly* tho' reluctantly: and the same motives which made me . . . give up all Hope of Reunion, make me most anxious, if it is to be given up, that it should be done *decidedly*, so as to avoid all future Risque of Enmity."[16]

A second line of thought also urged Shelburne toward moderation. Although Vincent Harlow may have pressed his argument too far, that historian is surely correct that Shelburne, drawing instruction especially from Adam Smith, valued international commerce more highly than territorial empire. Loss of sovereignty over the American colonies was far less important to him than establishing a climate in which trade might flourish. This second theme in Shelburne's views, like the first, drove him in the direction of compromise and concession. By the summer of 1782, George Dangerfield has sardonically observed, Shelburne was "prepared to apply a nostrum composed of equal parts of resignation, charity, and the principles of Adam Smith."[17]

In April, to open discussions with Franklin, the only

[15] John Norris, *Shelburne and Reform* (New York, 1963), p. 146.

[16] Harlow, *Founding of the Second British Empire*, 1:232.

[17] George Dangerfield, *Chancellor Robert R. Livingston of New York* (New York, 1960), p. 165.

American delegate then in Paris, the earl dispatched Richard Oswald, an aged, conciliatory, and naively open man. The choice may have been almost accidental on Shelburne's part, but once made it could not easily be changed, especially since Franklin went out of his way to give his personal endorsement to Oswald as a channel of communication. Oswald's softness of tone may have misled Franklin about Shelburne's intentions; more likely he craftily used the old man to establish understandings or apparent understandings that went farther than even Shelburne was prepared to—or could, for domestic political reasons—go.

Early in their discussions Franklin suggested that, if Britain truly wanted reconciliation, she ought to cede all of Canada to the United States. Oswald seemed sympathetic, and he even suggested that Shelburne was not opposed. But a statement of the ministry's position on various items, shown to Franklin toward the end of April, was silent on Canada, and Oswald did not explain to Franklin that the omission meant disapproval.

In July, after Shelburne had added leadership of the government to command of the negotiations, Franklin read to Oswald a list of "necessary" and "desirable" terms of peace. Regarding Canada, the "necessary" settlement was a return to conditions before the Quebec Act of 1774, to the situation under the Proclamation of 1763 when Canadian authority ended at the Nipissing line. But if Britain wanted a true reconciliation, it was "desirable" that she go as far as "the giving up of every part of Canada."[18] There matters stood when John Jay, newly arrived from Spain, joined in the discussions.

For present purposes there remain only a few points to emphasize about this phase of the negotiations beyond the obvious fact that they were exploratory and indecisive. Although Jay is generally identified with the break with France, it was Franklin who first defied the instructions of 1781 to be guided by French advice. While he did not conceal the existence of the conversations from Vergennes, who indeed approved of them, he did not ask the comte's advice before

<hr>

[18] Samuel Flagg Bemis, *American Foreign Policy and the Blessings of Liberty, and Other Essays* (New Haven, 1962), p. 114.

talking with Oswald nor did he report their contents afterward. (Neither did he apprise Adams, who was in Holland, or Jay, or the Continental Congress.) Beyond that, he constantly held out before Oswald, and through him to the earl of Shelburne, the prospect, if Britain granted favorable terms, of a reconciliation so complete that the French alliance would fall by the wayside. This did not square with the spirit of the alliance, certainly not with Congress's understanding of it.

Many American historians seem to feel that, at Paris, the nation's agents were ingenuous actors in a cast otherwise marked by an intriguing spirit. One is reminded of the stereotypical view of the principled Wilson struggling, in 1919, against the wiles of Georges Clemenceau and Lloyd George. Richard Morris goes so far as to say, "The peacemaking began as an encounter between innocence and guile, but the Americans rapidly acquired a measure of sophistication sufficient for the task at hand."[19] The events just described suggest that guile and sophistication were present from the outset. Rather than contrast American behavior with that of France or Spain, which was certainly convoluted and disingenuous, it is perhaps best to agree with a dispassionate historian who simply observes that "willingness to engage in double-dealing was characteristic of all parties."[20]

What followed almost defies clear description, for Jay lurched bewilderingly from one position to its opposite. First he cut off the talks with Oswald because he doubted British good faith. Then, developing at least equal doubts of France, he tossed aside his suspicions of Britain. To avoid French betrayal, he leapt eagerly into negotiations with England, not even requiring the assurances that he had previously said were essential. The whole affair is sometimes excused as a maneuver necessary to bring negotiations from generalities of the Oswald conversations to hard diplomatic bargaining, but, as we shall see, this argument is dubious. More tenable, although admittedly debatable, is the suggestion that Jay's

[19] Morris, *Peacemakers*, p. 459.

[20] Merrill Jensen, *The New Nation: A History of the United States during the Confederation, 1781–1789* (New York, 1950), p. 14.

maneuvers meant that the Americans had to fight battles, some of which they lost, that could have been avoided. Certainly the whole affair reveals the Americans—for Franklin went along and Adams supported Jay—as alarmist and ineffectually guileful.

From the beginning Franklin had demanded that Britain acknowledge independence before negotiations on details, including boundaries. Otherwise, he feared, England might demand a high price for independence or even break off negotiations altogether. He received what he thought were assurances in this regard.

But the ministry did not act, and Shelburne's opaque and contradictory speeches in Parliament, reflections of the slow death of his dream of imperial reconstruction, roused Jay's suspicions. When, early in August, a draft copy of Oswald's formal commission to negotiate—the early talks had nominally been informal—was shown to the Americans, they immediately noted that it avoided any mention of a nation calling itself the United States of America. Oswald's instructions, not shown to them, made it clear that the Shelburne cabinet wanted independence recognized in the treaty, not separate from or prior to it.

There is no evidence that the ministry intended to use recognition as a bargaining chip. Nor did the approach reflect any continuing life in Shelburne's dream. He had, however reluctantly, given up hope of reunion and now sought instead a peace of reconciliation. As he wrote Oswald at the time, "There never have been two opinions since you were sent to Paris upon the most unequivocal acknowledgment of American Independency." Nor was the language of Oswald's commission an indication of ill-will or trickery. Weeks before, Shelburne had told Oswald, "Commissioners will be named, or any character given to Mr. Oswald which Dr. Franklin and he may judge conducive to the final settlement of things between Great Britain and America."[21] Writing to Oswald at the time, the earl repeated that the form of the commission would cause no trouble. In short, the premier and his col-

---

[21] Morris, *Peacemakers*, pp. 294–95 (italics deleted); Harlow, *Founding of the Second British Empire*, 1:260.

leagues attached very little importance, if any, to the issue which alarmed Jay.

Jay exploded when he read the draft commission. Vergennes, for once consulted, argued that the style of Oswald's commission was unimportant as long as the latter accepted the Americans' commission, which of course gave them the character of national representatives. Franklin inclined to agree, but Jay dragooned the Doctor into his position. They passed word to London that, before they would negotiate, independence must be formally acknowledged and the commission revised. Jay drove the point home to Oswald: "I told him I would have no concern in any negociation in which we were not considered an independent people."[22] Shown a portion of the instructions that authorized recognition as the first article of a treaty, Jay refused to relent.

Within three weeks, London gave way. Changing the commission was easy, although an instinct to give no more than absolutely necessary meant that the new one was still equivocal. Prior recognition was more difficult because the ministry believed it could not be extended without Parliament's approval. Nevertheless, on August 29 the cabinet agreed to seek legislation if the Americans insisted. However, because of the political difficulties involved (recalling Parliament from vacation was only one of them), it directed Oswald to make a last effort to get the Americans to settle for recognition in the first article of the treaty. The Americans would have won their victories—over issues solely in their imagination—had not Jay swerved in another direction.

His suspicion of France, already strong, now became an obsession. Vergennes's advice that they accept Oswald's commission he considered evidence of French malevolence. "I am persuaded," he wrote in a report to Congress that broke a long silence, "that this court chooses to postpone an acknowledgement of our independence by Britain to the conclusion of a general peace in order to keep us under their direction."[23] French support of Spain's claims to land be-

[22] Bemis, *Diplomacy of the American Revolution*, p. 211.

[23] Francis Wharton, ed., *The Revolutionary Diplomatic Correspondence of the United States*, 6 vols. (Washington, D.C., 1889), 5:740.

tween the Alleghenies and the Mississippi and reports that France wanted to exclude Americans from the Newfoundland fisheries deepened his anger.

Then, early in September, Jay's agitation increased still more when he learned that Vergennes's closest confidant had left on a secret mission to Lord Shelburne. Jay had no doubt that Gérard de Rayneval, speaking for his master, intended to sell out the Americans, particularly on territorial issues. Although in their talks Rayneval let Shelburne know that France did not support all American claims, his instructions "scrupulously omitted the United States from the agenda"; his only real purpose was to explore chances of peace between Britain and her European enemies.[24] American issues were secondary, discussed almost in passing. The Rayneval mission had nothing like the character that Jay gave it.

Nevertheless, in his view, "no time was . . . to be lost in counteracting what I supposed to be the object of M. Rayneval's journey."[25] When Oswald, obedient to orders, made one last try before conceding on recognition, Jay (and Franklin) quickly agreed to drop the demand—the cause of the whole imbroglio—if a new commission to Oswald authorized him to treat with the United States. Then, behind his colleague's back, Jay sent an English contact, Benjamin Vaughan, to Shelburne with a message that, as he admitted, totally disregarded the instructions of 1781. Through Vaughan, he not only repeated a willingness to negotiate but broadly hinted that he was prepared to make a separate peace, an act prohibited by the alliance with France. Beyond that, he told Vaughan that while the United States would remain faithful to that alliance after the war, "yet it was a different thing to be guided by their or our construction of it."[26] By so acting, Jay far out-Raynevaled Rayneval.

Despite grumbling by a few colleagues, Shelburne quickly obtained approval of a new commission, something much

---

[24] Richard B. Morris et al., eds., *John Jay*, vol. 2, *John Jay: The Winning of the Peace: Unpublished Papers, 1780–1784* (New York, 1980), p. 333.

[25] Wharton, ed., *Revolutionary Diplomatic Correspondence*, 6:28.

[26] Morris, *Peacemakers*, p. 333.

less demanding than the independence legislation to which the cabinet had agreed in August. On September 21 it went off to Oswald. Received in Paris on the twenty-seventh, it proved acceptable to Jay and Franklin. The whole episode was over.

This affair sheds only unfavorable light on the two Americans, particularly Jay. In their original objective, to tie Britain on the issue of independence before negotiations began, they failed. They dropped the demand for prior recognition shortly after the ministry decided to arrange it, and the changes in Oswald's commission that they accepted left it filled with ambiguity. The cabinet approved a commission "enabling Mr. Oswald to treat with the Commissioners appointed by the Colonies, under the title of Thirteen United States," and the commission itself actually listed them one by one. To the ministry the commission did not "by any means amount . . . to a final acknowledgement of Independence, it only giving them during the negotiation the title which they wished to assume."[27] The Shelburne government had what it always wanted (but could have been induced to abandon), deferral of formal recognition of independence to the first article of the treaty of peace.

Even if Jay delayed serious negotiations for two months, perhaps the whole affair, by demonstrating American alienation from France, was essential in deciding Shelburne to seek a peace of reconciliation. Without it, he might have evaded negotiations or pressed the Americans hard. Earlier hints by Jay and Franklin that the United States could be induced to abandon France had been insufficient, and the Vaughan mission provided essential proof. Or so at least it might be argued.

However, at least as early as July, before the draft commission reached Paris, the ministry was prepared to negotiate on the basis of Franklin's "necessary" conditions. It is true that it also demanded American concessions to the loyalists and assurances regarding prewar debts owed by Americans to British businessmen. London also insisted that America show

---

[27] Bemis, *Diplomacy of the American Revolution*, p. 226; idem, *Blessings of Liberty*, p. 123.

its freedom from French control, and this was a major reason for the reluctance to make a free grant, in advance, of independence.

Too much should not be made, however, of these conditions. Even before the Vaughan mission, on August 29, the cabinet agreed, if necessary, to give prior recognition of independence via legislation. At the same time, temporarily dropping the debt and loyalist issues, it agreed to go ahead on the basis of the "necessary" propositions. Jay's démarche may have made clearer the breach with France, especially since he did not make it conditional on British concessions. But the decision to proceed, based on accumulated evidence rather than a single episode, came before the American took what he thought was the decisive step on the road to peace.

Even if unnecessary to bring Shelburne to negotiations, was the betrayal of France necessary to prevent French betrayal of the United States? So Jay and Adams argued. There were good reasons to be suspicious of Vergennes, who sought to break up the British Empire, not to create a new one, powerful and independent, on the American continent. To keep the new state weak and dependent on France, he wanted Britain to stay in Canada. "You know our system," he wrote a subordinate. "Whatever will halt the conquest of this country accords with our views."[28] Partly for the same reason, but also to please a more important ally, he supported most Spanish claims to land beyond the Alleghenies. In general he considered American claims to all lands as far as the Mississippi "foolishness not meriting serious refutation."[29] In addition, he may have wished to deprive the Americans of a share of the Newfoundland fisheries, although his convoluted maneuvers have also been explained as merely an effort to gain a share for France.[30] Finally, he did not want Britain to recognize independence except as part of a general peace. As Shelburne understood after talking with Ray-

[28] Morris, *Peacemakers*, p. 326.

[29] Ibid.

[30] Orville T. Murphy, "The Comte de Vergennes, the Newfoundland Fisheries, and the Peace Negotiation of 1783: A Reconsideration," *Canadian Historical Review* 46 (1965): 32–46.

neval, "The Point of Independence once settled, he appears rather Jealous than partial to America upon other points."[31]

The French minister usually tried to keep his views from the Americans, which made them seem more ominous when they became known. Although Franklin professed to disagree, Jay and Adams concluded, in Jay's words, that while France wanted to see America independent, "it is not their interest that we should become a great and formidable people, and therefore they will not help us become so." Or, as Adams more dramatically put it—early diplomats did not limit themselves to gray bureaucratese—Vergennes meant "to keep his hand under our chin to prevent us from drowning, but not to lift our heads out of the water."[32]

Vergennes was less malevolent than calculating. Certainly he was not the active enemy of American aspirations that Jay assumed. At no time did he try to jerk the Americans into line by reminding them that they had been ordered to obey him, although the instructions of 1781 had been written under the eye of his envoy at Philadelphia and were thus well known to him. He encouraged Franklin to talk with Oswald, merely desiring—as was plainly required by the treaty of 1778—that no separate peace be signed. On the whole his policy only took the form of oral exhortations; neither negatively nor positively did he seek to influence their success by material means, nor is it easy to see how he could have done so. Knowledge of France's position, through Rayneval and otherwise, may possibly have affected Shelburne's stance toward the Americans, but there is no clear evidence that the two were connected. The British minister determined his position on other grounds.

In the era of the American Revolution, as Bernard Bailyn has reminded us, conspiracy theories were in vogue.[33] Unfounded or not, they became real political forces. Excessive

[31] Bemis, *Diplomacy of the American Revolution*, p. 222.

[32] Gerald Stourzh, *Benjamin Franklin and American Foreign Policy* (Chicago, 1954), p. 174; Wharton, ed., *Revolutionary Diplomatic Correspondence*, 5:865.

[33] Bernard Bailyn, *The Ideological Origins of the American Revolution* (Cambridge, Mass., 1967).

suspicion of Shelburne and Vergennes disrupted and delayed the negotiations for peace. Whether delay affected the outcome, particularly regarding the West and Canada, is a question to which we now turn.

In simple terms, four provinces were at issue in 1782. The first, south of the Ohio River, was never contested for by Shelburne. Britain simply renounced any possible claims, in effect endorsing American ambitions there against Spain's. Between the Ohio and the Great Lakes lay the second cohesive territory. To the north were the third and the fourth. Taken together they make up the heart of modern Canada, but in 1782 they were quite distinct. These were the lands between the Lakes and the Nipissing line and those east of the Nipissing; the last was the only portion of Canada with any significant white population—the province of Quebec, taken from France during the Seven Years' War. In theory, any or all of these three latter areas—the Ohio country, the Nipissing lands, Quebec—might have fallen to either the British or the Americans. Put another way, the Americans might have gained the entire imperial patrimony or Great Britain might have held all the territory south to the Ohio. In the end, Britain lost only one, the Ohio country, and saved the other two, Quebec and the Nipissing. How this division was reached, how favorable it was to the Americans, and how well Franklin, Jay, and Adams pressed their country's case for each of the three areas—these are interesting questions.

Franklin had long coveted all of Canada, both Nipissing and Quebec. In his conversations with Oswald and when he passed on his outline of a settlement, he suggested "the giving up of every part of Canada";[34] if Britain did so, he argued, she would markedly improve chances of reconciliation and lessen American dependence on France. However, by placing Canada only in the "desirable" list, Franklin greatly weakened the force of his request, as Oswald recognized. Subsequently he never really pressed it, and with Jay's arrival it disappeared. The newcomer probably never considered it within reach, and he certainly felt the matter much less im-

[34] Bemis, *Blessings of Liberty*, p. 114.

portant than making peace before France could betray the United States. The commission question once settled, Jay prepared a draft treaty laying out the full extent of American desires; in it he did not, even for bargaining purposes, request all of Canada. In sum, the request for Canada—Canada including Quebec as well as the Nipissing country—was so feebly pressed as not really to have been an object of negotiation.

Nevertheless, at least during the period of informal discussions, Oswald thought well of the idea. More than that, he told Franklin that Rockingham and Shelburne were willing to consider it and that he himself was "not without hopes that it will be agreed to."[35] When his master disabused him, he did not tell Franklin. Oswald's personal views and his inaccurate report of his superior's are the only basis for any suspicion that, before conversations were derailed by Jay's intervention, there was a chance for the United States to gain Canada, both Nipissing and Quebec.

But Oswald of course was a tool, not a policymaker. No important British figure was ready to abandon all of Canada, and the political consequences of doing so would have been intolerable. Modern historians agree that "there was never any question from the British side of a surrender of Canada; and it does not appear that Jay or [the late-arriving] Adams thought that there was."[36] To this might be added that Franklin, too, came to see that his dream was unattainable.

Samuel Flagg Bemis argued, many years ago, that Jay omitted from his draft treaty any mention of Canada so as to gain British support against Spain in the Southwest. "Rather than let Spain clinch her claim to the Mississippi country," he wrote, "Jay—and Franklin, so it proved—preferred to let Canada go in [re]turn for British acknowledgment of the American boundaries of 31° North Latitude on the south [the Florida boundary, and] Mississippi on the west."[37] There

[35] Morris, *Peacemakers*, p. 277.

[36] Harlow, *Founding of the Second British Empire*, 1:303.

[37] Bemis, *Blessings of Liberty*, p. 60 (from an article published in 1937).

is an attractive symmetry to this argument. However, Shelburne was hardly likely to support a rival power against the Americans, especially since he aimed at a solid, not merely a grudging, settlement. The suggestion that Jay traded a claim to Canada for British support against Spain is supported neither by evidence nor logic. Moreover, Bemis does not make clear that abandoning Canada, in this context, meant only the relinquishment of claims to Quebec.

If the Americans never really had any chance to gain that country, there was scarcely more likelihood that they would lose the Ohio province. True, in 1782 British power there, such as it was, was greater than American. Further, the area was part of "Canada's natural hinterland,"[38] an area where Montreal firms dominated the fur trade, the only important economic activity. But the British ministers, and especially Shelburne, did not particularly value the territory,[39] and the earl later told parliamentary critics that he expected the fur trade to continue no matter who had dominion and that he positively welcomed the growth of American settlements that would provide markets for Britiah goods.

Late in July, in a private letter expanding on formal instructions Oswald was about to receive—instructions that accompanied the troublesome commission—Shelburne wrote that there would be no trouble over the Northwest, to which Britain laid no claim. At the important session on August 29, by accepting Franklin's "necessary" conditions, the ministry once again agreed to abandon all territory south of the Lakes and, for that matter, even more. Since this decision was taken before the Vaughan mission, it is not possible to excuse Jay's betrayal of France by arguing that this convinced Shelburne to surrender the Northwest to the United States.

Toward the end of negotiations, the British did briefly seek this territory. But they did so only in the context of the domestic political need to make some gesture in favor of the loyalists. As Franklin reported, "They wanted to bring their boundary down to the Ohio, and to settle their Loyalists in

---

[38] Burt, *Old Province of Quebec*, p. 331.

[39] Even the Rockingham ministry was ready to surrender the area.

the Illinois country. We did not choose such neighbors."[40] Even then, the British made clear that this was only one possible way to provide for the loyalists, and when the Americans objected, they readily dropped the idea. The area's fate was never in serious doubt.

Thus, with little difficulty, the Americans gained British recognition of their desires in the southerly two of the western provinces, that disputed with Spain and that between the Ohio River and the Great Lakes. Although boundary agreement with Spain did not come until Pinckney's Treaty in 1795, the settlements of 1782 clearly paved the way to national growth. Since in neither case had the commissioners overcome substantial opposition, few laurels are owing them. They did not win but rather accepted title to these vastly important territories.

On the other hand, they had given up, nearly as easily as Britain had abandoned the southern sections, their claim—perhaps one should call it Franklin's claim—for the fourth, most northerly one. This did not mean that they had lost hope for territory beyond the Lakes, specifically the third of the western areas, reaching north to the Nipissing line. They wished, in effect, to define Canada as comprising only the fourth region, the province of Quebec. If the Americans had lost the Ohio country, the loss would almost certainly have been only temporary, reversible with the growth of population. If the Americans had won the Nipissing country, on the other hand, there is a far greater chance that Canada's growth would have been permanently blocked, for this area, now the southern portion of Ontario, not only is Canada's industrial heartland but lies alongside water routes to the western plains and the Pacific Ocean.

Early in July, when Franklin outlined terms to Oswald, he demanded that Canada be restricted to her boundaries before the Quebec Act, "if not to a still more contracted state on ancient footing."[41] (This phrase referred to British claims against France when the latter held Canada.) In short, he

---

[40] Carl Van Doren, ed., *Benjamin Franklin's Autobiographical Writings* (New York, 1945), p. 589.

[41] Morris, *Peacemakers*, p. 287.

asked for—indeed, required—territory north of the Great Lakes, extending at least to the Nipissing line. While the British refused to consider giving up all of Canada, the cabinet twice endorsed cession of the Canadian backcountry by agreeing to accept Franklin's "necessary" demands.

The first occasion was late in July. The ministers unanimously agreed to Franklin's basic requirements, although they demanded additional provisions favorable to Britain. In a letter to Oswald, Shelburne emphasized the positive side of the government's position. If Franklin dropped his wish list, the premier wrote, the "necessary" points would be readily conceded and, in ways favorable to the Americans, even exceeded. Unfortunately for the latter, the argument over the commission prevented Oswald from presenting this position, and Franklin and Jay did not learn that the Nipissing country was theirs for the asking.

At the end of August, in another major statement of position not communicated to the Americans, this time because Jay's approach through Vaughan transformed the situation, the cabinet reaffirmed its earlier decision. A "Minute of Propositions" summing up its discussions stated, "We will settle the Boundaries of the Province and Contract the Limits of Canada as desir'd by Dr Franklin."[42] A leading historian of Canadian-American relations, one of few to emphasize this decision, writes, "The future of what is now the thickly populated portion of Ontario seems to have been trembling in the balance, without Franklin's or Jay's realizing that perhaps a little pull would bring it down on their side."[43]

We cannot of course be sure this offer would have been carried through. It was part of a package so generous to the Americans that the ministry might well have had second thoughts, if only on the basis of domestic political considerations, although revision of the package need not necessarily have meant a change with regard to the Nipissing. Further-

[42] Sidney Papers, William L. Clements Library, University of Michigan, Ann Arbor.

[43] Alfred Leroy Burt, *The United States, Great Britain and British North America from the Revolution to the Establishment of Peace after the War of 1812* (New York, 1940), p. 24.

more, news of the repulse of a Franco-Spanish attack on Gibraltar, news that reached England at the end of September, raised morale and lessened the urgency of peace when negotiations with the Americans resumed in October.

Still, a major reason for loss of the Nipissing territory lies in the refusal of Franklin and Jay—and Adams, when he joined them—to press for it. "It is a familiar chapter of history," Samuel Flagg Bemis has written, "how they [the British negotiators] finally succeeded in changing the Nipissing line to the actual boundary of today."[44] Familiar it may be, but only in the sense that we know it happened.

The Americans began well enough. The draft treaty prepared by Jay included an article fixing the boundary to Lake Nipissing and thence directly to the source of the Mississippi River. Oswald did not demur, even appeared favorable. Then Shelburne, previously so easygoing, pulled back. He sent an undersecretary of state, Henry Strachey, to stiffen Oswald's backbone and to seek various concessions. His motives were primarily political; he cared much less about the substance of his requests than about vulnerability in Parliament if he did not strike a harder bargain. Boundary questions came up only in the context of compensation for the loyalists, and for Shelburne either lands in Maine or in the West would have sufficed. Shelburne was much less stiff about the boundary than about the other issues he raised. Just before Strachey's departure the premier told him to fight hard on some issues and to get "as much as possible of Canada" but to give in to the Americans on this point, if necessary.[45]

Unaccountably the Americans backed off, although on other issues they fought hard. They offered a choice between two lines. One was an extension of the line of forty-five degrees (the northern boundary from the Connecticut River to the St. Lawrence) due west to the Mississippi; the other line followed the Great Lakes through Lake Superior, then ran westward to the source of the Mississippi. The forty-five de-

[44] Bemis, *Blessings of Liberty*, p. 126.

[45] Shelburne Papers, LXXXVII, Clements Libr., U. of Mich., Ann Arbor.

gree line, although it left territory for Canada beyond Lake Huron, would have sacrificed about half—the critical half—of the Nipissing country. Perhaps for this reason, but more probably because the Lakes line seemed easier to demarcate, Shelburne chose what is today's boundary. "Considering the immensity of the stakes," observes Richard B. Morris, "the struggle over the northern boundary and the 'back lands' was over rather quickly."[46] It was over so quickly because it was never really a struggle at all.

There is no record of the discussions that led to this settlement, either within the American commission or in sessions with Strachey and Oswald. In later reports to Congress the commissioners went on at great length about various issues Strachey raised, and we know the arguments were heated. About boundaries, including the one with Canada, their remarks are brief and, one feels, slightly defensive. Even the conclusion—"they appear to leave us little to complain of and not much to desire"[47]—hardly sounds like exultation.

How is one to explain this neglect, this lack of concern? Franklin alone had a real territorial vision, although Jay was staunch regarding the territory south of the Lakes. For Adams other issues, especially the fisheries, were more important. Possibly the Americans felt that if they gave way on the Nipissing, Strachey would be less demanding on other matters. Certainly no more than their adversaries did the Americans grasp the implications of the issue, especially for Canada. Still, as one scholar has observed, the boundary was "apparently as much the result of chance as of any deep appreciation of the vital issues involved."[48]

The Americans cannot be faulted for failing to foresee the future. They cannot, probably, be blamed for failing to divine the feelings of Shelburne and his colleagues, who until October were ready to cast away the Nipissing almost without thought. They can be criticized with specific reference to

[46] Morris, *Peacemakers*, p. 361. This comment pertains to discussion of the Northwest as well as the Nipissing country.

[47] Wharton, ed., *Revolutionary Diplomatic Correspondence*, 6:132.

[48] Donald G. Creighton, *The Commercial Empire of the St. Lawrence, 1760–1851* (Toronto, 1937), p. 79.

PEACE AND THE PEACEMAKERS

Canada's heartland for the great fuss they made over recognition. While they never really won on this point, they did put a stop to negotiations for two months. When negotiations were rejoined, Britain's position had improved. Even then, however, they well could have gained their point had they pressed it.

"Their insistence on 'the point of independence,'" A. L. Burt believes, "together with the resistance of the little garrison at Gibraltar, deprived the United States of the Nipissing line as a boundary."[49] These and the commissioners' appalling weaknesses meant that, when they might have blocked Canada's future and paved the way for American dominion over the whole continent, they instead settled for minimum American claims.

Since this paper focuses on the matter of "innocence and guile" and the Canadian frontier, more specifically the Nipissing boundary, the often acrimonious discussions during October and November may be only briefly described. Adams and then, at the very end, Henry Laurens arrived to take part. To the great surprise of Jay and Adams, who disliked and distrusted Franklin, the Doctor made no trouble and the delegation worked in reasonable harmony, albeit with differences of emphasis. There were very long arguments, Adams in the van, over the fisheries, especially since, when he mentioned the issue among his "necessary" conditions, Franklin had sloppily drafted his proposal. There were further disputes over compensation for the loyalists and over the rights of creditors, two matters that Shelburne had earlier been ready to pass over in silence. In the end, agreements were cobbled together, "trifling concessions and empty formulas,"[50] some so vague they caused trouble later on.

During these discussions the Americans did not keep Vergennes informed, as the instructions of 1781 certainly and the spirit of the alliance perhaps required. They still feared that he would come down on Britain's side; indeed, Adams believed that, as it was, some of Strachey's arguments came

---

[49] Burt, *United States, Great Britain and British North America*, p. 26.

[50] Hutson, *John Adams*, p. 128.

"piping hot from Versailles."[51] On November 29 Franklin, prudently used as a conduit because of his good relations with the French, told Vergennes that agreement had been reached. The next day the preliminary treaty of peace was signed at Oswald's residence, the Grand Hotel Muscovite, following which the Americans adjourned to Franklin's place in suburban Passy for a celebratory dinner.

Only then did the Americans provide the French minister with a copy of their handiwork, and they still withheld a secret article dealing with the Florida boundary. Vergennes was astounded. To Rayneval he wrote, "The English buy peace rather than make it. Their concessions exceed all that I should have thought possible."[52] Astonishment was succeeded by concern that the terms would lessen American dependence on France and annoyance that the commissioners had followed so independent a course, concluding what was, in all but name, a separate peace. With only marginal restraint, the foreign minister made his feelings known to Franklin, who sought to turn them aside with the blarney for which he was so well known. To his minister in America, Vergennes wrote, "I accuse nobody. I do not even blame Mr. Franklin. . . . [Still,] If we may judge of the future from what has passed here under our eyes, we shall be but poorly paid for all that we have done for the United States and for securing to them a national existence."[53]

On the other hand, the Anglo-American preliminaries broke a logjam and thereby served Vergennes's interest; his hope that all negotiations would move at exactly the same pace had never been realistic. This first settlement helped open the way to Anglo-French and, most difficult of all, Anglo-Spanish preliminaries of peace in January 1783. Only then did the American preliminaries formally come into force. Definitive treaties were signed in September 1783, but Britain and the United States did not exchange instruments

[51] Lyman H. Butterfield, ed., *Diary and Autobiography of John Adams*, 4 vols. (Cambridge, Mass., 1961–66), 3:72.

[52] Morris, *Peacemakers*, p. 383.

[53] Wharton, ed., *Revolutionary Diplomatic Correspondence*, 6:152.

of ratification in Paris until May 12, 1784, nearly a year and a half after the signing at the Grand Hotel Muscovite.

When he first departed from the instructions of 1781, Franklin did not report to Congress that he had done so. Nor did Jay, until after he sent Vaughan to London behind Vergennes's back. "Had I not violated the instructions of Congress, their dignity would have been in the dust," he boasted to a friend.[54] Adams, too, defended independent action, although at first he professed to believe—in direct contradiction of plain language—that Congress could not have meant to "oblig[e] us to agree to whatever the French ministers should advise us to do, and to do nothing without their consent."[55] (Franklin later rather sophistically argued that by naming five ministers Congress showed that it intended them to act independently of France; to follow orders from Vergennes, one would have been enough.) And all three argued, perhaps with more plausibility than accuracy, that they had not violated the treaty of alliance and its ban on a separate peace since their treaty did not come into force until European preliminaries were concluded.

In their formal report just after the signing, without concealing how they had acted earlier, the commissioners chose to concentrate on a narrower point, their failure to show the treaty to Vergennes before they signed it: "As we had reason to imagine that the articles respecting the boundaries, the refugees, and fisheries did not correspond with the policy of this court, we did not communicate the preliminaries to the minister until after they were signed, and not even then the *separate article*. We hope these considerations will excuse our having so far deviated from our instructions."[56]

When their report reached Congress, there was some grumbling, directed particularly at Jay. Robert R. Livingston, the secretary for foreign affairs, virtually invited Congress to order him to rebuke the commissioners. One delegate condemned them for "a mixture of follies which had no example

[54] Ibid., 5:810.

[55] Ibid., p. 839.

[56] Ibid., 6:131.

. . .[for] chicane and low cunning."[57] Others defended them because they seemed to have been so successful, and within only a few days news arrived of the European preliminaries, which in a sense made moot the question of betraying France.

Doubtless with regret, Livingston had to confine his rebuke, written solely on his own authority, to the ground the commissioners had chosen. He chastised them only for not showing the treaty to Vergennes before they signed it. Even Livingston, virtually in the pocket of the French minister, seems to have recognized that the supine instructions of 1781 could no longer be taken literally. In this he was somewhat like James Madison, who argued that the instructions were passé but nevertheless thought that to rescind them would be too great an affront to France.

The instructions of 1781 deserved to be disobeyed. In Congress, on the very day that Oswald presented his draft commission for inspection in Paris, Madison defended the instructions. While admitting that they were "a sacrifice of national dignity," he also argued, "but it was a sacrifice of national dignity to policy."[58] By 1782, at least, if not in 1781, the instructions were clearly a mistaken policy. Observed, they would have allowed Vergennes to slow negotiations to the snaillike pace of those between Britain and her European enemies, perhaps also to have prevented the Americans from even asking for some of the things they sought. It is, then, the manner of, the motives for, and the outcome of the commissioners' disobedience, not the simple fact of disobedience, that must be evaluated.

Franklin's confidential talks with Oswald, for example, seem fully justified, and they did not really trouble Vergennes although they would have done so had the foreign minister learned how broad were Franklin's hints that Britain had a chance to end American ties to France. On the other hand, failure to give Vergennes advance knowledge of the peace terms is hard to justify. Besides being a particularly blatant violation of the instructions, the failure to give notice

[57] Ibid., p. 320.

[58] Ibid., 5:647.

was a gratuitous insult to the French minister, who would have had no choice but to accept the inevitable at this point.

Most important was Jay's approach to Shelburne early in September. Jay was clearly unwise, disobedient, and dubiously loyal to the alliance when he outlined moderate terms of peace and suggested how close he would go to full betrayal of France. This lessened pressure on Shelburne to concede, threw away claims such as Canada that could at least have been used as bargaining points, and may have been at least a minor factor in the later effort, via Strachey, to tighten the terms. The cabinet had already decided on August 29 to go ahead, and, it must be hammered home, in the end the Americans got less than the ministry had then been prepared to offer—the Nipissing line and complete silence on tories and creditors.

Moreover, Jay terribly exposed himself. Shelburne could have ruined the Americans by passing details of the démarche on to Vergennes, and he could have been encouraged to raise British terms even higher. Irving Brant's judgment seems correct: "Not twice in human history, perhaps, has the safety of a victorious nation been made so dependent upon the integrity and good will of the head of an enemy government, and seldom have men held power who would have responded as the Earl of Shelburne did."[59]

Contemporaries, like later historians, considered the peace terms a great triumph for the Americans. And so they were, considering the relative power of the two parties. Shelburne fell under attack as soon as the details came before Parliament in January 1783, in particular for his failure to get hard promises regarding the loyalists and to gain better boundary terms. As Frederick the Great wrote to his ambassador at London, the criticism of the American and other treaties was unfair: "If the English make a bad peace, it should be attributed to the previous ministry, which set all the affairs of England in disorder."[60] This did not matter. Shelburne's

[59] Irving Brant, *James Madison*, vol. 2, *James Madison: The Nationalist, 1780–1787* (Indianapolis, 1948), p. 264.

[60] Marvin L. Brown, ed., *American Independence through Prussian Eyes* (Durham, N.C., 1959), p. 176.

government had always been weak in parliamentary terms. As soon as his enemies combined against him, he fell. The vehicle, a series of resolutions carried in the House of Commons on February 22, covered the whole range of peace settlements, not merely the one with the United States, and one of the resolutions explicitly welcomed the recognition of American independence. Shelburne cannot be said to have been cast out of office for making peace with America nor even for the generosity of his terms, although arguments against them strengthened an attack motivated essentially by domestic political considerations.

At the beginning of his classic study *The Diplomacy of the American Revolution* Samuel Flagg Bemis stated the theme of the pages to follow: "While pursuing the letter of the alliance with France, these bold plenipotentiaries broke their instructions and cut loose from French advice and control. To clinch their own country's advantage and independence, they took advantage of Europe's rivalries and distresses."[61] This chauvinistic tone, which still dominates discussions of the Paris negotiations, must be modified. The Americans did cut loose, as Bemis says. They did use, rather cynically use, European rivalries. But they were less in control of events than Bemis suggests. Such success as they gained depended on factors that they could hardly influence, some that they misunderstood.

The first was the extent of British war weariness. Like almost all successful colonial revolts, the American Revolution was not so much won by the rebels as abandoned by the imperial power; the rebels' essential success was simply in holding the field. The British after Yorktown, like the French after Dienbienphu or the Americans after Tet, still had a vast preponderance of military power. But they lost hope, a loss more critical than any battle casualties. The Conway Resolution of February 1782, like later pronouncements of Pierre Mendès-France and Lyndon Johnson, abandoned the goal of military victory. From then on independence was inevitable, and the terms of the resolution made plain that Parliament

[61] P. viii.

would oppose military efforts to improve the terms. Unaccountably, the Americans at Paris never really seem to have understood what this implied.

More problematic is a second factor growing out of the first. Once Parliament tacitly acknowledged American independence via the Conway Resolution, most details of that independence shrank by comparison with the terms of peace with France. Except for reparations for the loyalists, a matter of honor, specifics were unimportant. What was critical was that the United States show itself independent of France. So at least argues the historian John Norris, and his argument is plausible.[62] Franklin and Jay grasped the essential point that Britain, and more specifically Shelburne, could be tempted by evidence of a Franco-American rift, but Jay at least felt it necessary to go far beyond what was required and, if the flaccid retreats on Canada and then the Nipissing are evidence, wrongly believed that the Americans, in order to bring Britain to peace, would also have to concede some of their own desires.

Thirdly, none of the Americans really ever understood Shelburne. Admittedly he was difficult to understand. His early hope for a reconstructed empire, as well as the ambiguities of his statements even after negotiations had started, encouraged misunderstanding. Yet it should have been obvious that, whether before or after Shelburne lost hope for continued imperial ties, the last thing he would want was a definite breach in negotiations or, almost as bad, long and rancorous disputations. Finally, Shelburne's political weakness really drove him to peace. He could not hope to survive as a war minister; his only conceivable hope to remain in power lay in the conclusion of peace. Yet as late as November the Americans, especially Adams, suspected that Shelburne was spinning out the negotiations, seeking only an opportune issue on which to break them off.

The Americans saw none of these things. Instead of acuity, they brought to the negotiations, with the partial exception of Franklin, only "anger, suspicion, and resolve." And their suspicion was often either unjustified—as in that directed at

[62] Norris, *Shelburne and Reform*, p. 257.

Shelburne—or overalarmist—as in the case of Vergennes, who opposed American aspirations but could not effectively foil them. To this they added sanctimony, a sense of rectitude so strong that it justified almost any tactical behavior. Thus "the union of conscious virtue with deliberate deception was complete."[63] And this posture was largely unnecessary. The Americans having, all unwittingly, failed to settle when Shelburne was ready for silence on the loyalists and the creditors, later fought successfully to prevent stipulations for these unfortunates from being more than nullities. They recovered some ground Franklin had carelessly given up on the fisheries. But they failed to gain the Nipissing country and they settled for terms really probably not much different from those that might have been won by less suspicious men. They were, because of the factors in the air, bound to secure a peace and independence.

Few of America's peace negotiations have been sufficiently similar to those of 1782 and 1783 to suggest direct comparisons. The impact of cable, radio, and airplane; the personal intervention of presidents and secretaries of state; participation in multilateral settlements—these factors created new patterns. The Paris negotiations are most like those at Ghent in the summer and autumn of 1814. Even some of the issues were the same. Canada and the Northwest were again on the tapis, though as insubstantially as before. The American commissioners of 1814 never even presented their government's wishes, themselves feeble, for Canada. The British suggestion that an Indian "barrier state" be constructed south of the Lakes, although it drove the Americans into a frenzy, had only slightly more behind it than Shelburne's short-lived request for the same territory in 1782. The fisheries again caused contention at the end of the negotiations, and the settlement, like its predecessor, proved temporary rather than permanent; John Adams's son, the leading and sometimes almost the only spokesman for American claims, observed that there seemed to be some strange affinity between the history of his family and that of the cod. But it is

[63] Dangerfield, *Robert R. Livingston*, p. 164.

not so much the issues or settlements at Ghent that suggest comparisons as it is larger themes and issues, some also visible in other early negotiations.

First of all, in both negotiations the American representatives ignored the instructions of their government. At Ghent, even before negotiations began, they decided not to demand that Britain abandon the practice of impressment, a sine qua non in their instructions, and they not only never pressed their superiors' request for Canada but even had the effrontery to deny that Washington had ever considered such a thing. Thus the two issues—impressment and Canada—most often identified, although perhaps wrongly, with the coming of the War of 1812 passed out of the negotiations to end it. Nor were the acts of disobedience in 1782 and 1814 the only instances of such behavior. Negotiators at Paris in 1800 ended an undeclared war with France at the cost of throwing aside their orders to demand compensation for seized American ships. As late as 1848, in probably the most heroic act of all—not only because the protagonist, merely chief clerk in the Department of State, lacked the political stature of other truants but also because he actually had been recalled by his government—Nicholas Trist signed the treaty of Guadelupe-Hidalgo, which ended the Mexican War. Thus every peace settlement before midcentury involved defiance of orders. So did many other arrangements, among them the abortive Monroe-Pinkney treaty of 1806 and the Louisiana Purchase.

Probably no other Western diplomatic corps has ever been so disobedient, although freewheeling diplomats were not unknown in contemporary Europe. The conde de Aranda had to ignore his instructions so as to end the Anglo-Spanish part of the war of the American Revolution. A few very privileged men (for example, Sir James Harris, earl of Malmesbury) sometimes operated under very loose leads. But such independence was unusual. Disobedience was very rare, and when it occurred it usually led to dismissal and distrust, a fate befalling David Erskine, the Englishman who improvised a settlement with President Madison in 1809.

One explanation for American singularity may lie in the character of its diplomats. Trist being the exception that proves the rule, they were usually political figures, not career men. They were accustomed to lead and had allies at home who could be counted on to defend them. Often, indeed, they were selected precisely because of this political strength. While the envoys of European nations—Britain in particular—were sometimes political men, this was relatively uncommon in the case of the British and still more rare on the Continent.[64] Then, too, American negotiators were usually appointed only for a single task. They could give it priority and not worry overmuch about the personal consequences of departure from instructions.

The most obvious reason for the American pattern is the breadth of the Atlantic. Dispatches often took six weeks to cross the ocean in the days of sail, and when events moved rapidly Yankee diplomats could feel there was not time to ask their home government for new instructions and wait for a reply. (The same conviction led Erskine into error in 1809). Almost all truly important negotiations involving the United States took place abroad until 1842, when Lord Ashburton visited Washington to bargain with Daniel Webster. European diplomats in America, dealing with lesser issues, found it comparatively easy to hold to instructions they received. In by far the most important negotiations in Washington in the early years, those that resulted in the Florida treaty of 1819, the Spanish minister, Luis de Onís, exercised great freedom of action, but it had been authorized by his superiors; in this case at least, the usually rigid Spanish government gave him less restrictive orders than the American government almost always gave its own agents.

With the coming of the cable American diplomats, even those who were public figures, accommodated themselves far more closely to diplomatic norms. In the early years, however, their indisciplined ways were noteworthy. Jay and his colleagues had many successors, among them the men of Ghent.

Other patterns set at Paris and Ghent persisted, even to our own times. One was the practice of negotiating by com-

---

[64] Many diplomats were patronage appointees, but these had little or no stature of their own and were far more vulnerable.

mission; it was an approach by no means unknown in other countries and almost requisite during complex multilateral negotiations, but it was probably more frequently resorted to by the United States than other powers. In 1800 a commission arranged the end of the Quasi War with France. Five men represented the United States in negotiations, once again at Paris, that settled accounts after the Spanish-American War, although by this time improved communications meant that they were not so much bargainers as mouthpieces. President Wilson headed a five-man commission to Paris in 1919, although he never gave his lieutenants, except perhaps Colonel House, any real authority.[65] Peace conferences after 1945, commonly setpieces for signature of agreements already reached, usually saw the presence of more than one American representative. Nicholas Trist—and Henry Kissinger, negotiating to end the Vietnam war in the familiar environs of Paris—lie outside the usual pattern of plural representation.

Behind the consistent pattern lie evolving motives. The five men named in 1781 were selected in part to create a balance between conflicting views and contending sectional interests; thus the hard-line, antigallican Yankee, John Adams, was surrounded by colleagues believed to hold different views. Such was even more clearly the case in 1814, when the delegation included Republicans of four different political backgrounds (although two came from the same state) as well as one safely moderate Federalist. This commission, though bound by instructions it agreed to ignore, was expected to be a negotiating body, and the inclusion, for example, of Henry Clay was designed to ensure vigorous protection of Western interests, that of John Quincy Adams equally strong advocacy of those of New England.

James A. Bayard, the Federalist at Ghent, was mortally ill and played only a small role, but his nomination foreshadowed a shifting emphasis later on. Envoys came to be chosen, no longer to spearhead the defense of one interest or another, but rather to improve chances of Senate approval of any agreement that might be reached. In 1898 President

[65] The other major powers also employed commissions at Paris.

McKinley named representatives of various Republican factions for this reason, and the same sort of calculation explains the bipartisan delegations of more recent times. Wilson's failure to take any active Republican to Paris in 1919 was, on this ground, an unwise and much criticized departure from what was to become a national tradition. However, unlike most peace conferences of this century, the Paris meetings of 1919 were truly for negotiation, and the president was unwilling to share direction with anyone, least of all political rivals.

Wilson had difficulty enough with those he did include in his party both because they disagreed with his views and because, despite the incredible complexity of the issues before the conference, he tried to keep all important threads solely in his own hands. Permanent estrangement from two of them, Robert Lansing and Edward M. House, followed. Dissension also marked the delegation of 1898, to the degree that some of the negotiators did not share the administration's views regarding acquisition of the Philippine Islands, but their reservations were overborne.

Historians have made much of the quarrels within the delegations sent to Paris and Ghent. At Ghent there were sparks between Henry Clay and John Quincy Adams, the ebullient Westerner and the dour Yankee. Adams fought the rest of the delegation in an effort to be acknowledged the senior delegate, chief spokesman, and drafter of their official papers, but in the end, albeit with little grace, he recognized that the urbane Albert Gallatin could best play this role. At one point Adams became almost isolated from his colleagues, the issue being the familiar fisheries. On major issues, however, the Americans seldom differed. All agreed to drop impressment and not to talk of Canada. All fought resolutely against the "barrier state" idea and British proposals for boundary changes. Most important, they all agreed to stick to positions they firmly believed would end the negotiations. When London retreated, offering to settle for the status quo ante bellum, they all heaved sighs of relief and agreed to go ahead, with the result that a treaty was signed on Christmas eve, 1814. In the end John Quincy Adams, who had been at the center of such differences and policy clashes as did exist, wrote to his father, "Upon almost all the important questions, we have been unanimous."[66]

Three decades earlier there were differences between Franklin and his colleagues, differences exacerbated by the excessive suspiciousness of Jay and Adams. The latter considered Franklin lazy (they were not entirely wrong), weak, inattentive to national dignity, and above all too trusting of Vergennes. Adams hated Franklin, partly out of jealousy, and at first he found Jay difficult. Just after arriving in Paris, he wrote in his diary, "Between two as subtle Spirits, as any in this world, the one malicious, the other I think honest, I shall have a delicate, a nice, a critical Part to Act."[67] For his part, Jay, who alone faced Franklin during the imbroglio over Oswald's commission, hectored the old man, questioned his loyalty, and finally acted behind his back. The poisonous air lasted until nearly the end of the negotiations.

Jay's fight with Franklin deeply affected the negotiations. Still, Franklin did allow himself to be argued out of his initial position, and he must share with Jay whatever credit or blame attaches to the demands—for a revised commission, for recognition of independence—passed on to London. Similarly, he later joined Jay in reversing course, offering to negotiate without waiting for that recognition. Jay, of course, gave further force to the new departure by sending Vaughan with a message to Shelburne, and his suspicion of Franklin caused him to conceal it, but the Doctor had joined in the basic decision.

In the closing negotiations with Strachey the three Americans acted in close harmony, and their differences in emphasis and argument probably reinforced their effectiveness. Likewise there is no evidence that any one of them dissented—and we may be sure that Adams, at least, would have recorded argument—from the crucial decision to abandon the Nipissing country. Finally, Franklin, whether from prudence or gratefulness, usually so attentive to relations with Vergennes, even agreed to sign the preliminaries without showing them to the Frenchman. Adams, in whom forgive-

---

[66] Perkins, *Castlereagh and Adams*, p. 117.

[67] Butterfield, ed., *Diary and Autobiography of Adams*, 3:38.

ness was almost as rare as in his son, had to confess, "He . . . has gone on with Us, in entire Harmony and Unanimity, throughout, and he has been able and usefull, both by his Sagacity and his Reputation in the whole Negotiation."[68]

Admitting the importance of the Jay-Franklin battle, harsh but soon over, one can make too much of disagreements between the Americans at Paris as at Ghent. Diarists, and perhaps especially diplomatic diarists, tend to cherish disagreement and confrontation. John Quincy Adams's diary provides much of the evidence for disharmony at Ghent but passes almost silently over the more important community of views. His father's writings—and Jay's—perform a similar function for 1782. On the whole, such differences as existed within the two commissions were of little significance—troublesome and irritating to their members but not something that, even when glimpsed by their opponents, could be effectively exploited.

The men at Paris and Ghent deserve a place in history. Still, it seems possible to argue that they reacted rather than created, that their successes were largely negative and even less impressive because the pressures upon them were much less intense than they believed. The Americans modified but did not shape terms of peace molded elsewhere, primarily in the enemy's country. One might even maintain that Nicholas Trist, in 1848, did more to fix the terms of peace than his much more illustrious predecessors.

In 1782 and 1814 Britain's view of her own military and political situation was decisive. On the surface the picture was much more favorable in the later year. The war against Napoleon having ended, Britain faced only one enemy and she could dispatch veteran regiments across the Atlantic. In the summer of 1814 a large-scale raid on Washington torched the city and scattered the government. A combined operation against New Orleans was expected to do at least as well. In 1782, on the other hand, the effect of Yorktown was still felt, and Britain faced Spain and France as well as the United States.

But 1782 was perhaps not quite so bad and 1814 certainly

[68] Ibid., p. 82.

not so good as appeared on the surface. Yorktown had been won as a result of Franco-American cooperation unlikely to be repeated, Britain had a firm hold on New York and some strength elsewhere, and in 1782 military news from other fronts was encouraging. In 1814 London worried that Napoleon would escape from Elba to France (as he soon did), plunging Europe once again into war, and negotiations at Vienna had already shown that Britain and her allies had serious differences of view about postwar Europe. Finally, despite the sack of Washington, there were signs of improvement in the American military, made most apparent by British defeat in the West and on Lake Champlain. Taken as a whole, the good with the bad, the overall balances were not dissimilar.

The implications were clear. To defeat the Americans, if indeed such were possible, would require increased effort and unswerving persistence. Britain perhaps had the necessary resources; did she have the will? In 1814, in the intoxicating climate following Napoleon's first abdication, many strident voices called on the ministry to continue on, to chastise the upstart Madison, the jackal who had joined France's war with Britain when it seemed safe. By the fall of the year enthusiasm dwindled. Some even maintained that the raid on Washington had been punishment enough. Declining vengefulness, a concern over European tensions, problems in the domestic economy—all of these encouraged the Liverpool ministry, which had never seen much profit to be gained from the conflict, to seek ways to cast off "the millstone of an American war," as the foreign secretary described it.[69] Virtually impregnable in Parliament, it could proceed to make a peace that did not punish Madison but also did not give him anything for which his country had contended, save the very real satisfaction of having managed to resist British arms for more than three years.

In 1782 the picture was rather different, but the import was the same—British conditions were by far the most important factor in the equation. If Conway's Resolution showed, more clearly than any single event in 1814, that Brit-

[69] Perkins, *Castlereagh and Adams*, p. 152.

ain would not fight for victory, it did not suggest even the outline of a settlement. The general failures of the North ministry brought its fall, although Yorktown provided the coup de grace. Rockingham's ministry had no clear raison d'être, nor did it have a clear American policy. If, in that ministry, Charles James Fox had gained control of negotiations, a tougher line would probably have followed. But Shelburne won out and then, following Rockingham's death, headed his own ministry. He was even freer to act as he thought wise, and the result was a peace favorable to the Americans.

The Americans were surely lucky, as many have observed. Rockingham's demise put Shelburne in power at a key time. Yet in the long run his position was weak, probably impossible, and only the coincidence of a parliamentary recess protected him from immediate attack. He fell from power shortly after the peace. But it would be false to say that the American treaty cost him his position. Had peace not been concluded, Fox and North would have attacked him for prolonging the war.

In all of this the American negotiators played little part, and much of it they misunderstood. Franklin, Jay, and Adams did do well in fending off Strachey's rather feeble efforts, but otherwise they really let Shelburne frame the peace. Their major contributions were two: educating Shelburne to the fatuity of his dream of a reconstructed empire and removing beyond doubt the American desire to escape from France. These actions fixed the timing, letting peace go forward while Shelburne held power, and in this sense they were crucial. But the shape of the treaty was largely Shelburne's doing.

Americans and American historians sometimes magnify the success, wisdom, and purity of national figures. At other times, in a revisionist mood, they swing to the opposite pole and denigrate those who have guided affairs. Commonly, neither extreme is appropriate, although the proper interpretation need not lie precisely between the two extremes. But in the case of the men of Paris, it is now clear that the balance has tended too far toward the favorable side.

RICHARD B. MORRIS

The Durable
Significance of
the Treaty of 1783

IN A FOREWORD to a collection of peace treaties published a
decade or so ago, Arnold Toynbee spoke of "Anarchy by
Treaty" and assigned "the real weakness of a peace treaty" to
the fact that "the negotiators of it are under the mounting
pressure to conclude their work as speedily as possible, while
on the other hand the business that has to be transacted is so
voluminous, so important, and so difficult that, to be dealt
with properly, it would require much more" time to be given
to it than circumstances allow.[1] How true that is of these days
of "shuttle diplomacy," when so-called diplomats who are
named to represent a great power at a nuclear disarmament
conference publicly confess that they have no knowledge of
nuclear problems and have never even given thought to how
a limited nuclear war could actually be conducted.

In contrast to this contemporary experience with treaty
making, the treaty of 1783 was a triumph that was noteworthy both for its durability and its far-reaching impact. It
was a triumph not only because a sufficient number of Americans sustained the will to fight and continue fighting, backed
directly or indirectly by an ally and two cobelligerents, but
also because the Congress that had declared war had spent
years working out its peace aims and had sent to the conference table a group of four men who had been in the struggle
from the start. All of the four had participated in drawing
up the peace proposals and in urging their modifications

[1] Fred L. Israel, ed., *Major Peace Treaties of Modern History, 1648–1967*,
introductory essay by Arnold Toynbee, 4 vols. (New York, 1967),
1:xiii–xix.

where necessary, three had broad experience in diplomacy abroad, and the fourth had even spent time in the Tower of London—an experience that in retrospect might have been helpful to some modern-day diplomats who have been assigned to sensitive negotiations. They were learned, patient, and tough, prepared to ignore congressional instructions when they felt they ran counter to the national interest and equally prepared to ignore both the counsel of their ally and the various ultimata of George III.

If the Treaty of Paris of 1783 did not live up to Toynbee's characterization of "Anarchy by Treaty" but instead made possible the creation of a durable state, and if that treaty has only undergone the most trivial modifications since that day, the same cannot be said for the other treaties to which Toynbee is referring. Where today are the treaties of Utrecht of 1713, of Paris and Hubertusburg of 1763, or of Kuchuk Kainarji of 1774? Not to mention Vienna, the Versailles Treaty of 1919, and, of course, the Kellogg-Briand Pact to abolish war. They are all ghosts of a vanished past, along with the empires of the British, the Spaniards, the Dutch, the French, the Turks, and the Germans, a past associated with the departed, if not mourned, Bourbons, Habsburgs, Hohenzollerns, Romanovs, and Ottoman Sultans.

Not so the British-American treaty of 1783. While the map of Europe has been altered beyond recognition since the American and French revolutions, and that of the rest of the world since the wars of the twentieth century, the present bounds of the continental United States seem in retrospect to have been an inevitable outcome of the sensational territorial gains achieved by the American peacemakers at Paris in the fall of 1782. These concessions, it may be added, were won with little help at the diplomatic table from the courts of France and Spain but had the fortuitous assistance of an amiable Scot negotiator for Great Britain, his conciliatory prime minister, and the pro-American David Hartley, who succeeded Richard Oswald but was unable to achieve the second objective of the treaty negotiations—a treaty of commerce.[2]

---

[2] For the peace negotiations, see Richard B. Morris, *The Peacemakers: The Great Powers and American Independence*, new ed. (Boston, 1983).

PEACE AND THE PEACEMAKERS

Having secured generous boundaries that exceeded by far those of any republic since the days of Rome, the United States, spurred by the initiatives of continental-minded statesmen, quickly entered into a period of unparalleled creativity, establishing provisions for the admission of these newly acquired territories as states of the union on an equal footing with the original thirteen—not as dependent colonies. Thus was created a republic, not an empire, a republic born in a spirit of anticolonialism and capable of engrafting into its system some thirty-seven more states, two of them not contiguous and one of the two separated by vast stretches of the Pacific Ocean. So spacious a republic needed a unique kind of federalism to infuse the central authority with energy and operative powers, while conceding to the states and the people rights not explicitly granted the national government. These two creative pieces of statecraft—the Northwest Ordinance and the federal Constitution—were invented and put into operation within four years of the Definitive Treaty's ratification. Without this treaty their adoption would have had no meaning.

But the treaty itself was only a piece of paper, and almost every clause in it required explanation, interpretation, and implementation. If the boundaries lacked precision at certain points, the cause lay not in the carelessness of the treatymakers, who were meticulous in such matters, but in the defects of the geographical and cartographical knowledge of the day. Thus arose the controversy over the St. Croix River as a northeast boundary and the clause giving free access to the British to the Mississippi, a grant based on the erroneous assumption that the Mississippi's source was in Canada, not the United States. If the treaty assumed that the Americans had the right to navigate the Mississippi from its source to its mouth, that was due to the fact that the Americans claimed the easement that the British acquired from France in 1763 after their capture of the Floridas.[3] In fact, many of the difficulties that arose in the later implementation of the peace treaty stemmed from the fact that the Americans, having

[3] In Article VIII of the Definitive Treaty of 1783, based on Article VII of the Franco-British Treaty of Paris of 1763 (Israel, ed., *Peace Treaties*, 1:310, 350).

gained the victory, demanded the rights, sovereignties, and jurisdictions held by the British in North America after the Treaty of Paris of 1763. For example, the former colonists insisted on all the commercial privileges they had shared in the trading empire that the old British Empire had created.

The Americans had given considerable thought to trade ever since the war began. The general principles that were embodied in trade treaties proposed by the United States during and after the Revolution were derived from the Model Treaty of John Adams, drawn up for Congress in the summer of 1776. Recognizing the need to find sources for American trade other than Britain, Adams conceived of a treaty of amity and commerce as the vehicle whereby the United States would obtain recognition by the great powers as an independent state. While Adams used the term *alliance*, he had in mind, as scholars have pointed out, a commercial rather than a military-political connection. Adams's Model Treaty laid down what became the article of faith in America's longer-term negotiations: free ships make free goods. A policy espoused by little-navy nations, it would give neutrals the right to trade with belligerents while drastically restricting the list of contraband goods, even excluding naval stores and foodstuffs. The Model Treaty also embraced provisions for commercial reciprocity and unhampered trade with all countries.[4] At French suggestion, a conditional most-favored-nation clause was incorporated in the treaty of commerce of 1778 with France, and that clause was also included in the treaty with Sweden of 1783.[5] Two years later the treaty made with Prussia contained a most-favored-nation clause, but without the conditional provision of the French and Swedish treaties. It also embraced certain humanitarian fea-

[4] Felix Gilbert, *To the Farewell Address: Ideas of Early American Foreign Policy* (Princeton, 1961), p. 46; Gerald Stourzh, *Benjamin Franklin and American Foreign Policy*, 2d ed. (Chicago, 1969), pp. 124–25. The Model Treaty plan in Adams's hand is in the Papers of the Continental Congress, Record Group 360, Item 47, pp. 129–49, National Archives; Worthington C. Ford et al., eds., *Journals of the Continental Congress, 1774–1789*, 34 vols. (Washington, D.C., 1904–37), 5:576–89.

[5] Hunter Miller, ed., *Treaties and Other International Acts of the United States of America*, 8 vols. (Washington, D.C., 1931–48), 2:5, 125.

tures for which Franklin had been pushing for some years, such as immunity of noncombatants in wartime and decent treatment of prisoners of war. An article in the treaty providing that contraband goods on neutral ships could not be confiscated in wartime, but merely detained, with reasonable compensation for resulting loss to the proprietors, would raise pertinent issues as recently as World War I.[6] As for John Jay, who was now serving as secretary for foreign affairs, he would have preferred a policy distinguishing between "merely European" powers like Prussia and Sweden, and "partly European and partly American" nations—that is, those holding New World possessions—like Britain, France, and Spain.[7] Jay's growing isolationism may well have tinctured his diagnosis, but he was not prepared to press the point, and Congress ratified the Prussian treaty, seemingly not sharing Jay's lack of enthusiasm.

This treaty with Prussia was one of the very few diplomatic successes achieved by the United States during the Confederation's years. What is relevant to the Treaty of Paris of 1783 was that the frustrations suffered by the American negotiators in postwar diplomacy, particularly with Britain and Spain, proved major factors in the creation in 1787 of a federal union that endowed the nation with the muscle to get its treaties enforced, its foreign policy respected, and at least some, if not all, of its long-range diplomatic goals achieved.

Many people in Britain looked with unabated joy on the fact that the United States, by seceding from the empire, lost the valuable trade privileges that Americans had enjoyed during colonial years as well as the protection of the British fleet. No group was happier than the shipping interests.[8]

[6] Ibid., pp. 61–62, 164–65.

[7] John Jay, Report to Congress, May 17, 1785, Papers of the Continental Congress, Item 81; The Diplomatic Correspondence of the United States of America, from the Signing of the Definitive Treaty of Peace . . . to the Adoption of the Constitution, 7 vols. (Washington, D.C., 1833–34), 1:529–31.

[8] Vincent T. Harlow, The Founding of the Second British Empire, 1763–1793, 2 vols. (London, 1952–64), 2:254–55, 257, 266–67. For a balanced, if untraditional, treatment, see Charles R. Ritcheson, Aftermath of Revolution: British Policy toward the United States, 1783–1795 (Dallas, 1969), pp. 3–146.

One of the first acts of the British was to withdraw protection from American merchant ships operating in Mediterranean waters. The final year of the war had proved devastating both to the Continental navy and to the American merchant marine, and American ships and seamen were now totally vulnerable to North African piracy. During the peace negotiations with Great Britain, the American commissioners had sought to incorporate into the Definitive Treaty a provision pledging the British to interpose with the Barbary states in favor of the United States,[9] but the final draft failed to include it. The fact is that Britain saw every advantage in declining to assist her former colonies and new trade rivals in this and other ways.

As early as October 1783 an American ship, *Betsey*, and her crew were held hostage at Tangier by Moroccan pirates. By 1785 outrages had piled up, although the *Betsey* and her crew were released in mid-July, largely through the good offices of Spain and the energetic efforts of our chargé in that nation. Soon Algiers intercepted American ships, seized their cargo, and enslaved their crews. On the basis of information forwarded by John Paul Jones, Jay was obliged to inform Congress that Algiers had declared war on the United States.[10] Soon Congress was to learn the lurid details of the captivity of American ship captains and their crews and had to undertake delicate negotiations with each of the four piratical states—Morocco, Algiers, Tunis, and Tripoli.[11] When Algiers demanded the preposterous sum of 30,000 guineas, with a commission of some 10 percent to be exacted by their ambassador for himself, Jay refused but advised putting the matter to the states. "Until such time as they [the states] furnish Congress with their respective portions of that sum, the depredations of those barbarians will, in all probability, con-

[9] Richard B. Morris et al., eds., *John Jay*, vol. 2, *John Jay: The Winning of the Peace: Unpublished Papers, 1780–1784* (New York, 1980), p. 578.

[10] John Paul Jones to Jay, Aug. 6, 1785, New Jersey State Library, Trenton; *Diplomatic Correspondence*, 7:317–18.

[11] Jay to the president of Congress, Oct. 13, 1785, Papers of the Continental Congress, Item 80, 2:37; Ford et al., eds., *Journals of the Continental Congress*, 29:833–34; *Diplomatic Correspondence*, 7:316–17.

tinue to increase," he insisted. Needless to say, the states did nothing. The great question, as Jay put it, was "whether we shall wage war or pay tribute." As for himself, he preferred war to tribute. Jay was equally adamant, however, in his opposition to joining other maritime powers in a collective naval force to guard the Mediterranean. A nation that could not protect its frontier or pay its debts could hardly build and support a navy in distant waters.[12] And so, except for the treaty we bought from Morocco by Thomas Barclay, the consul-general in Paris in 1786, and ratified by Congress while the convention in Philadelphia was in mid-session, American seamen remained imprisoned or enslaved in the Barbary states until we had adequate force as a nation to put a stop to these barbarities.

Other diplomatic difficulties arose for the United States in carrying out the terms of the Treaty of Paris. Some Americans insisted that winning the war freed them of all prewar obligations. In turn, the British seemed to forget that they had lost the war. The results were an impasse over trade that, without a national government capable of exercising discriminatory tariffs, would not be settled under the Confederation, and the obduracy of the British in removing their troops from frontier posts. The Americans in turn—at least some of them—tried to block the payment of their debts to British businessmen and insisted on compensation for slaves that had escaped to the British lines.

Indeed, the reframing of British mercantilist policy in the postwar years may well have contributed more to the convocation of the constitutional convention of 1787 and to its success than, as Julian P. Boyd remarked, "many who sat in that august body."[13] The gravest threats to America were external in origin—not domestic insurrection or the possible secession of western territories, but British dumping and trade

---

[12] Jay, Report to Congress, May 29, 1786, and Aug. 2, 1787, Papers of the Continental Congress, Item 124, II; May 29, 1786, *Diplomatic Correspondence*, 2:343–46; Aug. 2, 1787, Ford et al., eds., *Journals of the Continental Congress*, 33:451–53.

[13] Julian P. Boyd, *Number 7: Alexander Hamilton's Secret Attempts to Control American Foreign Policy* (Princeton, 1964), pp. x, xi.

monopoly that contributed almost immediately to an acute depression in the United States. "I may reason till I die to no purpose," declared John Adams as early as June 1785. "It is unanimity in America in measures, which shall confute the British sophisms and make them feel, which will ever produce a fair treaty of commerce."[14]

Regarding the trade treaty, Adams ruefully confessed to Jay within six months of beginning his mission as minister to the Court of St. James's that he was a complete "cypher."[15] As Jay commented to Congress, unless Adams were given enlarged powers to retaliate, progress on the score of trade was purely speculative.[16] And Congress could not, restricted by the Articles of Confederation, give Adams such enlarged powers. Without a national government having authority over commerce, the United States lacked bargaining power to enter into a reciprocal trade treaty with Great Britain. Adams condemned the various duties imposed on tobacco and other American products imported into England and the prohibition of exporting tools and utensils made of British iron and steel: "It shews the spirit of this country toward the United States, and summarily comprehends a volume of politics for us." The prohibition on tool exports was designed "to prevent us from setting up manufactures in America." In trade matters, Adams concluded: "The Friends of America are reduced to Doctor Price and Doctor Jebb." The only answer to the "national prejudice in favor of their navigation acts," he urged, was to impose discriminatory duties on British products.[17]

To the extent that Britain's failure to move a trade treaty forward and, more especially, her refusal to evacuate troops

[14] John Adams to Jay, June 26, 1785, *Diplomatic Correspondence*, 4:224–27.

[15] Adams to Jay, Dec. 1785, Papers of the Continental Congress, Item 84, VI:39–49, 51–67; *Diplomatic Correspondence*, 4:467–74.

[16] Jay to the president of Congress, May 8, 1786, Papers of the Continental Congress, Item 81; *Diplomatic Correspondence*, 4:475–76.

[17] Adams to Jay, July 19 and Aug. 30, 1785, Papers of the Continental Congress, Item 84, V:534–38, 633–40; *Diplomatic Correspondence*, 4:241–46, 344–49.

from the northern and western posts were nonactions justified in British eyes by the alleged prior failure of Americans to pay their debts and treat the loyalist claims in accordance with the provisions of the treaty, Jay was moved to investigate. By correspondence with the governors he amassed enough data to conclude that nothing would be gained by pressing American claims for property removed by the British army during wartime so long as some of the states retained laws impeding British creditors from collecting debts as stipulated by treaty as well as other acts permitting actions at law for damages inflicted during the war under British military orders. By the fall of 1786 Congress learned from the secretary for foreign affairs that he had reluctantly concluded that the United States was the initial violator of the treaty's provisions, a view which he expounded in a searching and judicious report. In that document Jay made no effort to mask his antislavery views, telling the delegates that their insistence on the return of the blacks carried away by the British ran counter to humanitarian principles. Instead, he advocated compensation by the British government to their claimant owners, but even this demand he dropped as contrary to humanitarian principles when he served as minister plenipotentiary in the Jay Treaty negotiations in 1794.

This controversy and the facts that were brought home to John Jay over the extent to which the separate states were flouting the treaty of 1783 moved him to urge Congress to declare that treaties *constitutionally* made became "part of the law of the land, and are not only independent of the will and power of such Legislatures, but also binding and obligatory on them," and that state laws repugnant to such treaties must be repealed. In accordance with his recommendation Congress unanimously adopted a letter to the states, drafted by Jay, calling upon them to comply with the treaty.[18] This resolution may be considered the basis for the supremacy clause (Art. VI, sec. 2) in the federal Constitution.

On the issue of who had broken the treaty first, Jay seems

[18] Jay, Report to Congress, Apr. 6, 1785, Papers of the Continental Congress, Item 81; Ford et al., eds., *Journals of the Continental Congress*, 32:177–84, unanimously agreed to by Congress on Apr. 13, 1785.

to have been premature. Had he been privy to the correspondence between the home government and Canada's officials, he would have been astonished to learn that on April 8, 1784, Lord Sydney, secretary of state for home affairs in the Pitt cabinet, addressed a dispatch to Sir Frederick Haldimand, governor-general of British North America, instructing him that in view of the vagueness of the treaty's stipulation for evacuating "with all convenient speed," such a move might be delayed "at least until we are enabled to secure the fur traders in the Interior Country and withdraw their property."[19] *The very next day* George III proclaimed the ratification of the treaty and promised "sincerely and faithfully" to observe its provisions!

While alert to frontier dangers, Jay was not ready for war unless assured that France would join in on America's side, an assurance Thomas Jefferson could not obtain for him. He soon ascertained that Canadian officials, dissatisfied with the boundary settlement and responsive to their fur traders, were conducting a systematic program aimed at maintaining ties with possible western secessionists, a connection to be exploited at the propitious moment. "They hold the posts," he remarked to Adams, "but they will hold them as pledges of enmity."[20] Again, this matter was not settled until a military defeat of the Indians combined with the provisions of the Jay Treaty forced the British to evacuate from the northern and western territories of the United States.

The problem of debts to the loyalists and to English and Scottish businessmen was complex, and its moral aspects were overlaid with economic and political considerations. At the very start of the Revolution, American debtors owed the British in excess of £5 million. While this was not a huge sum, the debt was maldistributed and hit one region of the thirteen states hardest: most of the debtors were southerners, and Virginians stood in the front rank with a debt of over £2 million, or 40 percent of the national total. When the news

[19] Douglas Brymner, ed., *Report on Canadian Archives, 1890* (Ottowa, 1891), B, 50:142; see also Morris et al., eds., *John Jay*, 2:240.

[20] Jay to Adams, Sept. 6, 1785, Papers of the Continental Congress, Item 121; *Diplomatic Correspondence*, 4:228–30.

reached America that the treaty of peace provided that creditors on either side should meet with no lawful impediment
to the recovery in full value of their debts, a furor broke out
in Virginia. George Mason wrote Patrick Henry that the
question was frequently raised in conversation: "If we are
now to pay the debts due the British merchants, what have
we been fighting for all this while?"[21] While there were leading figures on both sides of the question, one investigator has
suggested that the anti–debt-payment group represented a
majority of Virginians, and to be sure, Virginians managed
by a series of legislative acts to make it difficult if not impossible for creditors to collect what was owed them.

At the start of the peace negotiations the British government seemed conciliatory on the point of the debts, authoriz-
ing Oswald to waive stipulating in the treaty both the
payment of debts to British merchants and compensation to
loyalists if he felt it necessary to do so. The British government counted on world opinion to bring about an equitable
settlement of both issues. The draft treaty that Jay drew up
omitted mention of both the loyalists and the debts. However, by the time the draft treaty reached the British cabinet,
that body was under insistent pressure from a variety of interests—Canadian fur traders, English fishermen, American
loyalists, and, not the least, English and Scottish creditors. A
new set of instructions to Oswald in October 1782 demanded
that he urge the Americans "as strongly as possible" to dis-
charge the prewar debts. Henceforth, the debts, along with
the fisheries and the claims of the loyalists, were the chief
points at issue between the British and American negotiators. Had the negotiations remained entirely in the hands of
Benjamin Franklin and Jay it is possible that the Americans
would have made no concession on the debt question. At the
very end of October, however, John Adams joined his
colleagues. At once, in what seems to have come as an off-
the-cuff and even impulsive gesture, made without advance
consultation with Franklin and Jay, who had been insisting

[21] W. W. Henry, ed., *Life, Correspondence and Speeches of Patrick Henry*, 3
vols. (New York, 1891), 2:187.

for months that both the commissioners and Congress lacked the power to deal with the subject, Adams blurted out: "I have no notion of cheating anybody." To save face, Adams's colleagues worked out a formula whereby Congress would recommend that the states open their courts of justice for the recovery of all just debts. Jay drafted the article as it appears in the treaty. It reads, "It is agreed that the creditors on either side shall meet with no lawful impediment on the recovery of the full value in sterling money of all bona fide debts heretofore contracted." And it was John Jay, more than any other man, who was to see that this clause was carried out, subsequently as chief justice of the United States and then, while still chief justice, as the negotiator with Lord Grenville of the Jay Treaty. Although his own court affirmed both the supremacy of treaties over state law and the right of a foreign creditor to collect a debt whose validity was sustained by the treaty, despite the legal impediments put up by a state to the contrary, Jay in his treaty did an extraordinary thing. He stripped the Supreme Court of jurisdiction over such cases and gave the creditors the right of appeal to a mixed commission; two of its members were to be named by the United States, two by Great Britain, and a fifth was to be selected by the appointed commissioners. The four commissioners selected the fifth member by lot, and the choice fell upon the British nominee. As a result the British insisted that interest on the debts should be paid for the period during the war; the Americans dissented.[22] A similar division occurred on the issue of restoring to the loyalists estates confiscated by bills of attainder; eventually, the Americans withdrew and the negotiations were halted. After Jefferson's victory in the presidential election of 1800, the dispute was settled by a compromise formula. In the Convention of 1802 the United States agreed to pay £600,000 sterling to the British government in settlement of all outstanding claims, an amount that was duly paid from the treasury of the United States in three annual installments. This was in fact less than

[22] See Richard B. Morris, *John Jay, the Nation, and the Court* (Boston, 1967), ch. 3.

a third of what the committee of British merchants had demanded of Grenville, but it closed the books on a major unsettled issue.[23]

The question of the disputed northeastern boundary commanded the attention of Congress almost immediately after the ratification of the Definitive Treaty. After reviewing reports of investigators on the scene seeking to fix the proper boundary, Jay recommended to Congress that a mixed commission be set up for that purpose.[24] This was another provision of the peace treaty that did not go into effect until the Jay Treaty, and its final settlement proved decades away.

Together, Jay and Adams, and the brief mission of Gouverneur Morris to London, failed to budge the British on any material unresolved issue. Winding up his affairs in London in 1788, Adams wrote Jay that "in preparing for my departure I have been personally treated with the same uniform tenor of dry decency and cold civility, which appears to have been the premeditated plan from the beginning, and opposition as well as administration appear to have adopted the same spirit."[25] A gleam of hope, in a closing conference the marquess of Carmarthen had implied that, once the United States established a new national government, a treaty of commerce would follow. That eventuality did not come to pass, however, for another six years, and then it was to be none other than John Jay himself who was to negotiate that compromise settlement. Thus, the Definitive Treaty of 1783 merely ended the war. It was that second settlement known as the Jay Treaty, so popular in England, so reviled in the United States, which for a decade brought real peace between Britain and her erstwhile colonies.

Finally, the fisheries: even the Jay Treaty was not able to

[23] For the discussion of the debt problems, see Morris, *Jay, the Nation, and the Court*, pp. 80–96; also see Morris, *Peacemakers*, p. 366, and Morris et al., eds. *John Jay*, 2:397–98, 402–3, 408, 429, 441, 547–48, 567–68n.

[24] Jay, Report to Congress, Apr. 21, 1785, Papers of the Continental Congress, Item 81; Ford et al., eds., *Journals of the Continental Congress*, 28:287–90.

[25] Adams to Jay, Feb. 14, 1788, Papers of the Continental Congress, Item 84; *Diplomatic Correspondence*, 5:357–59.

end this controversy. Again, the Americans had claimed all the rights that they had enjoyed as members of the old British Empire. It was the potential of the fisheries off the North Atlantic that had attracted the Pilgrims to Plymouth and the Puritans to Massachusetts Bay, leaving religious motivations out of this consideration. They had within a few decades developed a characteristic timetable with important legal and economic consequences. In the spring and summer, New Englanders took advantage of the location of the cod a considerable distance from the coast, notably on George's Bank, Jeffrey's Bank, and the Grand Banks, while in the winter, when the cod approached the shores to spawn, a home industry was pursued with great profit. Soon they expanded beyond the inshore waters of New England, operating off Nova Scotia and especially off the Grand Bank of Newfoundland.[26] Henceforth, New Englanders would play key military and political roles in acting to protect their fishing interests in the four intercolonial wars fought between England and France between 1689 and 1763. It was New Englanders, we must remember, who conceived the policy and demanded the expulsion of the French Acadian population that had refused to take an oath of loyalty to the British crown.[27] After 1763 France forfeited all her fishing rights in this area except for the northeast coast of Newfoundland and the fishing islands of St. Pierre and Miquelon. Otherwise, Frenchmen were confined to distances beyond three leagues from all coasts held by Great Britain, to fifteen leagues from the coasts of Cape Breton Island and thirty leagues from Nova Scotia. The fall of Louisbourg and the treaty of 1763 brought about the dominance of New Englanders in Nova Scotia, sometimes called "new New England."[28] By the outbreak of the Revolution fishing was a major New England industry. To Massachusetts alone, the value of the cod fishery was estimated at $1,300,000, with other fish raising the total

[26] C. L. Woodbury, *The Relationship of the Fisheries to the Discovery and Settlement of North America* (Boston, 1880), pp. 23–26.

[27] John Bartlet Brebner, *The Neutral Yankees of Nova Scotia: A Marginal Colony during the Revolutionary Years* (New York, 1937), p. 55.

[28] Ibid., pp. 11–12, 117.

not far from $1,800,000, with some 665 vessels and 10,000 men engaged in the fishing business.[29]

Accordingly, as John Adams learnedly expatiated during the treaty negotiations, the American negotiators considered fishing to be both big business and a basic American right claimed through usage and conquest. What Americans had long enjoyed, they had no intention of abandoning.[30]

Down to the signing of the Definitive Treaty the fisheries, along with the Mississippi, were central peace objectives. They also proved to be central political and economic issues in the first few decades in the history of the new United States. Ultimately, due to the backstairs efforts of French minister Conrad Alexandre Gérard and his cadre of pro-French members of Congress, the fishing rights were removed from the peace instructions as an ultimatum, and Congress substituted the negative assertion, "that in no case, by any treaty of peace, the common right of fishery be given up." This did not quiet the New Englanders, and finally Congress adopted a resolution to the effect that, if after the treaty of peace Great Britain were to molest the inhabitants in taking fish on the banks, Congress would deem it a breach of the peace. A careful reading of the revised instructions that went out to the peace commissioners shows that Congress had no intention of abandoning the claim of the United States to "continue to enjoy the free and undisturbed exercise of their common right to fish on the Banks of Newfoundland, and the other fishing banks and seas of North America," and an express stipulation to that effect was made a condition of agreeing to any treaty of commerce.[31]

The drafts of the treaty provisions relating to fishing went through various modifications. Jay's first draft called for fishing rights "of every kind" on the banks of Newfoundland and other places "where the inhabitants of both countries used formerly, viz., before the last war between France and

[29] Raymond McFarland, *A History of the New England Fisheries* (New York, 1911).

[30] Morris, *Peacemakers*, pp. 154, 373–74, 376–79.

[31] Ford et al., eds., *Journals of the Continental Congress*, 14:960–62 (Mar. 22, 1779).

Britain to fish," along with drying rights "at the accustomed places." Significantly this first draft, which was broader than later ones, had been hammered out by Jay three weeks *before* the arrival of John Adams, normally hailed as the savior of New England's cod. The second draft showed little change, except that places for drying rights were specified. In the final draft, save for omitting permission to Americans to dry fish on the shores of Nova Scotia, the British substituted "liberty" for "right" insofar as all fishing and drying claims were concerned. A compromise formula, after much heated discussion, was adopted whereby the Americans settled for a "liberty" to take fish on the "coast" of Newfoundland and the other coasts of British North America, as distinguished from the right that was acknowledged to them to fish on the banks and in the Gulf of St. Lawrence. What the Americans abandoned was the liberty of curing and drying on Cape Sable, as well as the explicit permission to be granted American fishermen to rent land for curing and drying their fish. Instead, the liberty of drying and curing was restricted to the period of time that these coastal regions remained "unsettled."[32] But since the fisheries issue was not settled in 1783, it represents another example of how further and extended negotiations were needed to make a durable peace between the United States and Great Britain.

Another clause of the treaty provoked litigation not only between the United States and Canada but also between the federal government and the states. Article II of both the Preliminary and the Definitive treaties, after tracing the northeastern boundary, added this clause: "comprehending all islands within twenty leagues of any part of the shores of the United States, lying between lines to be drawn due East from the points where the aforesaid boundaries between Nova Scotia on the one part and East Florida on the other, shall respectively touch the Bay of Fundy and the Atlantic Ocean, excepting such islands as now are or heretofore have been within the limits of the said province of Nova Scotia." While this description was intended to include offshore islands, it

[32] Jay's three drafts are found in Morris et al., eds., *John Jay*, 2:389–92, 400–404, 432–39.

did not delineate a seaward territorial boundary. As I have discussed elsewhere, neither of the two existent contemporary maps on the boundaries, the King George's map and the John Jay map, nor any of the others subsequently located in connection with the Maine–New Brunswick boundary negotiations, can be accepted as authentic evidence of the intent of the peace commissioners as regards the descriptions contained in the text of the Definitive Treaty.[33] What governs is the text: that *only islands* were comprehended by the line, not the seas, seabed, or subsoil, is self-evident from the text itself. This issue, insofar as the United States and the North Atlantic states were concerned, is definitely settled in the litigation over the seabed and subsoil in *U.S. v. Maine et al.* (1975).

The point should also be made that at no time was the twenty-league line in the boundary article of the treaty considered as imposing limits on the fishing, maritime, or other activities of the United States or of American citizens. The fishing banks, extending from George's Bank on the southwest to Flemish Cape on the east, stretch a distance of 1,100 miles and vary in width from 50 to 250 miles. Significantly, this area falls largely to the east of the twenty-league area stated in the second article of the treaty. As regards the fishing rights and liberties agreed upon in the final draft of the Preliminary Treaty, it is significant that in this final draft reciprocity disappears. No reciprocal rights were therein granted to Britons, Nova Scotians, or Canadians to fish along the Maine banks, the George's Bank, or other American fisheries locations.

The Definitive Treaty of 1783 was identical in wording on the boundaries and the fisheries to the Preliminary Treaty. As to the fisheries, the point should be made that, in their own negotiations with the French, the British learned of the latter's discomfiture with the fishing rights or liberties guaranteed to the Americans and of their wish to have a formal provision incorporated in the Franco-British treaty explicitly protecting French fishermen from the Americans. The Brit-

[33] Richard B. Morris, "The Treaty of Paris," *Fundamental Testaments of the American Revolution*, Library of Congress Symposia on the American Revolution (Washington, D.C., 1977), pp. 93–96.

246

ish gave the French an oral promise against such encroachments, but neither the preliminaries nor the definitive Franco-British treaty incorporated such a provision.

Significantly, the Treaty of Ghent in 1815, concluded at the end of the second war with Britain, reached no agreement on the fisheries.[34] The American commissioners insisted that none was necessary because the fishery "liberty" of the treaty of 1783 had been in the nature of an inalienable right, coming from a division of empire, which could not be extinguished as long as the independence of the inheriting nation, the United States, existed. For their part, the British contended that the fishery liberties had been abrogated by the effect of the war on all previous treaties. That abrogation was to be their compensation for the loss of the navigation of the Mississippi.

The result of the absurd impasse was the Convention of 1818, in which the United States was represented by Richard Rush and Albert Gallatin. The outcome was a grant by Great Britain of a permanent extension of the fishery "liberty" *forever* in common with British subjects, on certain specified coasts, while on others the United States formally renounced the liberty heretofore enjoyed to take, dry, and cure fish on or within three marine miles of any of the coasts, bays, creeks, or harbors.[35] In defense of this concession the American commissioners argued that the fishing ground off the coast of Nova Scotia, for example, was more than three miles from shore, while on Labrador, where the rights were retained, fishing was almost universally close to shore. Thus it is clear that the United States waived no meaningful fishing rights. Subsequently, fisheries issues between the United States and Canada dealt with such narrow problems as the

[34] Permanent Court of Arbitration, The Hague: North Atlantic Coast Fisheries Arbitration, *The Case of the United States before the Permanent Court of Arbitration at The Hague* (Washington, D.C., 1909), p. 16.

[35] Permanent Court of Arbitration, The Hague: North Atlantic Coast Fisheries Arbitration, *Proceedings in the North Atlantic Coast Fisheries Arbitration*, 12 vols. (Washington, D.C., 1912–13), 4:52–55; Harold A. Innis, *The Cod Fisheries: The History of an International Economy* (New Haven, 1940), p. 224; Lorenzo Sabine, *Report on the Principal Fisheries of the American Seas* (Washington, D.C., 1853), p. 161.

measurement of bays, procurement of bait, and rights of reasonable regulation by the Canadian authorities. Moreover, The Hague tribunal of 1910 ruled in accord with the 1818 convention.

No treaty with Great Britain signed in 1783 could be considered durable if one crucial provision were not carried out—the section providing for the free navigation of the Mississippi "from its sources to its mouth to be available to both the subjects of Great Britain and the citizens of the United States." Despite the American argument that the surrender by the 1783 treaty of Britain's western territory to the United States transferred not only the property but the servitude of the river as well, Spain denied that the servitude was valid any longer since it had recovered West Florida and owned both banks of the lower Mississippi. Furthermore, there could be no durable peace until the southern boundary of the United States was settled. Spain, which had been so cool toward John Jay's mission to that nation, now was confronted with its old foe since Jay was elected to the post of secretary for foreign affairs even before his return to New York in July 1784. Jay, inhibited by unyielding instructions from Congress and confronted by a series of hostile Spanish steps, including the revoking of privileges previously granted to Americans to navigate the Mississippi within Spanish territories, spent several fruitless years in negotiations with Don Diego de Gardoqui, a special Spanish plenipotentiary with the title encargado de negocios, whom he had known from his years in Spain. When Jay realized that a complete impasse had been reached on all issues *except* trade, he formally approached Congress with the idea of making a commercial treaty with Spain but proposing that the United States stipulate that it would forbear the navigation of the Mississippi for some twenty-five years. Despite hostile reactions by southern congressmen, Jay tried to persuade Congress of the advantages of this arrangement. Southerners argued that it would be an advantage to New England businessmen but would discourage the sale and disposition of lands in the western territory and would promote western secession. As a result of southern opposition Jay won a majority but not the two-thirds vote required under the Articles of Confederation.[36] Anxious to allay rising sectional tension and louder talk of western secession plots, he conceded that "a treaty disagreeable to one-half of the nation had better not be made, for it would be violated." Indeed, before quitting office he reversed himself and recommended that Congress reassert the nation's right to the Mississippi's navigation and its intention never to cede it.[37] Indirectly, Jay served the southerners' cause. The Jay Treaty of 1794 so alarmed the Spanish government that it yielded to Thomas Pinckney most of what it had withheld from Jay, and by the Adams-Onís Treaty of 1819 Spain renounced all claims to West Florida and ceded East Florida to the United States.

Of course, the "durable treaty" of 1783 had wonderfully expansive potentialities. The Convention of 1818 with Great Britain fixed the northwest boundary between the United States and British North America along the forty-ninth parallel from the Lake of the Woods to the crest of the Rocky Mountains, the boundary west of the mountains was established by the Oregon settlement of 1846, and the water boundary was defined in the arbitration award of 1873.[38]

But the greatest tribute of all to the durable character of the treaty of 1783 was the mutual disarmament of the United States–Canadian border, a move that started with the Rush-Bagot agreement of 1818, by which the Great Lakes were

[36] Ford et al., eds., *Journals of the Continental Congress*, 31:694–97; Edmund Cody Burnett, ed., *Letters of Members of the Continental Congress*, 8 vols. (Washington, D.C., 1921–36), 8:329–30.

[37] Jay, Report to Congress, Sept. 16, 1788, Papers of the Continental Congress, Item 81; Ford et al., eds., *Journals of the Continental Congress*, 34:530–34.

[38] Critics of the achievements of the American commissioners who claim that these negotiators should have insisted on the Nipissing line as our northern boundary, thereby obtaining southern Ontario for the United States, fail to appreciate the fact that the boundary agreed on provided this country with the basis for achieving an extension, by the Convention of 1818, of the northern boundary of the Lake of the Woods to the Rocky Mountains, and then a further basis for extending it along the line of the forty-ninth parallel to the Pacific Ocean by the Oregon Treaty. All in all, the United States would ultimately gain far more by the Line-of-Lakes boundary than by the Nipissing line.

disarmed, and was concluded by the Treaty of Washington of 1871, which provided the world with an example of the longest unfortified boundary on the face of the globe. If only that could serve as an example to East and West today and to a hungry Third World, where every boundary is contested, and where states seem obliged to spend so exorbitant a share of their meager annual income on an array of sophisticated weaponry that all of us pray will never have to be used.

Contributors
Index

Contributors

MARCUS CUNLIFFE is University Professor at George Washington University. English by birth, he is a graduate of Oxford University. Before taking up his present post he was a professor of American Studies at Manchester and Sussex universities, and he has held visiting appointments at Harvard University and the University of Michigan. His books include *The Literature of the United States* (1954; new ed., 1985), *George Washington, Man and Monument* (1958; new ed., 1982), *Soldiers and Civilians: The Martial Spirit in America, 1775–1865* (1968), and *Chattel Slavery and Wage Slavery: The Anglo-American Context, 1830–1860* (1979). His current research is concerned with the evolution in America of conceptions of republicanism and private property.

JONATHAN R. DULL is the author of *The French Navy and American Independence: A Study of Arms and Diplomacy, 1774–1787* (1975), *Franklin the Diplomat: The French Mission* (1982), and *A Diplomatic History of the American Revolution* (1985). Dr. Dull received his Ph.D. from the University of California and taught at the University of Texas. Since 1977 he has been a member of the staff of the Papers of Benjamin Franklin, where he is currently an associate editor.

JAMES H. HUTSON has been the Chief of the Manuscript Division, Library of Congress, since 1982. His most recent book, *John Adams and the Diplomacy of the American Revolution* (1980), won the Gilbert Chinard Prize for 1981. He is currently preparing a supplementary edition to Max Farrand's *Records of the Federal Convention of 1787*, to be published by the Yale University Press.

GREGG L. LINT received his Ph.D. from Michigan State University in 1975. Presently he is associate editor of the Adams Papers, with the primary responsibility for the *Papers of John Adams*, par-

CONTRIBUTORS

ticularly his diplomatic career. With Robert J. Taylor he has edited eight volumes of the *Papers of John Adams*, and he has contributed articles to *Diplomatic History* and to *America in a Candid World* (1977). His present research centers on Adams's diplomatic career and the influence of international law on the foreign policy of the United States between 1776 and 1826.

RICHARD B. MORRIS is Gouverneur Morris Professor of History emeritus at Columbia University and author of numerous books on American history, including *Government and Labor in Early America* (1946, 1983), *The Peacemakers: The Great Powers and American Independence* (1965), which won the Bancroft Prize, and the *Encyclopedia of American History*, now in its sixth edition. He has just published *Witnesses at the Creation: Hamilton, Madison, and Jay and the Constitution* (1985). He is also coeditor with Henry Steele Commager of the *New American Nation* series, a 40-volume reexamination of the history of the American people. He is currently cochairman (with James MacGregor Burns) of Project '87, an organization jointly sponsored by the American Historical Association and the American Political Science Association to stimulate nationwide study and understanding of the Constitution. He is editor of a multivolume edition of the unpublished papers of John Jay.

BRADFORD PERKINS, professor of history at the University of Michigan, was president of the Society for Historians of American Foreign Relations in 1974. He is the author of *The First Rapprochement* (1955), *Prologue to War* (1961), and *Castlereagh and Adams* (1964), a trilogy on Anglo-American relations from 1795 to 1823, the last volume of which won the Bancroft Prize. He is also the author of *The Great Rapprochement* (1968), an examination of British-American diplomacy from 1895 to 1914, and of numerous articles and reviews. He is currently working both on a broad interpretive study of American diplomatic history and an assessment of Anglo-American relations during the Truman administration.

CHARLES R. RITCHESON, until recently Lovell Distinguished Professor of History, is now dean and vice provost of libraries at the University of Southern California and Lovell University Professor. From 1972 to 1974 he served as cultural attaché at the United States embassy in London. His four monographs deal with various aspects of Anglo-American relations, and include *British Politics and the American Revolution* (1954) and *Aftermath of Revolution: British Policy toward the United States, 1783–1795* (1969), and he is the editor of *The American Revolution: The Anglo-American Relation, 1763–1794* (1969).

SAMUEL F. SCOTT is professor of history at Wayne State University. He has published articles and essays on civil-military relations in various American and foreign journals and collections. His book *The Response of the Royal Army to the French Revolution: The Role and Development of the Line Army, 1787–1793*, was published in 1978. He and Barry Rothaus have recently completed *A Historical Dictionary of the French Revolution*. He is presently working on a study of Rochambeau's army in the American and French Revolutions.

On retiring from the directorship of the Institute of United States Studies, London, in 1983, a post he had held since 1971, ESMOND WRIGHT became emeritus professor of American history of the University of London. He served from 1971 to 1975 as British editor of the Loyalist Publications Programme, a joint British-Canadian-American research project, and his *Red, White and True Blue* (1976) and *A Tug of Loyalties* (1975) are evidences of this loyalist interest. He is at present engaged in a major reinterpretation of the career of Benjamin Franklin. Among his other books are *Washington and the American Revolution* (1957), *The World Today* (1961; 4th ed., 1978), *Fabric of Freedom, 1763–1800* (1961; 2d ed., 1978), *Benjamin Franklin and American Independence* (1966), *A Time for Courage* (1971), *Europe Today* (1979), *The Great Little Madison* (1981), and *The Fire of Liberty* (1983). He has edited *Illustrated World History* (1964), *Causes and Consequences of the American Revolution* (1966), *American Themes* (1967), *American Profiles* (1967), and *Benjamin Franklin, a Profile* (1970).

Index